# 1

# Early Days

My mother always said I wanted to be an actress. I've often wondered how, in the middle of Assam, I could have known anything about acting.

Julie Christie

In the spring of 1940 meat rationing had just begun in England, as the country experienced the harsh economic realities of war. Hitler had chillingly paralysed Europe still further by invading Denmark and Norway, and the liner *Queen Elizabeth,* camouflaged in a drab grey to confuse German U-boats in the Atlantic, had just completed her secret maiden voyage, sliding into an anchorage off New York's Staten Island to remain there in safety until the war was over.

In London people took refuge from the uncertainties of war in the cinema. Advance ticket sales for the British première of *Gone with the Wind,* already billed as the greatest film of all time, reached a record £10,000. There was also a sense of pride that Vivien Leigh, a British actress born in Darjeeling, India, had on 29 February at a banquet at the Coconut Grove in Los Angeles won the Best Actress Oscar for her role as Scarlett O'Hara.

2

Forty-five days later, on 14 April, there was much cause for rejoicing for Frank and Rosemary Christie, a British couple living on a tea plantation in Assam in the north-east of India, with the arrival of their first child, Julie Frances, who would also one day win a Best Actress Oscar and star in another epic love story set against the background of civil war which would rival *Gone with the Wind.*

Julie Christie has frequently said that she has few memories of her early childhood on the near-isolated 900-acre tea plantation managed by her father. Like so many of those quintessentially British children who were reared in remote corners of the Empire, her early day-to-day care was often entrusted to nannies or *ayahs;* and one of her over-riding recollections of those years is of her terror at being tied to a tree by her nurse. The memory had such a nightmarish quality that Julie frequently wondered whether it had actually happened. 'I think it was real, but sometimes I just can't believe anybody did that,' she recalled during a rare appearance on a TV chat show when she was well into her forties. 'When I was naughty my Indian *ayah* took me out and tied me to a tree with my leather belt. "The tigers will come and get you," she said, and I strained against the leather belt and I screamed. I was out there for five minutes and I was never in any real danger but I have never forgotten it.'

When Julie was four, Rosemary Christie became pregnant again and duly gave birth to a brother for Julie whom they named Clive. With a new baby in the household, Julie was sent to the Convent of Loreto up in the mountains but already her parents were planning a very proper British education for her in England when she was a little older.

Prudently Rosemary Christie brought her daughter to England in 1948. There was a growing sense of unease among the British colonials as they witnessed at first hand the changes India was undergoing as it struggled to free itself from British rule. The whole country had been thrown into turmoil earlier that year when Mahatma Gandhi – the lifelong apostle of peace and the man who more than any other had striven to secure India's freedom – had become the victim of an assassin's bullet. Killed by one of his own countrymen, Gandhi was on his way to a prayer meeting when a fanatical Hindu stepped from a crowd and shot him three times. Gandhi's assassination, in the very year India gained independence, was followed a month later by the withdrawal of the last British troops from India. By the summer of 1948 Lord Mountbatten had handed over to Chakravarti Rajagopalachari as governor-general.

For the Christies and other British families living in India it was a fresh period of uncertainty and apprehension. Leaving for England with her mother, Julie, who by now could speak a little Hindi, understood little of these momentous events. She had uncertainties of her own to face.

The initial transition from comfortable colonial life to winter on the Sussex coast, staying with relatives in Brighton, was not easy for an eight year old. All the little things that had made up the fabric of her life so far – the servants, the warm climate, being able to run around barefoot – were suddenly no longer there. Most worrying of all, as her mother prepared to return to India, Julie realized that she would have to cope without her parents and her *ayah,* the people she had relied on thus far in her young life.

Uprooted and unable to settle, Julie proved too much of a handful for her grandmother, and her mother advertised for an 'auntie' to look after her young daughter while she herself returned to her husband and the tea plantation. Rosemary eventually settled Julie near Bexhill with 'Auntie Elsie', who adored the child placed in her charge and, in her mother's absence, Julie in return came to look upon Aunt Elsie as 'absolutely wonderful'.

Over the next ten years Julie was to leapfrog from school to school mostly as a boarder at convent schools. For a while, she seemed to be acclimatizing well to life at a local convent school until one day she told her fellow pupils a risqué joke that resulted in her expulsion. Nearly thirty years afterwards the incident still rankled. 'It's pathetic, really,' she told

Michael Aspel. 'I was expelled for this joke: a man and a woman were travelling in a train and the woman gets up and says: "Excuse me, I have to go and powder my nose." So she left the carriage and came back after a short while and then the man gets up and he says: "Excuse me, but I have to go and powder my nose." And he left and when he came back she said: "Oh, sir, you've left your compact open and the lipstick's showing."'

The innuendo may have evoked sniggers from Julie's classmates, but it was intended for their ears only. Unfortunately, one of the pupils then went home and recounted the joke to her mother who immediately demanded to know who had told her such a thing. The accusing finger was pointed at Julie and the mother complained to the head that she was sending her daughter to school to be educated, not for her mind to be 'polluted' by girls like Julie Christie. Once she had been named as the perpetrator, Julie's fate was sealed. The school deemed it had no alternative but to ask her to leave.

Rosemary was upset by her daughter's expulsion but she also considered the whole episode and its consequences somewhat silly. Julie was, after all, then only thirteen and still very much a child. Nevertheless it meant a new school had to be found and Julie was sent to the Convent of Our Lady at Filsham Road, St Leonards-on-Sea, Hastings, which meant yet another school uniform, this time of navy blue pleated skirt, light blue shirt, tie and hat.

To this day Julie is haunted by the memory of the nuns making her school years miserable. 'You are quite ugly enough as it is, Julie Christie, without making faces,' a nun once told her when she was clowning around in front of a mirror. What a thing to say to an insecure girl, Julie later recalled.

At fifteen, she says, she was self-conscious to such an appalling degree that she couldn't operate at all and never went to parties because she was so painfully shy. Even up to the age of sixteen she was so nervous when she went out with a boy that she was apt to stutter when talking to them. On the rare occasions she did attend parties she was so reserved and reticent that she would imagine people pointing her out and saying, 'Who's she? Isn't she odd?'

In an attempt to conceal her shyness and excuse herself from accepting party invitations she would make up lies about a jealous foreign boyfriend who wouldn't let her go out. One day she was offering just such an excuse and blaming some imaginary jealous Continental beau when the girl asking Julie to her party said, 'Oh the boys will be so disappointed. I told them about this beautiful girl who will be coming.' A nun had called her ugly but now, here was someone telling Julie for the first time that she was beautiful. It was a sweet moment for Julie: 'Wow, I thought. Wow!'

But generally, any natural exuberance, originality and independence Julie displayed at the convent were squashed out of her. 'I was always scorned, mocked or punished by the authorities for extremist behaviour. After I'd been humiliated enough I turned introverted.'

The younger, extrovert Julie had at one point earned herself the nickname SO, short for show-off, but her youthful passion and freedom of self-expression were gradually crushed, to be replaced by deep feelings of inferiority. She is of the firm belief that the stifling restrictions imposed by the nuns made it hard for her to recover any sort of unselfconscious look-at-me attitude later on.

Julie regularly found herself hauled up in front of assembly for various misdemeanours, so much so that she developed a dread of hearing her name called out. She wasn't always blameless and among her girlish pranks was putting maggots in the head-mistress's cereal; but when she was accused of tempting local boys by tucking her dress in the waistband of her knickers one summer's day, the warning she was given was a gross over-reaction. Julie had hitched her dress up in all innocence because it was a sweltering hot day and the school authorities read far too much into it. Many years later she remembered the incident and the reprimand with incredulity. 'Can you imagine how damaging that was, to force young girls to be so self-conscious about sex? As a result I fantasized about boys all the time though, in fact, I found mixing with them difficult.'

For a short time she attended a day school in Bexhill where, she was pleased to find, life briefly became quite normal. With her red swagger coat, red shoes, little red pochette, shocking pink lipstick – and boys – it was a far cry from the rigidity of boarding school. With her 'O' levels looming, Julie was transferred to yet another new school in 1954, this time to a sedate girls' school in High Wycombe in Buckinghamshire. Again it was a difficult time for her and contemporaries noticed how vulnerable Julie appeared to be. 'She seemed to want someone to love her all the time,' said one. 'Her family were in India and I think she missed them a lot. Nobody ever took her out on half-days and she never had many letters.' Whenever the end of term approached, Julie's friends would all be in high spirits packing up their belongings and counting down the days until they went home for the holidays and returned to the bosom of their families. But while her parents remained abroad Julie had to spend the holidays at the school with sometimes just one other girl for company. 'I learned to get along without my parents, without anybody,' she said.

Every three years when Rosemary travelled from Assam to England, she would rent accommodation in the school holidays at Cuckfield and at rural Chiddingly, areas of Sussex around Bexhill, which by now Julie had come to know well. They were conveniently located for Julie's brother Clive too. He had joined her in England and was a pupil at Mowden preparatory school in Sussex before moving on to top public school Tonbridge not far over the county border in Kent.

One year Rosemary took Julie to see her first Shakespeare play, *Coriolanus,* starring Richard Burton at the Old Vic. Burton's performance made a deep impression upon Julie and she returned to school with a photograph of the actor on the back of which she wrote a warning to other girls. 'Please don't touch. Very, very private property. Very precious property.' She signed off her cautionary words with 'Bugs', another nickname she had acquired at school because, like the cartoon character Bugs Bunny, she never stopped talking.

Even as a tiny tot, according to Rosemary, Julie had been highly imaginative and had always insisted that she was going to be an actress when she grew up. 'She thought up rather grim things,' Rosemary noted, 'not sweet little stories about fairies and elves but things about poor little Victorian boys. She loves cats, not dogs.'

Julie's ambition took on new significance when she saw an actor from the local Bexhill repertory company strolling through the village one day learning his lines. One day, thought Julie, she too wanted to be strolling around learning her part in that way.

As she continued with her education, Julie's growing inferiority complex among her contemporaries led her to her believe that everyone was smarter and prettier than she was. She tried to gain some sort of kudos by recounting to fellow pupils wild stories of how she had dramatically saved people from pythons and tigers as a child in India. In reality she had never seen a single snake during her early years on the plantation. The only time she felt like a person was when she was on stage in a school play. 'Then I could hide behind the character I was playing. I suppose that was why I made up all those stories about snakes and things with me saving people from them.'

Julie's happiest moments, then, were when she was performing in school productions because, as well as raising her self-esteem, acting offered a refuge from the loneliness she so frequently felt. A defining moment came when she was cast as a cavalier: suitably attired in doublet, high boots and plumed hat, Julie was required to make a swashbuckling entrance, seat herself at a table, slam down a tankard of ale on the tabletop and deliver a loud and hearty greeting to those around her. She knew then that she would relish becoming an actress.

In the classroom Julie excelled at English and History and went on to apply herself conscientiously enough to obtain seven 'O' levels. But she struggled with French and gave a poor account of herself in the exam, due to an unfortunate misunderstanding on her part. Asked to write a story on the theme of 'Un jour dans l'espace', Julie interpreted it as 'A journey into space', perhaps momentarily thrown by the fact that *Journey into Space* was one of the most popular, much discussed radio programmes of the day. Unfortunately, the exam paper was asking pupils to write about a day out in the country. Julie failed French miserably.

Rosemary Christie was particularly disappointed at this deficiency and when she came back to England on one of her visits she saw an opportunity to give Julie a complete change from her life and from everything she had known and was accustomed to in England. She arranged for her daughter to go and stay with a family in France for a year. The best way for Julie to improve her French, Rosemary reasoned, was for her to live in France and speak French every day. It would also allow Julie to spread her wings a little.

Julie was entrusted to a large family who lived close to the Pyrenees at Tarbes near Pau in Gascony. A middle-aged couple with three sons and three daughters, the family enjoyed a lifestyle that was so unconventional as to be bordering on the truly eccentric. Relics of the decaying aristocracy, they were worldly, intellectual people who lived under the volatile aegis of the head of the household who was compiling a dictionary of the Basque language.

At first Julie was desperately unhappy in their large, rambling and somewhat neglected home, lodging with a boisterous family who she quickly discovered were prone to tantrums and vociferous displays of emotion. Shyly she looked on aghast and embarrassed as one or other member flew into a rage and shouted at another openly in front of her. Such openly volatile and erratic conduct was all so different from the restrained behaviour of the people she was used to.

Julie also physically felt distinctly uncomfortable in their home with its sombre velvet and brocade décor and its dark, frequently unlit, shadowy and shuttered ambience. Every morning Julie would wake up after a night of nervy anxiety, nursing a splitting headache and thinking she couldn't bear to spend another minute there. She would pass much of her day weeping, feeling lonely and deserted.

On tear-stained writing paper Julie wrote repeatedly to her mother pleading to be allowed to return to England. One letter begged: 'Please let me come home. Another week will kill me.' Rosemary was sad to read from Julie's letters how dispirited she appeared to be but she wrote back explaining that there would be many unpleasant things to be faced in life and that she should at least stick it out for three months. She strongly advised Julie to stay, assuring her cheerfully that she would not come to regret it.

There were several more days of misery for Julie to endure before the gloom began to lift when she encountered another English girl who had come to stay close by. Now she had someone with whom she could chat and have a giggle, go out for walks, and take days out to go mountain climbing. Suddenly her surroundings began to look very different and, buoyed by having found a friend, Julie began to warm to the French family who had tried to welcome her into their midst in their own unconventional way. 'I saw the mad family I was living with for what they really were. I grew up in a cold family and was an undemonstrative child. But I got used to kissing people, being more open, displaying my feelings more easily.'

Always a tactile race with a kiss on each cheek the norm for a greeting at any time of day, the French did not seem so alarming to Julie any more. She started going to dances and balls where her blossoming sex appeal coupled with her more relaxed demeanour inevitably caught the eye of the French boys. Most of the boys who were attracted to her and gave her their attention were in their early twenties. 'I had a lot of flirtations,' she confided when she got back to England, 'although nothing actually happened there. I wasn't seduced or anything in France. But I had left England a gauche, awkward young girl and returned a self-confident young woman. The person I was after I returned to England had no relation to the person I was before.'

Picking up her life back in England, Julie enrolled with Brighton Technical College to take her 'A' levels but, by her own admission, she was undisciplined and didn't knuckle down to work as much as she should have done. Her French sojourn had broadened her horizons and she was eager for new experiences beyond the strict confines of boarding school.

With a friend, Julie landed herself a holiday job in a Sussex hotel where the management worked her hard as chambermaid and washer-up. The hotel was close to a lunatic asylum and she found herself working alongside some of the asylum's more trusted members. Julie's immediate task was cleaning the rooms and making the beds, but at lunch-time she would be pressed into service in the kitchens, washing the dishes. After further chambermaid duties she was back at the kitchen sink for another stint of washing up. It was a long day.

Later on, she took another brief holiday job cleaning bottles for Schweppes and the aroma of decaying bitter lemon residues put her off the stuff for years afterwards. During term-time Brighton offered many distractions, not least the beach – and boys. Julie mixed with lots of other teenagers and students like herself, a beatnik crowd who spent many an hour in the seaside coffee bars listening to the latest Elvis Presley records on the juke-box. They were youngsters full of hope and optimism as they looked to their future. 'I wanted to go to university but I met a boy called Joel in Brighton, my first *real* boyfriend,' she recounted.

Joel was all for pushing Julie's acting ambitions. He could see the way other boys enviously eyed his girlfriend and he could imagine her up there on the cinema screen breaking hearts. Julie would entertain none of that heady nonsense. If she was going to become an actress she wanted to be a serious actress on the stage. When Julie revealed to her mother her ambition to act, Rosemary was inadvertently condescending. 'She thought of acting and movies as something like modelling. She'd say, "Oh you'll do well, you're pretty." ' But that was not really what Julie wanted to hear. What she desperately wanted was not to be thought of as frivolous.

Encouraged by Joel and their immediate circle of friends, Julie applied for a place at the Central School of Speech and Drama in London and also at the Bristol Old Vic, two highly respected training grounds for actors. Julie was delighted to be summoned for auditions with both and more than a little surprised but elated when both wrote to say they were prepared to offer her a place.

Both establishments had much to commend them but the Central School had the greater pull for Julie. It was at that time more prestigious and was more accessible from Sussex. Besides, the capital seemed to offer many more exciting opportunities than Bristol. Julie was living with her mother, now separated from her father, at Chiddingly, a charming little village in the country. But with a mile to walk to the nearest bus stop, the house was isolated, and Julie was ready to trade the tranquillity of village life for the bright lights of London. 'I hated the quiet of the country then,' she confessed. 'I never met any boys and those I did know didn't want to drive 100 miles every time they took me out on a date.'

The Central School of Speech and Drama was founded in 1906 by Elsie Fogerty, a small but determined woman. She went on to earn a formidable reputation among her drama students, who were either in awe or simply terrified of her, not least for her resolute insistence on the clearest of diction among her pupils. In 1956 the School moved from the Royal Albert Hall to its current location at the Embassy Theatre, Swiss Cottage, a fine late-Victorian playhouse which in 1899 housed the first set designed by the influential stage designer Edward Gordon Craig. It was here that Julie, brimming with enthusiasm, enrolled the following year for a three-year course.

Swiss Cottage was too far away for Julie to commute daily from Sussex but finding somewhere to live in London posed immediate problems. Because her father owned a tea plantation, Julie was considered ineligible for a grant. Despite her truthful insistence that she had precious little money, the Central School could not see how this was possible given her father's colonial assets. So, for the first term in London she spent an anxious time turning up at the addresses of fellow students or friends clutching a blow-up air mattress and begging floor space for the night. In return she would cook meals for her accommodating friends, 'my mates' as she liked to call them, rustling up recipes from a cookbook she had diligently compiled in her own handwriting.

Over the next few months Julie's nomadic life bedding down on her blow-up mattress in cupboards, attics, box-rooms or wherever she could find floor space, became a source of admiration and mild amusement among her mates. Even among students, it was not a lifestyle everyone envied, especially when one balmy late summer's night Julie's network of friendly floors failed her and she slept on her air-filled mattress in a park. From time to time she also incurred the wrath of landladies who discovered her unscheduled presence in the morning on premises which had been let to young men. They would look Julie up and down demanding explanations and tut-tutting, unable to comprehend that such an attractive girl could stay up all night with her friends innocently drinking coffee and listening to records.

Julie accepted her gypsy lifestyle – her 'air-mattress era' as she herself described it – cheerfully enough. 'I learned how to adapt to different environments. For six months, every night I had to search out a new place to sleep. That sort of thing builds self-reliance in a girl. All this shifting around when I was young going from school to school in India, England and France and being broke as a drama student has been a good thing for me. It has made me independent. I feel I can cope with almost anything that comes along. It has made me practical. I can cook – or live on bread, chips and spaghetti if I have to.'

At weekends Julie would head home to Sussex with bags of washing and return to London with a sack laden down with food, as much as she could carry. There would be hot meals available in the drama school canteen but while other students queued up, paid, and tucked in, Julie would delve into her sack and produce something to eat. By the end of the week as Julie's provisions ran low, she would be seen digging ever deeper into her sack and pulling out suspect chicken bones, or the most unappetizing slices of days-old roast beef and gnawing on them.

While her diet may have been poor and her erratic no-fixed-abode existence tiresome, she found the actual drama lessons thoroughly rewarding. She was introduced to and learned to love Bertolt Brecht, and the entire process of studying without the pressure of having to earn a living was proving enjoyable. She also found herself mixing with students from very different backgrounds. She had grown up conservatively and, until she started mixing with the Brighton beatniks and the Central School students, she found going out with anyone with any sort of an accent was intolerable. But that snobbishness inherited from the convents and genteel Sussex country circles soon disappeared when she arrived in London.

Even at drama school, Julie's blossoming good looks were starting to determine what direction her early acting career was to take. One of her teachers, whom she regarded as rather good in a forceful sort of way, suddenly turned on her in class one day after she had said something which annoyed him and snapped: 'Well, you'll be all right. You'll go into films anyway. You've got that sort of face.'

Julie was shocked. 'I remember bursting into tears and rushing out in front of the whole class. I was crying and crying and then a friend said, "I don't know what you're crying about. I'd be jolly pleased if someone came up to me and said that about me." ' The aspirations of all the drama students then were totally focused on the theatre but Julie had to admit that it did put the teacher's remark in perspective.

Barry Justice, a Central School contemporary, said Julie's potential as a film actress was quite clear to almost everyone at this stage: 'She was immensely intelligent, hopelessly untidy, deliriously scatty and possibly one of the most generous people I have ever known. She was quite devastatingly beautiful. We all just accepted the fact that she would be a film star one day.' But at the Central School the world of films was then regarded by the more intense students as something infra-dig. It was the theatre that they and Julie aspired to.

In 1960 Julie and the other third-year students mounted, as was the custom, a production at the Embassy Theatre. This performance was partly intended as a showcase for budding talent to which many influential producers, directors and agents were invited by the school in the hope that their leavers would quickly find work. Their production of *The Diary of Anne Frank* – the wartime story of a Dutch Jewish family who concealed themselves in an attic for two years before being discovered by the Nazis – featured Julie wearing a dark wig in the lead role of Anne, the teenager who recorded the Frank family's ordeal in the pages of her diary.

In the audience, casting interested eyes over the production, were John Schlesinger, who was then making a documentary about the Central School for the BBC, and TV director Michael Hayes, both of whom were later to become hugely instrumental in the development of Julie Christie's career as an actress. Hayes at the time was planning a new science fiction series for the BBC, *A For Andromeda,* and he had made it known in television and acting circles that he was on the look-out for a stunning young actress, a girl who was quite out of the ordinary, to play a vital role in his series. Tipped off by an agent about 'an English Brigitte Bardot' at Central School, Hayes was persuaded to take a look at her in the final-year production.

Hayes liked what he saw and arranged a meeting with Julie at which he very quickly decided she was perfect for the key role of a laboratory assistant, a striking brunette who is killed and by some molecular reconstruction recycled as a blonde android via a menacing computer controlled from outer space. *A For Andromeda* was to be a seven-part series which guaranteed Julie Christie eleven weeks' work, four on location in Pembrokeshire and the remainder in a London studio.

For a young hopeful who was just leaving drama school *A For Andromeda* was a heaven-sent opportunity that drew congratulations from her mates and no little envy from her fellow students. But Julie appeared to take it all in her stride, unaware of its significance and her good fortune. She also reckoned that landing the role had little to do with any acting ability she might have. 'I don't think they wanted an actress,' she said self-deprecatingly. 'They wanted somebody who was blonde and looked stupid. I was perfect.'

*A For Andromeda* was well received when it was screened by the BBC in the winter of 1961 and the first of many fan letters for Julie Christie began arriving at Television Centre.

Julie's entry into television and the accompanying exposure prompted other offers of TV work including a J. B. Priestley play, *Dangerous Corner,* essentially a four-hander with Julie in one of the main roles. But she was still anxious to pursue stage work. That was what she had been trained for, she kept telling herself, and when an offer came from Frinton-on-Sea repertory company in Essex she grabbed it straight away. The Frinton foray offered Julie a new range of roles from serious drama to light revue but she found some of the challenges beyond her.

A play called *Live Like Pigs* provided her with one of her most embarrassing moments. It consisted of dozens of short scenes and required intense application and clear thinking from the cast to ensure that their exits and entrances were timed correctly. Prone to wavering concentration, which was already preventing her from passing her driving test despite many lessons, Julie managed to get herself into a fearful muddle. 'Suddenly the house lights began to fade and there I was in the middle of a scene I should not have been in. I just curled up on the floor and pretended to be a rug. The actress in that scene, who was supposed to be seducing the man next door, nearly died of shock.'

If all was not going entirely smoothly on stage for Julie Christie, she was still attracting the attention of TV producers and, by a natural progression, film producers too were wondering whether she might have what it takes to be a movie star. She was making better progress than many of her Central School contemporaries with whom she desperately tried to keep in touch as their working lives threw them all in different directions.

On the round of auditions, Julie's name was put forward for a film called *A Kind of Loving,* which was to be produced by Jo Janni and directed by John Schlesinger. But the director had been unimpressed by her Anne Frank performance and Janni felt there was no role for Julie in their film.

There was more disappointment awaiting her when she was interviewed for a major new big-budget movie called *Dr No,* to be based on Ian Fleming's best-seller about the womanizing

British secret agent James Bond. Sean Connery had already been cast in the role that was to make him a huge star all over the world, and the Bond film producers Cubby Broccoli and Harry Saltzman were searching for an exciting young actress to play Bond's love interest, the provocatively named Honeychile Ryder. They knew exactly the kind of girl they were looking for and the impact they wanted her to make on screen.

If there had been one scene in Fleming's book that had convinced the two men that *Dr No* was perfect for the screen, it was the one where Bond meets the girl for the first time. Bond is taking a nap on Crab Key beach in Jamaica when he is woken a woman's voice singing a Jamaican love-ballad; getting to his feet he sees a beautiful woman wearing only a leather belt with a hunting knife in a leather sheath. She is striding out of the surf like Aphrodite and stands in front of him on the shimmering sand, lissom, bronzed and glistening. In his book Fleming likened her to 'Botticelli's Venus seen from behind'.

Julie was just one of dozens of hopefuls up for consideration for the role of Honey after Cubby Broccoli had seen her on television, and she read several times for director Terence Young who thought she was very striking. He was impressed enough with Julie to arrange for her to be introduced to Broccoli at his London offices in South Audley Street, Mayfair. But Julie arrived for her meeting with the powerful producer looking dishevelled and wearing jeans. Saltzman liked her but to Broccoli the girl in front of him did not seem anything like the voluptuous heroine he envisaged would sizzle on to the screen in the crucial beach scene. The actress who played Honey would spend much of the film in a skimpy bikini and a wet shirt and Julie did not have what Broccoli was looking for. As he succinctly put it to Saltzman later that day, 'She's great but she's no good for us. No tits.'

Ursula Andress, an unknown Swiss beauty, was eventually chosen for the role of Honey after Broccoli spotted a photograph of her in clichéd starlet pose wearing a man's T-shirt – and soaked to the skin. Ursula's spectacular entrance in *Dr No* was eventually to set the standard for the beauties who would decorate the Bond films to follow. From her role as Honeychile Ryder, Ursula was able to build a film career based almost exclusively on glamour. Denied the chance to be James Bond's first fantasy girl, Julie Christie was to build a very different career.

# 2

# Reluctant Starlet

It drove me mad, all that doing your hair up and wearing make-up and posh clothes, no matter what was happening, with people keeping you looking like a china doll. I couldn't have borne that, if that was what film-making had to be.

Julie Christie

In 1962 Julie was still living largely hand-to-mouth clutching her trusty air-mattress until she finally found some sort of permanence by moving into a flat in Earls Court which she rented with four mates and where she was given the attic room. Her friends were mostly impecunious artists and, like her, usually cat-lovers. She was happy to cook for her flat-mates and they in turn gave her lifts and accompanied her to the cinema. An avid reader of film reviews, Julie was especially interested in innovative cinema and would track down the latest French films, even in the most out-of-the-way cinemas.

In 1962 Julie was still living largely hand-to-mouth clutching her trusty air-mattress until she finally found some sort of permanence by moving into a flat in Earls Court which she rented with four mates and where she was given the attic room. Her friends were mostly impecunious artists and, like her, usually cat-lovers. She was happy to cook for her flat-mates and they in turn gave her lifts and accompanied her to the cinema. An avid reader of film reviews, Julie was especially interested in innovative cinema and would track down the latest French films, even in the most out-of-the-way cinemas.

Her own screen debut, however, was as far from the French 'new wave' as it was from the Bond films. In the spring of 1962 Julie was sent to Beaconsfield Studios to be interviewed by film producers Julian Wintle and Leslie Parkyn who were planning a series of light comedy movies. Julie gave a good account of herself in the interviews and in her screen tests but there was no wholehearted commitment to sign her up until, astonishingly, there had been much debate about Julie's bottom lip. Perversely, the movie men were concerned that it was too big or too obvious and in close-up it might make her look sulky. Julie survived such detailed scrutiny. The movie executives may not have reached agreement over the merits of her bottom lip, but they were all agreed that Julie was certainly sexy, and different. The upshot was the offer of a contract with Independent Artists for three movies, which included the promise of promoting Julie Christie as a new star.

The ink was barely dry on Julie's contract with Independent Artists when she was plunged straight into her first film, *Crooks Anonymous.* At the helm was director Ken Annakin who was turning his hand to comedy again after scoring a resounding success two years earlier with his exciting adventure movie *Swiss Family Robinson,* much of which he had shot in Tobago. *Crooks Anonymous* was very different: a comic, low-budget yarn to be shot at Beaconsfield about a group of ex-convicts who set out to reform and watch over their less fortunate brothers and return them to the straight and narrow. Wilfred Hyde White played the head of this unlikely welfare team, aided and abetted by a competent British cast including Stanley Baxter, Michael Medwin and Pauline Jameson. The main object of the team's attentions was safe-breaker and jewel thief, Captain 'Dandy' Forsdyke, played by Leslie Phillips.

Julie was cast as Babette La Verne, a striptease dancer and Forsdyke's despairing girlfriend who refuses to consider marrying a man who won't even try to go straight. Forsdyke is finally persuaded to take the cure from the society of ex-convicts and is subjected to a series of tests. After several twists in the plot, he eventually emerges to marry Babette. Julie made a ravishing bride when the wedding ceremony was filmed at the old church behind the market square in High Wycombe, Bucks, not far from where she had been a nervous, lonely schoolgirl some five years before. Quite a crowd gathered to watch the filming which went ahead in a near gale, showering the onlookers with confetti.

At the end of shooting *Crooks Anonymous* Ken Annakin, beating the drum for his film and his new star, was moved to say, 'In my many years in films I've never before met a complete newcomer who has shown such talent. Here is a girl who has done no more than one television serial since leaving the Central School of Speech and Drama. She arrived for a test and I knew that here we had someone out of the ordinary. In fact, it was on the strength of the test alone that she was considered for star billing and awarded an option for two further pictures with Independent Artists at Beaconsfield. Julie is intelligent, talented and a bit of a rebel. She knows what she wants and will very probably get it. She has two more films to make for us, I'm happy to say, and it will be damn good experience.'

Despite this glowing accolade from the director of her first film, Julie was under no illusions. 'When I emerged from drama school I think I was considered especially good looking, and people were always on the look-out for the good-looking girls just as they are with models today.' And she was far from sure that the next two films would be 'damn good experience'. Julie found Ken Annakin to be a kind man, but she says they were on totally different wavelengths. 'I was crazy on French film and, if I was to be in a film, I wanted it to be a Nouvelle Vague film. Instead, there I was in a bikini, my hair piled up on top of my head and wearing a hundred pounds of lipstick.'

The notices for *Crooks Anonymous* were predictably less than glowing but Leonard Mosley in the *Daily Express* in August 1962 did have a good word for

Julie. He said it used to be that the perpetual moan from film producers was that young British actresses of talent simply didn't exist. 'I am pleased to announce,' he wrote, 'things are improving since this week I have had an advance preview of a new girl with looks, poise, personality and potential. Her name is Julie Christie and, at 21, she is a girl to watch.'

Producers Wintle and Parkyn, patiently trying to build Julie up as a bright new young star oozing with sex appeal, now cast her in a follow-up romp, *The Fast Lady,* in which the lady of the title was a vintage Bentley motorcar and Stanley Baxter and Leslie Phillips were again the main stars. The story centred on Murdoch Troon, a dogmatic Scot played by Baxter, who is the honorary secretary of a cycling club. On one run he decides to exert his right of the road when challenged by a large car driven by an impatient tycoon, Charles Chingford, and finishes up in a ditch. Murdoch chases Chingford, played by James Robertson Justice, to his house where he falls head over heels for Chingford's daughter, pretty car-mad Claire played by Julie. Egged on by his fellow lodger, racey car salesman Freddie Fox (Leslie Phillips), Murdoch sacrifices all his worldly wealth to buy the Fast Lady, a vintage Bentley, in order to impress Claire. The plot now called for Claire to have developed a great liking for Murdoch but Chingford will not agree to his daughter going out with him in the Fast Lady until he has tested Murdoch's driving ability. Unhappily for Murdoch in the middle of his test he gets caught up in a bank-robbery chase, but still manages to get around in the Fast Lady – with Claire as his driver.

It most certainly wasn't Shakespeare, but instead of treating *Crooks Anonymous* and *The Fast Lady* as a valuable learning experience, Julie came to regard them almost with disdain. 'I didn't find them instructive at all,' she confesses. 'I was far too snobby for that! I thought I was much too good for them, you know, and didn't talk to anybody. I'd go roaring away from the studio on a motorbike every evening, thinking I was just the last word in unconventionality! I was in that sort of state and I wasn't learning anything from anybody. It was intellectual snobbism. I was very young and young people are apt to be snobs of one kind or another.

'I found myself in what I despised. I despised it in theory and I didn't know I despised it until I found myself in it. It was a blow to my pride and I wasn't learning anything. I who was one of the biggest intellectual snobs suddenly found myself in this.'

What Julie loathed most of all was being made up and dressed up for glamorous publicity pictures. Her hair was teased into different coquettish styles for photo-shoots where she would be asked to pose in anything from a baby-doll nightie to a tight sweater, holding a hula-hoop, a fashion fad of the day, or in a white pill-box hat and matching just-decent mini-dress and ankle-high white boots underneath a Christmas tree. Julie resented the emphasis that was continually placed on her sexuality.

'It drove me mad,' she said, 'all that doing your hair up and wearing make-up and posh clothes, no matter what was happening, with people keeping you looking like a china doll. I couldn't have borne that, if that was what film-making had to be.'

Julie made no secret of her feelings or her beliefs. She hit the headlines when she chained herself with handcuffs to actor friend Cy Grant at a service to commemorate Human Rights Day at the Church of St Martin-in-the-Fields in Trafalgar Square. She wasn't going to be subjected to a Hollywood-style grooming for stardom in the established film studio method. She would arrive at Beaconsfield Studios in the most unstarry fashion on the back of a mate's motorcycle, which irritated those who expected her to act like a celebrity. She was also admonished for daring to turn up at a press showing of the film wearing a sombre grey suit. Julie thought it was fabulous, mainly because it had been copied from a French design. 'But they said it was all wrong, that I should wear black. I told them I'd give up films first. I like money and what it can buy – clothes mostly. But I don't want to be part of any organization that I cannot control.' And there was no doubting she meant it.

*The Fast Lady,* an attempt to duplicate the 1953 success of another British movie, *Genevieve,* about a vintage car entered in the London to Brighton rally, was released in February 1963 and did reasonable business in spite of mainly unflattering reviews. The film emerged as a reasonably brisk situation comedy in which the cast of experienced farceurs did their best to exploit comic moments ranging from the pratfall variety to *double entendres. The Times* decided that the movie encapsulated elements of British humour down the years but the *Observer* declared: 'This is British comedy at its conventional and vintage motorcar worst.' And *London Evening News* film critic Felix Barker agreed: 'This hits a new low in the flourishing weed garden of British Rot.' In general Julie was rarely mentioned in the notices, although Leonard Mosley told his *Daily Express* readers: 'The girl in the story is, by the way, a nuzzlesome newcomer named Julie Christie.'

After the filming of *The Fast Lady* the future looked bleak for Julie Christie and she began to wonder what was wrong with her, old feelings of inferiority springing up again. 'I was considered just another horrible little starlet on the make. It was awful.'

At this low point of self-doubt in her professional life, Julie's personal life was about to be brightened by one of Britain's hottest young stars.

By today's standards, a glossy magazine cover showing a pretty girl in an open blue denim shirt holding a Sten gun might be considered nothing more than mildly provocative. But back in 1962 when a stylish new magazine called *Town* featured Julie Christie on the front cover in just such a brazenly decorative pose, it generated heated controversy about the effect such images might have on public morals.

It should be remembered that at this time Australia's yodelling export Frank Ifield was top of the pop charts, the Beatles had yet to release their first hit 'Love Me Do' and the capital was some years away from becoming known as 'Swinging London'. So, *Town*, as it expected and probably hoped, received a number of complaints from its readers about the blonde's indecorous image. But that full-colour photograph of Julie taken by the then up-and-coming photographer Terence Donovan was destined to have a remarkable and unforeseen impact on both Julie's personal and professional life.

As well as objections from some of its readers, Julie's photograph inevitably attracted much male admiration, not least, unbeknown to Julie, from a rising young actor by the name of Terence Stamp. The moment he saw *Town'* s magazine cover, Stamp was so enamoured of the blonde vision staring from the glossy cover that he decided he simply had to meet her. Meeting pretty girls was not exactly a problem at that time for Stamp. The son of an East London merchant seaman, Stamp was twenty-three, the same age as Julie, tall, slim, with a perfect masculine face and extraordinary, penetrating, almost translucent blue eyes, all of which combined later to earn him, at the height of the fame that was to come his way, the dubious title of 'the world's most beautiful man'. Moreover, quite apart from his physical presence, Stamp possessed a rough Cockney charm which the opposite sex mostly found magnetic especially since his rapid rise to fame in the film *Billy Budd.*

Peter Ustinov had made an instant star of Stamp by choosing him for the title role in his movie based on Herman Melville's allegorical tale of the clash between an exceptionally good-hearted foretopman and an inhumanly sadistic master-at-arms aboard a British fighting vessel in 1797. As the angel-faced Budd, Stamp played the embodiment of good to co-star Robert Ryan's embodiment of evil as Claggart, earning not only critical praise but also a romantic and heroic image since the film hinged on the issue of moral justice that arises when Budd is condemned to hang for killing Claggart though recognized even by those who sit in judgement upon him as being morally innocent.

The film opened to critical acclaim in London and the reception in New York was no less cordial. Stamp was hailed as an exciting new discovery on both sides of the Atlantic and won an Oscar nomination for Best Supporting Actor. One of the first of a new breed who set out to change the image of the young actor, he was working class, ambitious, irreverent and funny. By the time Julie Christie appeared as *Town'*s cover girl he was enjoying his success by living in some considerable style in a London flat he shared with his dear friend Michael Caine, another actor destined for great things, who had gone off to South Africa for three months to appear in *Zulu* with Stanley Baker.

On Caine's return to London after shooting *Zulu,* he discovered Stamp rhapsodizing about a stunningly beautiful girl he had seen on a magazine cover and desperate to find out who she was. Caine took one look at Julie's picture and said, 'I know her.' Stamp refused to believe him at first although he fervently wanted to. But Caine insisted that he really had met her and as the realization dawned that Caine was not pulling his leg Stamp eagerly pressed his friend to tell him more.

Caine explained that he had indeed met Stamp's fantasy girl while they were rehearsing different plays at the BBC. He recounted how he had spotted this very beautiful blonde sitting on her own at a corner table in the BBC canteen while he was queuing up at the buffet counter. He was intrigued that she was sitting alone at a table for ten in what was otherwise a full canteen where spare chairs were at a premium. 'She was stunning,' Caine recalled, 'so stunning that she had actually frightened everybody off.' Never one to be scared of a pretty girl, Caine picked up his tray and made straight for her table. When she looked up on his approach, he fixed her with a direct gaze and enquired in a deadpan voice whether the nine empty chairs at the table were taken. He was greeted, he remembers, with a toe-curling smile and an invitation to sit himself down.

With Stamp absorbing every detail, Caine told how he had learned over lunch that she was not long out of drama school and was working on her very first television show, a science fiction series called *A For Andromeda,* in which she played a mysterious, heavenly body from outer space. The casting was absolutely perfect, Caine had thought to himself, and when the girl had played down the importance of her role by stressing that she had no dialogue, Caine thought – but chose not to say so – that, in her case, words were not necessary since her face and figure spoke volumes in every known language. He took an instant liking to this beautiful young woman but soon realized that the chances of his becoming romantically involved with her were slight and, although he saw her around on several subsequent occasions, they were nothing more than vague friends.

As Caine spun out the story, Stamp became more and more enthralled and finally begged Caine to tell him her name. 'Julie Christie,' said Caine, which unsurprisingly meant nothing to Stamp. But the fact that his best friend knew her name and had actually met her on a few occasions was enough for him to insist that Caine engineer a date for him. Caine protested that it wasn't that simple. 'I didn't know her well enough to ring her up and say come round and be ravished by my best friend,' he says. 'But I did bring about the meeting and subsequently a massive romance between the two of them.'

While Caine promised to think of some way of arranging a date for his friend, Stamp wasted no time trying to track Julie down himself. He telephoned *Town* magazine to see if they could put him in contact with her but without success. Stamp was further frustrated by the fact that he did not at that time know Terence Donovan, the photographer who had taken the striking picture of Julie, so that route was also balked. But Stamp was not in the mood to give up the chase of the young woman who had so beguiled him from the cover of a glossy magazine. When word reached him that Julie had been spotted at a new club called the Discotheque in Wardour Street, he persuaded Caine and another actor friend, Doug Sheldon, to accompany him to the Discotheque that very night in the hope that Julie might turn up there again.

Stamp was in for more disappointment once he and his friends had descended into the club's dimly lit Wardour Street basement. Peering through the semi-darkness, he remembers, he saw model Christine Keeler but no one who resembled Julie Christie among the girls gyrating on the cramped dance floor. There was no sign of her either among the girls sitting out on the old brass bedsteads with bare mattresses which served as the Discotheque's seating area. Forlornly Stamp headed for home, wondering if he was ever going to meet this dream girl.

He had almost abandoned the idea when Caine invited the actor and writer Derek Marlow round for a drink at their apartment. During the evening the conversation inevitably progressed to the current London showbusiness scene and when Marlow mentioned an actress called Julie, Caine caught Stamp's eye and silently signalled that Marlow was talking about Julie Christie. Whenever Julie's name was mentioned after that, Stamp found Caine motioning to him out of Marlow's eyeline and it gradually became clear to him that Marlow had to be talking about Julie Christie. The evening ended full of promise for Stamp with Marlow promising to introduce him to Julie.

Marlow was as good as his word. He went away and subsequently mentioned to Julie that Terence Stamp was keen to meet her. Julie was intrigued but needed some persuading. She had seen *Billy Budd* and had been impressed by Stamp's performance in the film and, she told herself, he was undeniably good looking. But she was nervous as usual of meeting anyone new. Marlow impressed upon her that if she agreed to meet Stamp for a meal then he would go along as well to help break the ice. Finally, after several false starts, a date for this momentous meeting was eventually arranged. It was agreed that Marlow would bring Julie to have dinner with Stamp at the Seven Stars restaurant in Coventry Street in London's West End. It would be dinner for the three of them.

For Stamp, the Seven Stars held the advantage of being almost on home ground. It was a restaurant he was familiar with since he had eaten there on many occasions once he had left drama school and was able to afford it. Stamp knew he would feel at ease in its familiar surroundings. He arrived at the restaurant well before the appointed hour and settled himself at a table in a horseshoe-shaped booth from where he could have a commanding view of the restaurant and a clear sight of the door so he could observe Julie's arrival.

Julie was a bundle of nerves before the date as her familiar shyness took hold. A part of her was flattered that a rising star with Stamp's striking good looks should want to meet her but she also told herself that she would not be bothered if nothing came of it. It was the latter view that eventually made Julie decide to treat the date as nothing special and she dressed accordingly.

When Marlow ushered Julie through the door of the Seven Stars, Stamp immediately noticed that she was hardly attired to knock him dead. Her simple clothes were in stark contrast to Stamp's carefully chosen trendy jacket, shirt and trousers and the gold Rolex watch, given to him by film producer James Woolf, which he had slipped on hoping to impress Julie. Now he was acutely aware that compared with Julie he had over-dressed for the occasion.

Stamp's first impression of the glossy magazine cover girl he had dreamed about as she seated herself at his table without so much as a word was that Julie Christie looked fierce. In her state of anxiety Julie kept her head down, gazing at the white tablecloth, only infrequently lifting her eyes to meet Stamp's. When she did manage to do so, Stamp noticed that they glittered with defiance which he was not to know was down to sheer nerves on Julie's part. While Julie studied the menu, lit up and tensely tapped her cigarette on the ashtray in between puffs, Stamp tried to inject some warmth into their meeting with small talk. At that stage all Stamp knew about her was that she had studied for three years at the Central School had appeared in the TV series *A For Andromeda* and had worked for a while as casual labour at the Post Office.

When the meal arrived Julie toyed with her food, ate little and said even less. In the more comfortable moments when Julie unfroze enough to engage in a little conversation, she and Stamp talked of what each would do when their boat came in. Ever reluctant to blow her own trumpet, Julie played down her acting ambitions but said the only luxury she would indulge in if she was ever lucky enough to earn decent money as an actress would be to go out and buy herself a rocking chair. By the time he called for the bill Stamp was beginning to think the evening was all a bit of a disaster.

Leaving the Seven Stars, Julie, Stamp and Derek Marlow stepped out into the night and threaded their way through the bustling crowds towards Piccadilly Circus. At the steps leading down to the Tube the trio paused to say their goodbyes and, under the statue of Eros, Stamp asked Julie for her telephone number. She willingly gave it but when Stamp said that he had nothing to write it down with and that he would simply trust his memory, Julie was sceptical. She imagined this was simply his way of hinting that he was not interested in her and that he would conveniently be able to forget it. It was with this thought that Julie, with Derek Marlow escorting her, headed for home.

Not wishing to appear too keen, Terence Stamp allowed several days to elapse before Julie Christie received a call from him asking her out to lunch. She was genuinely surprised to hear from him, fully expecting that he would have forgotten her number anyway. She was pleased he had called and she told Stamp she would be delighted to have lunch with him. He suggested they meet at the Casserole, a stylish new eating establishment which had just opened in the King's Road, Chelsea, and when Julie turned up at the restaurant she was relieved that Stamp was not as sharply dressed as he had been for their first date. This time she felt more at ease and a pleasant lunch was in prospect.

Half-way through the meal Julie was astonished and thoroughly puzzled when a man in what looked like a cricket umpire's white coat suddenly entered the restaurant and politely enquired via a waiter if there was a Miss Christie in the house. He explained that he had a large package for her waiting outside.

Julie was soon located by the waiter and the delivery man but she protested that there must have been some mistake. She said she was simply dining at the Casserole and certainly wasn't expecting any sort of a delivery. Becoming flustered and, desperate as ever not to draw any attention to herself, particularly in a crowded restaurant, Julie accepted Stamp's suggestion that he accompany her outside to sort out the confusion. There on the pavement Julie saw a large package immaculately wrapped in brown paper which the delivery man again insisted was for a Miss Christie. Julie was more perplexed than ever when the delivery man said the package had been ordered from Harrods.

Julie had no idea what it could be or why it had been delivered for her until Stamp stepped up to the package and gave it a gentle nudge whereupon it proceeded to oscillate gently to and fro. 'Oh you!' she said, with a grateful smile. It was the start of a seesaw romance.

Physically Terence Stamp and Julie Christie could hardly have made a more striking couple, Julie's fresh-faced blonde sex appeal contrasting sharply with Stamp's virile, dark good looks and hypnotic blue eyes. But their worlds at that time were very different. Although the same age as Stamp, Julie was all too aware that while she was still only just starting to make her way as an actress, her new boyfriend and his flat-mate Michael Caine were already names to be reckoned with in movie circles. Following on from his success in *Billy Budd,* Stamp was embarking on another major movie, *Term of Trial,* playing a class-room Casanova, with Laurence Olivier, no less, as a middle-aged schoolteacher who is compromised on a trip to Paris by a fifteen-year-old pupil played by Sarah Miles. Caine's struggle for recognition was about to end with the imminent realease of *Zulu.* 'It was painful,' said Julie of her contrasting fortunes, 'because

Michael and Terry were just hitting it and I wasn't. I was earning my own living, but only just. I had no confidence at all.'

The disparity between Julie's spartan lifestyle and that of the two actors also hit home with her the first time Stamp took her back to the apartment he rented with Caine spread over three storeys above a hairdresser's salon at No.5 Ebury Street in Victoria. They even had the Queen as their near neighbour, the two men joked. Caine was quartered on the top floor and Stamp had the second floor while the third was communal. Compared with the portable air-mattress existence Julie had known, Stamp's home was the veritable height of luxury, all plush red velvet with its big double beds, ornate trappings and tassels, pink ceilings, oval mirrors, cushions scattered around the thick oriental carpet, and white wine stacked up in the larder. The comfort appealed to Julie although it quickly became clear to Stamp that she did not aspire to any such grandeur for herself. What she did relish, however, was that Stamp and Caine shared a good cook whose speciality was steak and kidney pudding and Julie's diet improved considerably once she had made their acquaintance. 'What heaven it was to go down there and eat this wonderful steak and kidney pudding,' she said.

As they got to know each other and became lovers, Stamp was concerned at Julie's lack of self-confidence and the way she viewed her prospects as an actress with something akin to despair. He was amazed, too, at how frugally she lived, although he fully appreciated that life as a struggling actress was no picnic. 'When I first met her she was about as depressed as you can get without opening your wrists,' he recalled. 'About her only possession was an old air-bed which she carried everywhere hoping to find a mate with some spare floor space where she could kip down for the night.

'She'd been out of work for so long she was about to chuck it in and get a job in the Post Office. She said it was either that or starving to death and she meant it. I told her to starve to death but stay in the business. You've got to be around when the phone rings.'

If Julie often felt out of place in the sumptuous surroundings of her new boyfriend's flat, Stamp for his part felt similarly uncomfortable when Julie took him back to her tiny abode in Fulham for the first time. He couldn't believe how cramped it was, how menial and Bohemian her surroundings, nor the way that the broken window offered an eagerly accepted open invitation to stray cats to come and go as they pleased. Julie seemed to mind not at all, rather she was delighted. Stamp was no stranger to impecunious student flat-sharing but he recalls that Julie's lifestyle at that time was a forerunner of the hippie communes and contrasted sharply with the lifestyle he was then aspiring to.

None the less he found Ruby Crystal, as he liked to call her, delightful and for a while Julie moved in with Stamp and he introduced her to a different side of London life which she had never seen before. There were nights out at the Ad Lib, the trendiest disco in town – situated in a penthouse behind the Empire cinema in Leicester Square with huge windows and a spectacular view of the West End – where Julie would find herself on the dance floor doing the shake and rubbing shoulders with the Beatles or the Rolling Stones, who were just starting their meteoric rise. It was a microcosm of a vibrantly youthful new London, a reflection of its relaxed atmosphere, its cultural vitality and sexual revolution.

There were leisurely lunches at Alvaro's on the King's Road, and dinners at trendy eateries like the Pickwick in Great Newport Street, the first of the London club-cum-restaurants to become the in place for the famous in the sixties. Other haunts included the Arts Theatre Club, also in Great Newport Street, but much more up Julie's street was the Studio Club off Swallow Street where artists mingled with fringe actors.

A serious examination of Julie's willingness to step up into Stamp's newly acquired celebrity lifestyle came when Stamp was invited to a London film première. Naturally he asked Julie to accompany him but she had never been to one before and her initial reaction was one of terror. It was to be a grand, star-studded, black-tie affair followed by a champagne dinner at the prestigious Savoy Hotel and Julie was none too sure she wanted to go. She knew that being the girl on

Stamp's arm she would inevitably be the focus of some attention and besides, she told Stamp, she did not have a coat to wear.

One week before the event Julie was still dithering over whether to go to the première or not and Stamp decided he would help make up her mind by offering to buy her a coat. He told her she would look lovely in a fur coat and generously gave her an open signed cheque to pay for one. On the night of the première Stamp was adjusting his bow tie when Julie arrived at his Ebury Street home looking dazzling in a fur coat. Stamp told her how beautiful she looked then asked where she had got it. 'In the Portobello Road. It was a fiver. Was that all right?' she replied nervously.

Even though she could now cloak her nerves in a fur coat, Julie was still in a state of agitation about being involved in such a glittering affair as a movie première. 'I was terrified that because I was with a big star I'd be looked at and have to talk.' she said. 'But you could buy Valium or some calming sedative sort of thing across the counter in those days so I bought some and took about a hundred.

'The première was all right, then we went to the party and I was feeling fine. But I started to drink champagne and it ended up with me collapsing. Me, who didn't want anybody to look at her, who didn't want to attract any attention. Me, collapsing in the midst of all these bright, sparkling people in the middle of the floor.'

Fortunately for Julie, Sarah Miles, another rising young actress, rescued her and whisked her off to the ladies to help her recover. Stamp's final recollection of the evening was of Sarah Miles berating him for not looking after Julie.

Julie's affair with Stamp was never destined to last. He was understandably ambitious and his filming commitments were taking a toll on the time they spent together. In hindsight he said he believed Julie didn't like him very much and that she found him a bit bossy. When some years later they met up after not having seen each other for a while, Stamp says Julie seemed astonished when she asked him how he was and he replied that he wasn't well because he had an ulcer. 'My god, you're normal,' was Julie's reaction. Stamp concluded: 'The fact that I had an ulcer meant I ticked over like anybody else. She hadn't really been aware of it before. She thought I was a robot.'

The end of their affair effectively came when Julie was unexpectedly signed up for a role in a new British film called *Billy Liar* alongside Tom Courtenay. Location filming in Bradford was to take Julie up north and Stamp turned up at King's Cross railway station to watch her film a night scene for *Billy Liar* before their enforced parting. Stamp remembers Julie looking so cold and forlorn that he wrapped her in his sheepskin coat to keep her warm and told her to take it with her when she travelled north.

*Billy Liar* was to change Julie Christie's life for ever and when Terence Stamp received a letter from Julie indicating that he was not going to be the great love of her life, he knew the film had indirectly altered his path too. Charitably Stamp noted in his book *Double Feature* that their parting was his loss because she was one of the most lovable creatures he had ever met. 'She would have made a steadfast friend,' he said. The love may have died but Julie's and Stamp's paths were to cross again when they co-starred in the film *Far from the Madding Crowd.*

# 3

# Billy Liar

Who can forget the famous entrance in *Billy Liar?* Before she had spoken a single word, fame and fortune were hers if she wanted them. She walked and walked along a soot-shabby street in a northern industrial town, turning it, by her mere presence, into a place in the sun.

Frederic Raphael

The director who rescued Julie Christie from the light comedy glamour-girl roles with which she was rapidly becoming associated was the man who had overlooked her for *A Kind of Loving,* John Schlesinger.

The eldest of five children born to a paediatrician, Schlesinger grew up in a Queen Anne house in Inkpen, Berkshire, was educated at Uppingham public school and did National Service with the Royal Engineers before starting out as an actor on leaving Balliol College, Oxford. Schlesinger then began making amateur 16mm films but, after the BBC had rejected him for their directors' course, he was subsequently taken on by the Corporation's current affairs department. There Schlesinger began his career with a straightforward film account of Petticoat Lane for the popular news magazine programme *Tonight,* but by the time he had moved on to Huw Wheldon's arts programme *Monitor,* he had progressed to making documentaries focusing on a wide range of subjects – Russian acrobats at Harringay circus, the Cannes Film Festival, the experiences of Italian opera singers in London, and a documentary called *The Class,* the programme that had taken him to London's Central School of Speech and Drama in 1960, when Julie was in her final year. Although she did not feature in Schlesinger's film, he did notice her as an actress who possessed striking looks.

Schlesinger's growing reputation as a skilful film-maker was enhanced greatly when in 1961 he was asked to create a film for British Transport and he turned in a 30-minute study of people passing through busy Waterloo station, which not only captured the hustle and bustle of a busy railway station, but poignantly encompassed the very human aspect of lost children and escorted prisoners. Although he shot *Terminus* in just two weeks, Schlesinger spent six months on the editing and his painstaking care paid off because the film earned a Gold Lion Award for Best Documentary at the1961 Venice Film Festival, a British Academy award and the attention of Jo Janni.

Janni was a London-based film producer of Milanese extraction, an enormously cultured man who had studied films at the government-sponsored Centro Sperimentale, the film university in Rome, where he won a cup for the best-directed film of the year. He left Italy for England in 1939 just before the outbreak of war and formed a company called Victoria Films in 1947 through which he went on to produce several interesting movies in the 1950s, notably *A Town Like Alice* in 1956 with Peter Finch and Virginia McKenna which was a resounding success. Despite frequent overtures to live and work in Hollywood, Janni was so attached to Europe that he insisted on staying put in London and was to remain in the same Chelsea house for forty years.

Janni had admired Schlesinger's *Monitor* item on the Italian singers in London and now *Terminus* confirmed his view that he and Schlesinger might make films together. Accordingly he sent Schlesinger a copy of Stan Barstow's novel *A Kind of Loving* with a view to making it into a film. He also enclosed a postcard saying, 'I would like to discover you.' Schlesinger recalled: 'The book, when I read it, made a great impression on me. I sent it back with a postcard with the words: "Please discover me with this." ' It was the start of an adventurous collaboration which was to create some of the most influential British films of the era and which would have a marked effect on the life and career of Julie Christie.

With Janni as producer, Schlesinger as director, and a screenplay by Keith Waterhouse and Willis Hall, *A Kind of Loving* hit the screen in 1962 telling the bitter-sweet story of a young draughtsman attracted to a typist in the same factory in a Lancashire industrial town. His is a physical attraction that he

cannot resist but she has a deeper feeling for him
and when a fumbling romance ensues and she becomes pregnant, he grudgingly marries her.

Schlesinger's shrewdly observed film gave an appealing debut to young British actress June Ritchie
as the bewildered Lancashire lass and Alan Bates
proved a likeable hero who largely held the audience's
sympathies despite his weaknesses. Importantly,
Schlesinger won plaudits for handling the film with a
sharp documentary eye, with wit, and with tact,
always mindful that he was unfolding a piece of
fiction.

*A Kind of Loving* was both critically and financially
successful and earned a Golden Bear award at the
Berlin Film Festival. Greatly encouraged, Janni and
Schlesinger were understandably keen to consolidate
their successful collaboration and towards the end of
1962 they eagerly joined forces once more on a new
film project, *Billy Liar,* based on Keith Waterhouse's
novel.

Keith Waterhouse had originally intended his novel
about a young man who lives through his fantasies
to be called *Saturday Night at the Roxy,* until
publication clashed with another gritty novel about
the provincial working class called *Saturday Night and
Sunday Morning.* Waterhouse swiftly gave his novel
the snappy new title of *Billy Liar.* It had become both
a popular book and a successful stage play by the
time Janni and Schlesinger saw the screen potential
of the story of Billy Fisher, a young day-dreaming

undertaker's clerk leading an irresponsible life trapped in a drab North Country town. Billy fiddles the petty cash, is at war with his parents and is involved with two girls who share his engagement ring. Above all, Billy is an incorrigible liar and inveterate dreamer, who retreats into an invented world, seeking escape in fantasies set in the imaginary state of Ambrosia. After failing to hitch his star to a visiting TV comedian to whom he has sent some scripts, he sees the chance to trade his drab existence for the bright lights of London when he meets a kookie, free-wheeling girl called Liz. She is the only one who appears to understand him and urges him to escape with her to London, but at the last moment he lacks the courage to do so.

Tom Courtenay, who had taken over from Albert Finney in the hit West End stage production, was a natural to play Billy in the Janni–Schlesinger film of *Billy Liar* and the remainder of the major casting appeared to be falling smoothly into place with the very popular Wilfred Pickles signed to play Billy's hectoring father and Mona Washbourne as his dim mother.

The only casting that taxed Janni and Schlesinger was the part of the free-roving, sophisticated girl-of-the-world Liz, a role that both men saw as crucial to their film. No young actress sprang immediately to mind and together they spent weeks thumbing through casting directories and mulling over various names.

One morning Schlesinger and Janni were sitting in Janni's office three floors up at 33 Bruton Street, Mayfair, when their attention was drawn, just as Terence Stamp's had been, to the picture of a very striking girl, gun in hand, on the cover of the newly published *Town* magazine. And there were more pictures inside. 'Very good pictures,' Schlesinger remembered. 'Rather provocative. She looked scrumptious, absolutely marvellous. I said, "Well that's the kind of girl we want." I didn't connect the girl with Julie Christie at the time. Then I suddenly remembered that this girl on the magazine was the one I'd seen when I'd made the documentary for the BBC about London's Central School of Speech and Drama. She wasn't in the film but I'd noticed her, a very striking girl.'

When he and Janni discovered who she was, they called Julie's agent and asked for her to come in for a reading with Tom Courtenay. Julie was only too pleased. She had read the book of *Billy Liar* and was aware of the critical acclaim that the play had received and she saw the possibility of working with Schlesinger in a film version as a means to escape the frothy films she was currently saddled with.

Fresh from a holiday in Spain – tanned, relaxed, lithe, fit and with her hair lightened by the sun – Julie arrived at Janni's offices looking stunning. The contrast with the student who had underwhelmed the two men as Anne Frank could hardly have been greater. In the course of conversation, however, it quickly became apparent that she was indeed the same girl. Although both men were impressed with the bronzed beauty who now walked through the door, Schlesinger remembered Julie's performance as unexceptional, and Janni, as he always did, cautiously insisted that further tests should follow. And so it was that Julie was taken off to Hampstead Heath to be screen-tested along with several other actresses including Topsy Jane who had played the role of Liz on the London stage.

'I did a very bad reading and followed it with three very bad screen tests,' Julie recalled. 'I had to do a test run on Hampstead Heath, the scene where I try and persuade Billy to leave his small town and come to London. But I couldn't do a damn thing. My throat constricted and my voice went dead.'

It was simply a bad attack of the nerves. Julie was in awe of Schlesinger and Janni and unsure quite what they wanted from her. 'The part called for a nice, ordinary North Country girl, an earth-mother figure and I was too bony and intense,' she reflected. Unfortunately for Julie, Schlesinger agreed. He felt that Julie came across as terribly cold. 'She wasn't very good in the tests. She was nervous and looked a little hard. It was difficult to break down her nervous resistance. We did everything. A cameraman took her to dinner to make her feel easier. But she was terrified.' Schlesinger had to admit, however, that 'she still looked marvellous – too good to be true'.

Knowing she had not done herself justice in the tests, Julie could not hide her disappointment. She was desperate to work in a respectable film and it was with a sense of gloom that she returned to *The Fast Lady* at Beaconsfield, wondering if she had blown her big chance. 'I tried not to let myself hope for the part, but after three tests you can't help hoping. I was just dying to do something I wasn't ashamed of.'

Just to reassure himself that he wasn't making a terrible mistake in passing up Julie for his screen Liz, Schlesinger told Janni he would go to Beaconsfield Studios and watch Julie at work for himself. But on arriving on the *Fast Lady* set, Schlesinger remembers how shocked he was at the way they were doing her hair and make-up. 'Her hair was very ordinary and little film star and there were inches of pancake on her face,' he said. 'We wanted her to look pretty with her hair matted – which gave Julie no problem at all. But she looked dreadful. She put me off.'

Helpless in the hands of the *Fast Lady'* s hair and make-up team, Julie was uncomfortably aware of the impression she must have made on Schlesinger that afternoon. 'I think he was rather appalled because I was made up so much. You could see him thinking: "Ho, ho, that's not what I want at all." ' Julie's cause wasn't helped by a make-up man taking Schlesinger aside to make derogatory remarks about Julie's mouth, 'that strange, rather butch mouth', as Schlesinger himself has described it. 'You'll have trouble with that mouth,' the make-up man warned him darkly. The director's mind was further swayed when one of the cast whom he knew well gave the opinion that Julie was 'hopeless' and that there were dozens of pretty girls like her who could do just as well. Schlesinger drove back to London ready to tell Janni that he had decided Topsy Jane, not Julie Christie, must play the role of Liz.

Hopes were high for *Billy Liar* as it swung into production in Bradford. Schlesinger had deliberately chosen Bradford for his setting, not for the usual image of cobbles and smoke belching from factory chimneys but for the newly rebuilt centre of the city where the back-to-back terraced houses were being torn down to be replaced by supermarkets and shopping piazzas, symbols of a Britain in transition. This environment, established during the opening credits of *Billy Liar,* was to provide the provincial suburban atmosphere from which Billy's flamboyant fantasies blossom. It was also intended to show the conformity against which Schlesinger was to maintain the film was set, thus making it a middleclass rather than a working-class drama.

Unfortunately, by the end of the first week of filming, *Billy Liar* was facing a major crisis. Topsy Jane had fallen ill and been forced to withdraw, leaving Schlesinger and Janni to start the search for Liz all over again. Together they took time out to sit down in a little viewing room in Wardour Street to rescreen the tests of the other candidates. When they re-ran Julie's it suddenly seemed to outshine all the rest. 'I thought: why on earth didn't I start with her in the first place?' recalls Schlesinger. Julie's film *Crooks Anonymous* had just come out and was playing at the New Victoria cinema that week and Schlesinger and Janni debated whether they should go and watch it before making their final decision about Julie. But time was so pressing they decided it would be better if they disregarded it and simply backed their own instincts.

Schlesinger himself made the call to Julie at her flat. Convinced that she had missed a great opportunity, Julie was ecstatic at this unexpected reprieve. 'When the call to say I had the part came through on the pay phone in the corridor it was like a dream come true,' she said. 'I couldn't believe it. I just didn't know whether to jump up and down, whistle or shout. Imagine, I was going to work with the great John Schlesinger!

'At last I was in a New Wave film, an English equivalent to the French stuff, so that I was realizing my ambitions to be in class – in this case working class! – films, something that aspired to be a reaction against the status quo, which is what I wanted to do most of all because I thought myself a rebel. I told my friends, "I'm going to be in one of those nouvelle vague films," and let it go at that. I didn't want to talk about it.'

Julie was asked to head north for filming at once and Schlesinger resolved to do his utmost to smooth Julie's late arrival in *Billy Liar.* He could see for himself how nervous she was. Julie goes further: 'I remember absolute terror because I hadn't a clue what I was supposed to be doing from beginning to end, although John Schlesinger was very good to me.'

The sudden drafting of Julie into *Billy Liar* meant Schlesinger had to reshoot all Topsy Jane's scenes, which were already in the can. But he knew that one scene would prove impossible to re-create. The centrepiece of the movie was a march-past of Billy's imaginary Ambrosian army while Billy takes the salute from the Leeds town hall balcony with Liz alongside him. The Ambrosian army numbered several hundred and Schlesinger knew it would be asking too much of the local authorities to block off the city all over again to accommodate a reshoot. Besides it would have been too expensive. In the event, Schlesinger was able to shoot close-ups of Julie for the march-past scene but there was nothing he could do about the long-shots. He would have to use the footage he already had.

In terms of dialogue Julie Christie's role in *Billy Liar* was no more than an extended cameo and her screen exposure amounted to just four scenes. Liz is first introduced returning to her home town in the cab of a lorry, having hitched a lift. Billy spots her in the lorry and says to his friend Arthur Crabtree, played by Rodney Bewes, 'She's crazy. She just enjoys herself. She works until she gets fed up then goes somewhere else. She goes where she feels like.' This teasing description of Liz afforded Schlesinger the opportunity to follow up with what he envisaged as a key scene for Julie, encapsulating Liz's free-wheeling attitude to life. She would be filmed bounding breezily down the high street without a care in the world and into Billy's life.

Schlesinger accordingly devised a long camera tour following Liz down the main street as she joyfully skips, hop-scotch fashion, over lines in the pavement, dodges in and out of the traffic, pulls a face at her own reflection in the window of C&A, looks idly at the scaffolding and architecture of new buildings, glances at the ornate façade of old ones, and watches a celebrity ribbon-cutting at the opening of a new super-market. All the while she is gaily swinging a duffel bag that obviously contains all she owns.

Schlesinger saw this sequence as largely requiring no dialogue. He hoped Julie's walk would simply speak volumes about Liz's *joie de vivre,* her peaceful co-existence with the world and her glowing innocence.

Although it eventually looked seamless when it was screened, Julie's relaxed and confident, jaunty walk was in fact pieced together bit by bit. 'I'd had a long argument with the cameraman about the use of the cinemascopic zoom lens,' Schlesinger explained. 'He said it couldn't be done in winter, in that light. He just wouldn't use that bloody zoom lens. So we shot rather unsatisfactorily for a week in Bradford. I still wasn't satisfied. I didn't have the sequences I wanted.' When the weather improved Schlesinger chose to finish off the sequence in London. A feature of his documentary-making training was his understanding of location filming and his keen eye led him to an area around Tottenham Court Road where extensive rebuilding was taking place and which looked much like Bradford. There he was able to gather the remaining footage he required. 'Finally one morning we had all the material we needed,' he says. 'We had a smashing sequence and we knew it.'

When Schlesinger came to look at the rushes, the fluidity of movement and expressiveness of Julie's walk thrilled him. Julie seemed to float down the street oozing happy self-confidence and sexuality. Everything about her walk said that Liz was free, emotionally and sexually, free in spirit and free of care. 'I knew that the introduction of this girl was the key point,' says Schlesinger, 'although I didn't realize it was going to make such a big difference to Julie Christie's career. It's easy to be wise after the event but we watched her and said: "By God, we have a star!" '

In all, Julie Christie worked for just two weeks on *Billy Liar* culminating in a mere 11 minutes of screen-time in the 98-minute film. After her extraordinary entrance, Liz meets Billy on the balcony at the Locarno dance hall and there they dreamily discuss marriage before going off to the park to make love. In the park Liz persuades Billy to meet her at the railway station to catch the midnight train to London with her. Once they are settled into their seats in the railway carriage, however, Billy's nerve fails him at the last moment and he seeks a way out by rushing off to get some milk from a machine on the platform. The train moves off spiriting Liz away to London and leaving Billy behind clutching two milk cartons, icy little reminders of his entrapment. Liz has thoughtfully left his suitcase on the platform and Billy, unable to follow, has no option but to trudge off home to his parents' semi-detached.

Tom Courtenay, on screen for much of the film, rightly garnered some excellent reviews when the film was released in September 1963 and Julie won praise for investing the ending with emotional force. But it was her carefree stroll through fictional Stradhoughton that had the critics drooling.

At the time, however, Julie was largely oblivious to the impact she had made and she felt that, anyway, she had gained a measure of recognition by default. 'Taking over from Topsy Jane was like wearing someone else's clothes,' she said. 'When Billy was finished I had no idea if I was good or bad. When the reviews came out I just thought, "They're good, that's a relief." When friends called up to congratulate me I couldn't really see what the excitement was all about.'

Some twenty years after making *Billy Liar,* Julie was able to form a very different view when she sat down and watched the film on television. 'It really is a beautiful film,' she exclaimed then. 'Oh my god, wasn't I lucky? Who knows what would have happened if Topsy Jane hadn't become ill. My career might have been like a million other actresses, constantly struggling for jobs that never come along.'

If Julie could not get very excited about it at the time, excitement there most certainly was among the film critics. According to Cecil Wilson in the *Daily Mail,* 'Julie's frank, sunny smile warms the whole film.' While the *Express'* s Leonard Mosley continued his enthusiastic chronicling of Julie's film career with a prediction: 'Julie lifts her shapely ankles another rung up the ladder to stardom as the lovable will o' the wisp and almost infiltrates Billy's daydreams. She makes herself at home on the screen in such an easy, unforced, natural way that we would be very surprised if she did not become a star.'

Even *The Times* of 14 August 1963 enthused wholeheartedly. 'Miss Julie Christie is very glamorous as the one girl who understands Billy ... She has that rare quality of obliterating everything else from the screen whenever she moves across.' And William Hall in the *London Evening News* confidently announced: 'For Julie Christie, the only girl of the three he loves, it is a part that will bring the offers tumbling in. Her gamine face and exciting personality are destined for big things.'

When *Billy Liar* became a box-office hit the limelight fell unerringly on Julie for the first time and, inevitably, she had to contend with questions as to whether she shared Liz's approach to life. 'I can't say I did,' she said. 'Despite the fact I thought of myself as a rebel, I was very shy, and Liz wasn't shy. She was also of a very different class from me, so that when she got lifts from lorry drivers she had that confidence of equality, whereas I would have been absolutely paralysed by my awful middle classness and unable to say anything at all. In a way it was her class that gave her strength and I didn't have that class.

'I thought a lot about Liz. That's how I know how different from me she was. Liz loved life, everything was a thrill for her. Not for me. There's a damned lot in life that doesn't thrill me at all. There's a lot that worries me.

'Liz had this quality of restfulness, or repose. Not me. Oh god not me! I'm nervousness itself. And she has this quality of being incredibly at ease with everyone. Not me. I'm struck dumb when I'm with people who are famous or important or witty. For a while I went out with a boy who was very well established and so were most of his friends and they were extremely witty and bright. I finally had to break off the relationship. Whenever I was with them I sat in a corner with my mouth shut. I was a bore.

'I suppose I move more easily than some people. Liz wants to go on finding things out. She doesn't want to be tied down. She retains her freedom. She assimilates then passes on. This is all fine. But you have to have friends. You can move if your friends move with you. But that's all. You can get lonely so quickly. All the time I was moving around with my little mat. God it was awful. I never want anything like it again. Liz kept drifting away from Strad-houghton for long periods then returning to try to persuade Billy to leave with her.'

Both *A Kind of Loving* and *Billy Liar* remain celebrated examples of the new wave of realism of British cinema in the early 1960s. Both are notable for infusing an element of comedy into gritty portrayals of working-and middle-class life. But *Billy Liar,* quite apart from the distinction of rating among the best 100 films chosen by the BBC and the British Film Institute to celebrate the centenary of talkies in 1995, is also remembered as the film that launched Julie Christie to stardom. Her poetic entrance lingers long in the memory and whenever John Schlesinger is asked to discuss his movies, the topic of Julie Christie and *Billy Liar* is always a favourite among his inquisitors.

Julie earned £1,000 for *Billy Liar* and the film was a turning point for her. 'I got marvellous reviews for it,' she reflected. 'I know it was my looks. I was so bad, it couldn't possibly have been anything else. I felt I was terribly lucky. I wanted to go into theatre but I thought if I was going into cinema at all, it had to be the respectable side of it, the "new wave". Everybody who was anybody in the cinema in the sixties wanted to be in "kitchen sink new-wave".'

*Billy Liar* also won Julie the Variety Club's Most Promising Newcomer of 1963 award and, crucially, it introduced her to American audiences where, as in Britain, the critics were quick to acclaim her. 'Julie

Christie is beautiful, graceful, sweet and would make even a television commercial worth seeing. Just to watch her open a beer can would be a pleasure,' said *Newsweek,* and *Time* magazine described her as 'an actress so brimful of careless charm that she parlays a few scenes into instant stardom'. The highly influential showbusiness magazine *Variety* noted: 'Miss Christie turns in a glowing performance that will ultimately signpost a very successful career.'

Seizing on the soon-to-be-famous walk scene, Archer Winston of the *New York Post* reflected: 'Afterwards, contemplating it, you realize it's the kind of thing that will someday be lifted out of context and studied for its technical virtuosity.'

Prophetically, the *New Yorker'* s critic expressed the hope that Julie Christie, in her next role, would be in London in a charming flat wearing exquisite clothes and speaking sentences that parse. He could not have known that John Schlesinger and Jo Janni had by now commissioned Frederic Raphael to write a screenplay for a new Schlesinger–Janni film about a London fashion model called *Darling* with Julie firmly pencilled in for the leading role.

Raphael was just one who had recognized the significance of those eleven minutes of Julie Christie screen-time and particularly the now legendary walk. 'Perhaps it was a contrivance of the cameraman but she looked positively incandescent,' he later recalled. 'The swing of the sixties came to life during that lyrical parade. She chimed with the times so perfectly that she seemed to have brought them into being. The old theme of "the girl can't help it" was renovated so miraculously in her casual ability to stop the traffic that Venus seemed to step down from the half-shell to make way for her.'

Julie was more circumspect and put her *Billy Liar* walk down to John Schlesinger. 'John's direction was everything,' she said. 'It was a beautiful walk to lovely music.'

*Billy Liar* changed Julie's life irrevocably on both a career and a personal level. She was alarmed at the level of attention that was being focused on her and fearful that celebrity status might rob her of her identity and private life.

Working with Schlesinger gave Julie a totally new perspective on film-making after her less than fulfilling experiences in *Crooks Anonymous* and *The Fast Lady.* Until *Billy Liar* Julie confessed she had not been seriously interested in film acting. 'In fact,' she admitted, 'I rather looked down on it. Films were an inferior way of expressing your art.'

Her training at the Central School, she stressed, had had nothing to do with films whatsoever. 'I can't remember any of the process of learning or unlearning specific techniques for the cameras. All I can remember is that awful business of having my hair done and so forth, which I couldn't stand. And there was the business of photographers and being taken to parties, none of which was on the cards for me, because all I wanted was to get on stage and be an actress. It wasn't till I made *Billy Liar* that at last nobody gave a hoot what I looked like. That was outside the system, and the people who made those films felt themselves to be outside the system and they didn't approve of that kind of fabrication of stars at all.'

Inevitably *Billy Liar* prompted numerous enquiries about Julie's availability for other film projects. One came from no less a Hollywood luminary than Cary Grant, then one of the most worshipped of screen idols. Grant had spotted Julie's photograph in a magazine and was anxious to learn more about her for a film he was helping to cast. Grant asked the British Hollywood-based showbusiness correspondent Roderick Mann to contact Julie for him. Mann duly passed on the message that Grant was anxious for her to call him but Julie was clearly unimpressed. 'The greatest name in showbusiness, the man hundreds of girls would crawl through a mortar barrage to meet – it meant nothing,' Mann reported. 'She never did ring him.'

Under the terms of Julie's contract, however, there was still one last film for her to make for Independent and producers Julian Wintle and Leslie Parkyn were already mapping out a new movie, this time a light-hearted romp set on the Continent, with Julie as the inevitable glamour girl. But having sampled a taste of 'new wave' filming Julie was now reluctant to slip back into such lightweight fare and she made no secret of her views.

Eventually the Independent producers saw no point in holding Julie to her contract against her will when she was now so clearly intent on taking her career in a very different direction. With commendable generosity they allowed her to walk away still owing them one more film.

By this time, final editing of *Billy Liar* was under way and Jo Janni had seen for himself that Julie Christie was destined to become a star. When the film was released he organized a meeting with Julie at which he proposed a four-year contract loosely based on the old tried and trusted Hollywood studio system of control, except that in this case there was no major studio, just Janni himself calling the shots. In effect it meant that Janni would pay Julie an annual salary and in return she would appear in his movie productions or other movies he personally chose for her to star in. For the latter, Julie would pay him 50 per cent of her fee. A projected income of £50 a week sounded an attractive proposition and Julie was happy to sign, although the money side of the contract did not specifically register high on Julie's list of priorities. Much more interesting to her was the promised screenplay by Frederic Raphael. *Darling,* however, would not be going into production for some months and Julie decided to put that time to good use.

# 4

# Birmingham, Moscow, New York

It was obvious straight away from Julie Christie's test that here was a formidable actress, a girl who knew how the camera loved her, as they say. She was absolutely exceptional. But the producer thought she was a B-picture actress.

Michael Winner

One person who was not surprised by the impact of Julie Christie's performance in *Billy Liar* was Michael Winner. Around the time in 1962 that John Schlesinger had passed over Julie Christie for *Billy Liar* in favour of Topsy Jane, Winner, then at the beginning of his career in films, was screen-testing young actresses for a movie he was planning to direct called *West 11*, a serious drama with, coincidentally, a screenplay by the *Billy Liar* scriptwriting team of Keith Waterhouse and Willis Hall.

There was an important role in the film as the central character's girlfriend and Julie was one of three actresses whom Michael Winner tested. The others were Suzanne Farmer, at the time starring in Hammer horror films, and Kathleen Breck. When he looked at their tests, Winner felt Julie was outstanding and there was no doubt in his mind that hers was the best by a very long way. Eagerly Winner showed the test on screen for his producer Daniel Angel and said it was patently obvious that of the three girls it had to be Julie Christie. But the wind was taken out of Winner's sails when the producer turned to him and said, 'You can't possibly use her. She's a B-picture actress.' And besides, he added, who would fancy Julie Christie? 'Well I would for a start!' replied Winner. It was clear to him that Julie was much more than a pretty face and, indeed, he considered her a formidable actress. But from the producer's point of view there was much weighing against Julie. She had recently lost out to Millicent Martin for a major role in Clive Donner's film *Nothing but the Best* and she had come second-best to Topsy Jane for *Billy Liar.* Swayed by what he saw as other filmmakers' lack of confidence in Julie, the *West 11* producer would not permit Winner to cast her in his film and the role went to Kathleen Breck instead. It was a major disappointment for Winner who was also thwarted in his attempts to cast Sean Connery in the leading role and James Mason as the villain.

Denied the three leading actors of his choice for *West 11,* Winner decided then to become a producer and for his next film, *The System,* he immediately turned to Julie Christie. He told her that this time he was the producer of his film as well as director and that he wanted her to play the lead in his movie. Julie replied, as Winner remembers, 'Well, they thought I was so awful in *Billy Liar'* – the film at that time had not been released – 'that they've told me I mustn't do any more films for now and that I've got to go to Birmingham Rep and learn how to act.' So Winner ended up without Julie Christie in *The System* either.

After the excitement of filming *Billy Liar,* Britain's newest young star was determined not to be swept off her feet by the movie world. She knew, in spite of her early screen success, that she had not yet served her genuine acting apprenticeship in the theatre. And for that reason in the summer of 1963 she plumped for a six-month contract with the prestigious Birmingham Repertory Company. It certainly wasn't for the money: she was paid £16 per week and £5 of that went straight away to pay for her homely digs with her landlady Mrs Cetti, in Forest Road, Moseley.

Mrs Cetti, a large affable Italian woman, gave Julie a room on the top floor. There Julie was often joined by the house cat, a piebald kitten called Kitchen which quickly recognized Julie as a cat-lover. To make the room cosy Julie personalized it by pinning up a montage of her favourite newspaper and magazine illustrations. There were one or two of herself but mostly they were pictures of Rudolph Nureyev, Terence Stamp, Peter Ustinov and two drawings by friends. She took along some of her favourite books, including Sartre's *Age of Reason* and her portable gramophone was soon blaring out her choice of jazz records, with Mose Allison a frequent favourite on the turntable. Mrs Cetti, 'dear, sweet landlady', as Julie called her, remained very proud of her most beautiful lodger long after she had left. She ran her spotless boarding house until the late seventies and her tenants gradually changed from actors to students. But every new arrival was always shown 'Julie Christie's room' and if they were really privileged they got to sleep in it.

Julie was very lonely at first in Birmingham and her mother went to visit her to check on her digs. 'They're marvellous,' she was happy to pronounce. 'Her landlady looks after her just like a mother.' But Julie came to miss London and her friends and initially found the tightly knit company a shade suspicious of their exotic new member. Most young actors were desperate to shrug off the badly paid slog of rep and make it big in movies. Julie, it seemed, was anxious to do exactly the reverse.

She was auditioned by the director John Harrison and confided afterwards that she had been more nervous beforehand than for any of her screen tests. On her arrival in Birmingham, she explained that she was determined to learn. 'I wanted to work in the theatre in Birmingham because at the moment my freedom is more important to me than my future. I'm not going to let the success of one film suddenly turn me on my head. I want to get better and better as an actress and tougher as a person, too. I suppose I'm lucky in a way to have the guts to decline the big offers with thanks.

'I came because I knew it was a good rep, and I wanted the experience. In the normal run of things I would have stayed in rep after drama school. After this last film I probably have more opportunity of getting good parts, but I know that stage work will help me as an actress generally. It means that I will be better equipped for more trying parts. Maybe I have been too lucky too soon. I could have done with this experience before. I could spend a year here in Birmingham but I know I won't.

'After the money I got for *Billy Liar* the theatre pay is pretty small beer. But I was rather careless with it and it has all gone anyway. You know what it is in our business. One day you've got the cash and your friends haven't so you dole out a bit. The next minute you're the one on your beam ends and it's your friends who have to chip in. What I need', she said mischievously, 'is a real super boyfriend so when I next make a killing, he can turn the stuff over as they say, and make it grow.' She admitted happily that she had not been short of offers but said, 'I would like to fall in love. But the bloody nuisance is, I can't. Boys say they're in love with me, but that's not the same, is it? I'm looking for the real, bang-on super relationship.' More hesitantly Julie admitted: 'Yes, I suppose I do want to be a star. But I don't see myself as the kind of star who gets there just on fame. I don't want to be one without having the ability. That's a dodgy thing. If it did happen I know I wouldn't change. I mean, I have had quite a bit of luck so far, and I haven't changed. I am too lazy to make any concessions to other people, and I don't want to be anyone's property but my own. I am mad about fashion but I am just not the furs type.

'My idea of getting that far is being free to make good films with people I respect. I wouldn't mind working in France for that reason, because they make good films there. But I am more interested in my own dramatic integrity than just making films.'

Julie had proved she was as good as her word by turning down film and television offers to go to Birmingham. Her day consisted of rehearsals from 10.15a.m. to 6p.m. with an hour for lunch which she usually skipped in favour of a nap or a walk and she spent the tea-break mostly on the phone to friends or to Jo Janni in London.

Gradually she made friends with the other actors, especially Sheila Gish and Christopher Bidmead, and as pals from London visited she soon felt much less lonely. But there was certainly no star treatment. Julie travelled by bus, stayed and drank stout in the bar after work and was delighted to be regarded as 'just another member of the company'. In June she found herself playing Alithea, number eleven on her debut Birmingham Rep cast list, in a production of Wycherley's Restoration comedy *The Country Wife* at the Station Street theatre. She was prepared to work hard, even if her insistence on always rehearsing in bare feet did raise a few eyebrows among some of the older members of the company.

Julie made much more of a contribution in *Thark,* by Ben Travers, and in *The Good Woman of Setzuan* by Bertolt Brecht she acquitted herself with distinction – 'I love it. I'm playing a pregnant Chinese lady – not a part of great importance' – before going on to play the only female part in James Saunders's *Next Time I'll Sing to You,* for which she was widely praised.

Fortunately, her career did not depend on her ability to sing. In a revue by Malcolm Bradbury, Jim Duckett and David Lodge, she sang a blues song alone on stage. Next day the *Birmingham Post* theatre critic observed cruelly: 'Julie Christie should never, ever, be allowed to sing unaccompanied on stage again.'

At least through Birmingham Rep Julie was discovering what she could and couldn't do, what she most favoured and what kind of role suited her best. She had fun portraying a hostess in a Wild West saloon in a comic revue but felt inadequate when pressed into playing a beauty contestant, Miss USA, which required her to parade in a figure-hugging one-piece swimsuit and high-heeled shoes. 'My legs are too short and my bosom is too small,' she commented, dismissively.

At the end of August she returned briefly to the glittering film world when the company gave her two days off as she was required to fly to Venice where *Billy Liar* was launched with some impact at the film festival. But Julie refused to have her head turned by the jet-setting plans. She told the local paper the week before: 'Next Thursday morning I fly to Venice for the film festival where *Billy Liar* is one of the entries. I shall not stay long there. On Friday I shall fly back and on Saturday I shall again be on stage at the Birmingham Repertory Theatre.'

Julie was as good as her word and thoroughly professional in her approach but Michael Winner received a postcard from Birmingham saying, effectively, 'What on earth am I doing up here?'

When *Billy Liar* opened in Britain and America with much acclaim for Julie, she found herself giving interviews to American journalists who wanted to know exactly the same thing. They were intrigued that such a striking bright new young film star should be closeting herself away in a provincial town, living in one room in digs and treading the boards for such a menial salary. They were intrigued too by Julie's scatty nature and her desperate efforts to try and get herself organized. 'I keep trying to put everything in life into little boxes with titles on,' she confided. 'It's all a desperate attempt to keep everything under control. But they keep getting out of control. My little room is very tidy. I get home after the theatre dead tired and I empty my handbag and put everything in little piles – this to be done tomorrow, this to be put away and in five minutes my room is in a frightful mess.

'I had a boyfriend once and he got furious with me. "You live in little boxes," he said, "Do you have to put labels on everything for Christ's sake?" On the other hand I never look into the future or worry about the future.'

Birmingham theatre director John Harrison was, of course, delighted that he now had a beautiful new movie star in his company and it certainly did the box office no harm. 'As a movie actress I should think she has arrived,' said Harrison. 'As a stage actress, I think she is still in the early period and it would be six months anyway before one could advise how large a talent she could in time become. She has warmth, energy, a fine intelligence, a very real feeling for the stage. She's a marvellous girl.'

Productions at the Birmingham Rep were regularly attended by talent scouts from nearby Stratford's Royal Shakespeare Company and Julie was thrilled to receive an offer to go on a world tour with the RSC in *A Comedy of Errors.* The tour was to mark the 400th anniversary of Shakespeare's birth, and, following the scouts' favourable reports, Julie was offered the not insignificant but far from starring role of Luciana.

The tour would stretch across five months, take in several countries behind the Iron Curtain and finish up in America. It was a thrilling prospect for Julie who had long harboured ambitions to appear in Shakespeare and she could also look forward to working with the illustrious Stratford director Peter Brook. But most exciting of all was the thought of travelling with the company to Eastern Europe and the chance it offered to explore its great cities. On the itinerary was Berlin, Prague, Moscow, Leningrad, Warsaw, Helsinki, Bucharest, and Budapest. Then it would be on to America taking in Washington, Boston, Philadelphia and New York. It would be a grand adventure but the tour would also, to her relief, distance her from the mounting pressures of coping with film executives, agents, promotion and publicity officers, at least for a while.

After rehearsals at Stratford, *A Comedy of Errors* moved to London in mid-January for more rehearsals and a dozen performances at the Aldwych Theatre. By the time the 55strong company was ready to head off to Europe in early February, the play was being staged in tandem with *King Lear* starring Paul Scofield and Julie had found herself a handsome new boyfriend among the cast and was embarking on a fun-filled liaison. Shortly before she joined the RSC Julie had openly revealed that she was frequently lonely and longing to meet a smashing young man, as she put it, to share some good times and he emerged in the tall and handsome person of Peter Tory.

'I'd been in Sheffield Rep as a juvenile lead,' he says, 'and after I'd auditioned for the RSC I was taken on for the tour of *King Lear* and *Comedy of Errors*. I was carrying a spear and saying, "Edmund is dead, my lord," in *King Lear* and I was literally carrying spears and being just one of the crowd in *A Comedy of Errors* which Julie was in.

'I was just one of several young chaps who were playing the parts of lazy drunken knights whom King

Lear surrounds himself with. So we were all fairly ruggerish, and of course we all fancied Julie Christie like mad.

'With a company like that, where there were young lusty actors and actresses, it became, as it always does, an insular unit especially since we were all going behind the Iron Curtain and could make only little excursions. So the whole company became rigid with sexual tension and there was a lot of pairing up going on including quite a lot of homosexual relationships.'

Competition became fierce among the company's virile young males to see who could pair off with Julie Christie. So fierce that the young men all placed bets about getting her into bed. 'We actually had a wager,' recalls Tory, 'that the first person who stepped out with Julie, or set up with Julie or became her boyfriend would get $10 from each of the other spear-carriers when we arrived in America.'

For Peter Tory, the wager was immaterial. He was very attracted to Julie and was entranced by her breathy enthusiasm for everything. 'She was very lively and scatty but delightfully so,' he says. 'She had that husky voice and was enormously enthusiastic and fun, and very affectionate and terrific company. She was very Bohemian. She had a kind of gypsy soul, she was unconventional and very much her own spirit and what came across was a kind of whacky scattiness. She was such fun to be with.'

Tory was delighted to find his feelings of affection were returned and he became the envy of his actor rivals when the company left for Europe. They were both young and single and now Julie had suddenly found someone she liked enormously with whom she could share the five-month adventure that lay ahead for both of them.

'It was the height of the Cold War and so going behind the Iron Curtain was fascinating for all of us,' says Peter. 'Wherever Julie, I or the others went we were followed and our suitcases were gone through. But we had great fun. Julie wanted to go and see everything, all the museums, the art galleries. She was just so full of this breathy enthusiasm and if she wanted to go to some shop or some museum, then we just had to go and find it. In Leningrad we went to the Winter Palace and spent hours in the Hermitage looking at all the wonderful works of art there. Everywhere we went Julie bought posters and she was terribly upset at the end of the tour when I lost them all at one of the airports.'

Like other couples in the company, Peter and Julie frequently found it a challenge to spend nights together at the Russian hotels where the company was quartered. 'We regularly had great parties after the show in one of the hotel rooms,' he says, 'but the problem was you were not allowed in other people's rooms. On each floor of the hotels there were women with a bunch of keys sat at desks so they could see down the corridor. So in order to have a party we had to distract them. Someone would run down the corridor and distract these women and then one room would fill up with fifteen or twenty actors and a great party would ensue.'

It was obvious to the whole company that Julie and Peter were very close but after one such jolly gathering in his hotel room when a cold, snowy dawn was coming up over Bucharest at five in the morning, Tory found himself alone, apart from another actor sitting on the end of his bed. It was clear from his colleague's tone that he wanted to sleep with Tory, who made it equally clear he was simply not interested, not that way inclined in the slightest. Julie Christie's would-be rival was clearly miffed. 'Call yourself an actor? You should try every experience,' he scoffed before leaving the room in disappointment.

One actor in the company whose friendship both Tory and Julie did come to value, however, was John Laurie. A genial Scot with a sharp sense of humour, Laurie was to become a firm TV favourite some five years later in the BBC TV sit-com *Dad's Army* as local undertaker Private Frazer with his mournful catch-phrase, 'We're doomed, we're doomed.'

'He became a great mate to all us youngsters,' says Tory. 'In *King Lear* he played the Duke of Gloucester in a broad Scottish accent which rather confused everybody. But he hated the whole business of Peter Brook and that kind of intense direction and improvisation and nearly resigned and went home.'

On stage it fell to Peter and one or two other young knights to help bring about the blinding of Gloucester and they were hard put to contain their laughter when Laurie screamed out his agony in a guttural Scottish accent. 'I used to corpse every time it happened,' says Tory. 'Even though we were performing the play in front of all these grand people everyone would assemble in the wings just to watch and hear John Laurie uttering "aaaarrrrghhhh" in a Scottish accent as he was blinded.

'One of the most popular Beatles tracks of the day was "All My Loving" from the LP "With The Beatles" and the plane carrying the company from city to city would resound to us all singing our own special version of the chorus inspired by John Laurie. When Gloucester is blinded and John has given his guttural "aaarrrghhh", in the text it has "O my follies" and Regan says, "Out vile jelly" as his eye is taken out. Our version of the Beatles hit was "Close your eyes and I'll blind you, Regan's behind you, aaarrrghhh my follies" sung in a broad Scottish brogue. It was often sung lustily and clearly on the Eastern bloc aeroplanes, which we were forced to fly in. John Laurie who hated Peter Brook and the production was enormously entertained by this.'

One night in Moscow Julie was in the wings purely as an interested onlooker when Laurie went through his usual Scottish histrionics as he was blinded. But that particular night Laurie had a heavy cold and, with two gauze patches placed over his eyes to simulate his blindness, he waited as usual for a pat on the back from Peter Tory which signalled his cue to go on. But due to his cold he was snuffling and spluttering in the wings and Tory proceeded to pat him on the back trying to help him clear his coughing fit. Laurie unfortunately thought this his cue and with fake blood all over his face staggered on to the stage and roared out his by now familiar 'aaarrrghhh' just as Edmund was delivering his famous 'Now gods stand up for bastards' soliloquy.

Realizing his mistake, Laurie then stumbled across the stage and exited into the wings – but on the far side, stage left. Now, with two gauze patches on his eyes, he had to feel his way rapidly around the back of the stage to take his position in the wings ready for his proper entrance, stage right.

'Peter Brook's extraordinary set', Tory remembers, 'included 30-foot high metal sheets all interwoven and hanging. They had big handles on them and in the thunder scene the stagehands would shake them and it produced totally authentic, loud thunder. When John Laurie was finding his way round the back, he got mixed up in all these thunder sheets so there was this totally unscheduled thunder storm in the middle of Edmund's soliloquy.

'After the performance all of us, including Julie and me, went to a reception at the Kremlin where there were all sorts of Russian ballet people and professors who probably knew Shakespeare better than any Englishman does and who had studied *King Lear* and knew every nuance of the text. Julie and I were standing chatting together, when a Russian professor with a huge black beard came over and said, 'Wonderful! Wonderful! Wonderful! The thunder in Edmund's "Stand up for bastards" speech – a masterpiece!'

Together Julie and Peter explored as much of Moscow and Leningrad as time and Russian security would allow. 'Those of us who were not doing very much had all the energy and lack of responsibility which meant we could really explore these places and the nightlife and museums,' says Tory. 'But it was very, very cold as it was the winter. I can remember us looking out on to these old roof tops in places like Prague and watching the snow being blown off in great flumes and people shuffling around in huge fur coats slithering everywhere on the ice and women in Moscow with pneumatic drills on road gangs.

'Like Julie, I was fascinated by everything. We had a lot of fun. Julie didn't express any intellectual views about politics at that time. She was just full of enthusiasm for everything. When we were in Romania, Julie and I went off to the mountains and spent a wonderful weekend not skiing but on sledges. We had to get there by night train and the following morning we got into the back of a lorry and were taken right up this dark valley to the top of the mountain illuminated by the sun and there was a chalet there and a restaurant. It was magical.

'Julie was just lovely. She didn't glamorize herself at all. In fact she could be quite scruffy. She had brownish hair and when she coloured it lighter she never minded if the roots showed. She bit her fingernails too. She wouldn't spend hours in the mirror and she'd just chuck on a woolly jumper. She was just a very lively, scatty, Bohemian, lovable, rather scruffy girl. Unselfconscious, un-vain, impulsive, slightly scatterbrained.

'She had great qualities as a person and all of that was divined by the camera. She made no impact at all in *A Comedy of Errors.* Her performance was so small and underplayed, a very muted performance. But the camera finds an inner mystical and magical quality. I was absolutely amazed, mesmerized by her charisma on screen. It's like many great screen actresses. It's something that the camera does. There's some inner thing that connects with the camera but doesn't necessarily connect with people in everyday life. I've always been stunned by the internal quality and depth that comes through with Julie and as far as I can tell she has never been spoiled by the movie world. She's shunned it in a way that shows she's tremendously human.

'When we got to America it was an amazing contrast – from Cold War Europe to Washington. We hired a car and drove down to Cape Cod with Julie with her feet up on the dashboard in the passenger seat singing along to the radio. Behind the Iron Curtain no one had known who Julie Christie was, but because her *Billy Liar* fame had by now reached America, we were descended upon by journalists. She was so much the centre of attention, so much wined and dined. She wasn't really ambitious. She was just enjoying herself. She enjoyed the attention of the newspaper-men in America but she didn't in any way become intoxicated by it. It was "This is fun. Fancy me, Julie Christie, having all this attention." I think she enjoyed it but she rejected it in the end – that was what was so interesting.

'Our relationship had never been that serious, although it was great fun, and at that point we drifted apart. We went our separate ways. But when we got back to England the Queen asked for a Royal Command performance of *A Comedy of Errors.* So we all gathered again for the performance at Windsor Castle. I hadn't seen Julie for a while and it was nice to meet up with her again. Afterwards there was a party we all went to with the royal family and I spent most of the time like a spear-carrier holding an ashtray for Princess Margaret. She never addressed me at all. I just held the ashtray.

'I was living in west London at the time and so I said to Julie, "Why don't you come and spend the night with me?" The coach taking everyone back into London from Windsor stopped at Hammersmith and let us off and we walked across Hammersmith Bridge down Castlenau to my flat where Julie spent the night with me.

'I had told my flat-mate Robin that Julie Christie had been a great friend while we were on tour and I think he thought this was very much a tale brought back from Russia and America and wasn't sure whether he really believed it or not. The following morning he and I were having breakfast in the kitchen – I had said nothing – when suddenly in walked Julie Christie to join us wearing just one of my shirts.'

Not long afterwards, Julie's and Peter's careers took them in different directions. In fact, Peter very quickly realized he did not want to cope with the press hoo-ha now surrounding Julie and admits he would not have been able to compete anyway. 'We lost contact, sadly, when she went off to be a big movie star,' he says, 'though she did send me a postcard from the set of *Doctor Zhivago.* She also sent me a movie star-style photo of herself across which she had written: "To the man I'd most love to spend a night in a Romanian train with. Love Julie".'

Peter Tory, now a distinguished and much respected writer, still treasures the great friendship he had with Julie Christie and there is neither envy nor malice when he says he was more than a little surprised when Julie later embarked on a lengthy liaison with Hollywood star Warren Beatty. 'I think Beatty may have been a bit surprised when he got to know Julie that she wasn't really a movie star at all. And I can't believe Beatty was her style at all either. That whole glitter and glamour and smoothness, power, and huge amounts of money, gliding motorcars and swimming pools and artificiality of Hollywood. I can't imagine she really liked that. She liked people who were a bit like her, unconventional, and had the Bohemian spirit. She is an enigma, an icon despite herself and she remains so.'

During the course of their romance Tory says he did get around to informing Julie that the RSC spear-carriers had had a wager about her. 'She was highly amused,' he says. 'In fact she came off-stage one night into the wings and went up to one of them and said: "You owe Peter Tory ten dollars!" ' As it happens, all Julie and I had done was to have a bath together in a room on the fourteenth floor of the Ukrainian Hotel in the middle of Moscow. Come to think of it, ten dollars wasn't enough. It should have been twenty.'

# 5

# Darling Julie

I don't think men see any lusty sexiness in me.
The appealing thing is an air of abandonment. Men
don't want responsibility and neither do I.

Julie Christie

The idea for a film about a beautiful, amoral girl
who sashays into the upper echelons of London society
by moving with blithe assurance from one bed to the
next sprang originally from a conversation John
Schlesinger struck up with broadcaster Godfrey Winn
during the making of *Billy Liar.*

Winn had briefly appeared as himself at the very
start of the film. He was featured as the radio host
introducing the popular BBC programme *Housewives'
Choice* and then rewarding a lucky Light Programme
listener with Kenneth McKellar singing 'Song of the
Clyde' over the airwaves. During pauses in filming
Winn happened to be chatting to Schlesinger about a
woman he knew who was moving upwards in chic
society by hopping from one bed to another and living
the fantasy that there is always something – or
someone – better around the next corner.

From that conversation emerged the framework
of an idea for a film about a woman whom everyone

calls 'darling', the kind of woman who is sexy, fun-loving, amusing, good company, driven but aimless, and very firmly on the make as she flits from man to man. Initially Schlesinger, Janni and Raphael, who had read philosophy at Cambridge and had had his first novel published shortly after leaving university, were basing their proposed film on a well-known lady who was kept in luxury by a syndicate of gentlemen. 'In Italy,' said Schlesinger, 'it would have been a funny story of the men's various relationships with their mistress. Set in London it was just ugly and rather nastily sexual.' But within the original frame-work the three men spent the next eighteen months trawling through their own experiences to create a composite picture of a sixties girl whose gorgeous looks guarantee her a place in any social group and a taste of any new sensation she chooses. The character they came up with was a fashion model to be called Diana Scott and for the film title they settled on *Darling.* 'The word means nothing,' Schlesinger pointed out. 'Everyone uses it. It's just a sound now and only rarely is it used to communicate affection.'

Frederic Raphael, Jo Janni and John Schlesinger had begun to plan *Darling* in November 1962 but round about the time Raphael had completed his script, in the summer of 1963, a national scandal erupted which almost caused the entire *Darling* project to be abandoned. Britain was rocked by the Christine Keeler sex scandal in which John Profumo, Secretary of State for War, resigned after confessing to a relationship with a call girl who was also having a liaison with Soviet naval attaché Eugene Ivanov. The trial of Dr Stephen Ward, a key figure in the Profumo affair, on charges of living off immoral earnings, lifted the lid on a twilight world where the famous and wealthy consorted with prostitutes, perverts and drug addicts and attended parties at which women of loose morals were brought together with important and influential men.

The details emerging from the court hearings of orgies, two-way mirrors and black magic went far beyond anything that Raphael's imagination had dreamed up for *Darling,* thus making his story-lines look positively pale by comparison. But, rather than jettison the entire project, it was felt that the central concept, a modern film about a modern woman, still remained and Raphael and Schlesinger duly closeted themselves together to adjust the story-lines. Further problems then arose when the revamped script turned out to resemble too closely the life of someone they both knew. Raphael set to work on a third version and finally the script was done. The movie would unfold in flashback with 'darling' giving a hypocritical version of her life to a reporter from a woman's magazine. The 'darling' girl's amatory climb up the social ladder would finally gain her a title of nobility but bring with it bitter loneliness and disillusionment.

The final synopsis presented this 'darling' as a model who has grown up to accept the undeniable fact that she is a darling and knows that her beauty gives her the power to unlock doors closed for ever to the mere ordinary. A lovely child, she has been pampered and spoiled and, as a young woman, has improvidently married an unsophisticated boy her own age. When she later finds him boring and immature, he is swept carelessly aside in Diana's headlong rush towards what she thinks of as 'experience'. In a London street Diana is interviewed by television journalist Robert Gold and her reaction to this chance meeting is strong and immediate. It grows into a love-affair and she leaves her husband as Robert's conventional marriage pales into insignificance against the strength of his feeling for Diana. That they should decide to live together is inevitable. Robert leaves his family and starts sharing a flat with Diana.

As Diana's career as a model advances and her face becomes a familiar image of sophistication, she begins to feel that she needs other stimuli. Restlessness, boredom and a determination to enhance her modelling career drive her into the cold and comfortless bed of Miles Brand, top executive of a large industrial firm whose product she has been advertising as his company's Happiness Girl. Cool, callous and worldly, Miles fascinates and almost mesmerizes Diana. He takes an amused and unemotional hand in her career, introduces her to society, and then helps find her a small part in a Gothic horror movie that boosts her ego. After the première, which she attends with Robert, she tells him she is pregnant. Robert is delighted and regards it as a permanent binding guarantee and even Diana is at first intrigued by the prospect of motherhood.

But although happy at first, she eventually fears responsibility and realizes it is going to impede her career. She enters a private nursing home and blithely undergoes an abortion, an operation which she tells herself is a 'miscarriage'. The experience leaves her miserable and riddled with self-pity. Her one desire is to escape from London, from responsibility, from Robert and she goes to stay temporarily with her married sister in the country. But after a comfortable and unexciting few days there and her family's heavy-handed efforts at match-making, Diana goes scurrying back to London and Robert.

But Robert is still not enough and she quickly bores of his quiet, scholarly life. In search of new excitement she again seeks out Miles whose worldliness and complete assurance continue to cast a spell over her. She tells Robert she is going to Paris to make a film and in reality she spends time there with Miles who shows her the seamier side of Paris, introduces her to a decadent crowd and forces her to attend a wild party and share his perverted tastes. She finds them repugnant at first but Miles's cynical amusement soon drives her into accepting them without a qualm. Returning to London, she resumes her pretence with Robert but she is careless. He can no longer ignore her indiscretions and walks out, leaving her crushed and bewildered.

For companionship and consolation and as a diversion, Diana befriends Malcolm, an effeminate fashion photographer whose platonic sympathy soothes her wounded pride. She travels with him to Italy for the filming of a commercial at the ancestral villa of Prince Cesare Della Romita, a wealthy widower with six children. Diana is flattered by his courteous attention and even more flattered when he proposes marriage. But she refuses and she goes with Malcolm on holiday to Capri where they both sleep with the same young man. She treats the prince's proposal as a delicious joke and returns to London and Miles. This time Miles's lack of warmth, genuine feeling and depravity nauseates her. She finds herself alone and loneliness is something that Diana finds insupportable. She opts for the security of married life with the prince in Sicily. Her marriage makes Diana an international celebrity and now she has every material thing she could possibly desire but discovers that she is still alone. Preoccupied with travel and business, her husband cannot give her the real affection she craves.

Diana soon tires of her opulent but empty life and in desperation returns to London and Robert. After their reunion at London airport Robert and Diana go to a hotel to make love. Diana feels that nothing has changed and that she has been given a second chance, but while she makes plans for their future together, Robert is already booking her a return flight back to Italy. The drive to the airport is bitter. Diana threatens to kill herself but Robert is unshaken in his knowledge that there is no future for them, no second chance and he sends her back to Italy where she must resume her lonely, boring life. At the airport Diana composes herself to meet the press before boarding her plane. She puts on her rich international celebrity face for the photographers and returns to rejoin her husband, a prisoner of the world that she has conquered.

Schlesinger was convinced that the role of Diana, the epitome of the callous selfish modern girl who wanted something for nothing, was the best written for a British actress for a decade. But his and Janni's efforts to get *Darling* off the ground proved to be fraught with problems. The major movie distributors showed little interest in backing their project. They said that Diana Scott was too cold, or too bad, or not bad enough. But their principal objection was that there was no big name in the cast. Why is the lead being played by an unknown starlet, they queried. Why is there no established American star, they repeatedly demanded.

In New York Schlesinger tried to approach the American film mogul Joe Levine for backing. Levine was a natural target because in the late fifties he had formed Embassy Pictures to exploit European spectacles. But Schlesinger's attempt ended in confusion and farce when it turned out that Levine had completely mistaken him for another man also called John

Schlesinger. Janni was having no luck either. 'They all said I must be mad wanting £400,000 with an unknown girl as a star,' moaned a frustrated Janni. 'But you can have your money, they said, if you use Shirley MacLaine or someone like that.' It was the classic catch-22. Janni could not afford a Shirley MacLaine and no one seemed prepared to risk bankrolling *Darling* unless Janni could parade a star of MacLaine's stature.

Schlesinger and Janni listened to all the arguments but, since they were determined to stick with Julie Christie, they now had to consider whether they could persuade a top-name actor to star in *Darling*. The two men felt this might be only marginally easier than persuading a Shirley MacLaine to join the movie but they did eventually manage to broker a fragile finance deal which carried, however, the proviso from the prospective backers that a film actor of genuine status should take the male lead.

Robert Gold, the central male character in *Darling*, was originally written as an American journalist working in Europe so it was logical that they should try first for an American star. Boldly they went first for Paul Newman whose stock in Hollywood at that point could hardly have been higher following a string of successes in movies like *The Hustler, Sweet Bird of Youth, Hud* and *The Prize*. It was no real surprise when Newman turned it down.

Still setting their sights high, Janni and Schlesinger then pushed for Gregory Peck, a durable and likeable

American actor with a good movie track record, who had won an Oscar in 1962 for *To Kill a Mockingbird.* Despite his youthful looks, Peck was almost fifty and might have been just too old for the role in any case, but it never became an issue because he too declined. Even Cliff Robertson, then very much a second division Hollywood film actor, turned it down and Schlesinger found himself resorting to interviewing cowboys from TV serials but again without any success.

Despite these setbacks Schlesinger pressed ahead with as much preliminary pre-production work as he dared and he flew to America to visit Julie who was in Philadelphia in the final stages of her tour with the RSC. On arrival he decided not to see *A Comedy of Errors* since he had heard that Julie was not brilliant in it and he concluded that it would be counter productive to observe her limitations on stage when he was planning to cast her in a modern, very different, very glamorous movie role. He preferred to think of Julie as the actress who had so lit up the screen in his *Billy Liar* and he wanted to convince himself she could do it again in *Darling.* He also decided he couldn't face seeing Julie in a role that his youngest sister, Susan, had played at Stratford. It would have been too painful for him, Susan having recently committed suicide aged only thirty over the death of her lover from cancer.

Julie was delighted to see Schlesinger and they spent three days working together at his hotel reading Frederic Raphael's screenplay and going over it in detail. Schlesinger outlined what he expected of Julie explaining that Diana was a woman who is impatient to experience everything, not greedy for anything in particular, just for sensation, for something different, new and exciting. The omens were not overly encouraging when Julie indicated that she was not sure if she was capable of playing a part of such magnitude. It was a long and exacting role and she feared that she simply wasn't up to it. But Schlesinger was full of encouragement and assured her she could pull it off. He promised to give her his full support during filming and flew home to England with only minor reservations about Julie's ability to carry the role. He was concerned that Julie would find it difficult to portray Diana when she matured from flighty model to wealthy wife of an Italian prince, although his fears were later to prove unfounded. 'I knew she would be right and that she would be very good for the series of bitchy moments but not so good for the comedy,' he said. 'We had to tone that down a little.'

Schlesinger conveyed to Janni his thoughts that he was more than ever convinced that Julie must play the lead despite the common cry from potential backers that she was merely a little-known starlet. 'I said to myself, this girl Diana has to be always changing clothes. Who would look at home in fifty radically different costumes? She's got to slouch around a flat in London in sweaters and skirts. She goes to bed a lot. She has to model. She wears funny hats and knee socks. She's got to be a girl who goes back to nature in Capri in bikinis, shifts, jeans, T-shirts. She has to be elegantly velvet as the wife of an Italian nobleman. I could only visualize our Julie carrying it off.'

Back in London the search for a top name opposite Julie was, however, still proving fruitless. In addition to Robert Gold, Schlesinger and Janni had another important male role to fill, that of suave ad-man Miles Brand, a further rung on Diana's sexual ladder. It was a significant part and there was, therefore, much encouragement for the project as a whole when Laurence Harvey accepted the role. Harvey, an ambitious 35-year-old Lithuanian-born actor, had been slowly working his way up from British second-feature films, and he was keen to play the manipulative Miles. Soon afterwards Roland Curram filled the role of effeminate photographer Malcolm with whom Diana competes for a lover on a working holiday.

With Harvey on board, Schlesinger now turned to Dirk Bogarde and offered him the male lead. Bogarde, then forty-five, had begun to achieve international distinction as a character actor after achieving much success in lightweight home-grown films, but he could detect an unmistakable air of desperation about the *Darling* project when he met Schlesinger for the first time and the part was officially offered to him over lunch. Bogarde recalled that Schlesinger told him in no uncertain terms that it was not going to be a prestige picture and added: 'By that I mean there is no money, and really no one wants to make it except me and the girl and Jo Janni.'

It wasn't a promising start but Bogarde had been impressed by the script he had been sent and he was intrigued enough to enquire who 'the girl' was. Schlesinger told him he would not know her since she was only just starting out in movies and went on to say that although he thought she was brilliant and had a big future, the problem was that they could not find a leading man for her. Schlesinger was honest enough to tell Bogarde that he had tried several big names, including Gregory Peck, but each approach had been unsuccessful. Bogarde's assessment was that he was being offered the role of Robert Gold as a very last, reluctant, choice.

'But who *is* the girl?' Bogarde asked once more. When told it was Julie Christie he said he did indeed know who she was because he had seen her on TV in *A For Andromeda.* This came as a pleasant surprise to Schlesinger, especially when Bogarde followed up by telling him he would love to work with Julie. 'She's The Young. I want to be with the young,' said Bogarde. 'I like the script and I'll do it.'

Bogarde's enthusiasm, however, did not mirror Schlesinger's at that precise moment. The actor's recollection was of Schlesinger giving a shrug, getting on with his soup, and telling Bogarde that if he did star in *Darling* then they wouldn't get the backing they needed for the movie. But, no matter, said Schlesinger, they would at least do some tests, a suggestion which was met with injured indignation from Bogarde who felt that after appearing in forty-five films he hardly deserved to be subjected to a screen test.

Schlesinger hastily explained away this slight to Bogarde by stating that he meant 'tweedy tests' since he envisaged the character of Robert Gold in *Darling* as being a less formal man than the carefully groomed and be-suited actor he saw sitting across from him at the lunch table. 'You're so frightfully soigné,' said Schlesinger delicately. The lunch ended cordially enough, however, with Bogarde resolving to go away and purchase some knitted ties and present himself in 'unsoigné' fashion to *Darling'* s director next time in old gardening clothes with his hair newly washed. He duly landed the part of TV interviewer Robert Gold, Diana's first important conquest on her way upwards in London's chic society. The role of Estelle Gold, who loses her husband to Diana, was given to Pauline Yates, an accomplished actress with whom Julie had worked on a J. B. Priestley drama for Granada TV. The major casting was thus complete.

While *Darling* edged ever nearer a starting date, producer Jo Janni agreed to loan his contracted star briefly to MGM, and Julie went to Ireland in August 1964 to film a small role for the great Irish–American director John Ford. This, she felt, really was a step in the right direction and she jumped at the chance to work with such a distinguished film-maker even though she was aware that she had once again been hired largely for her looks.

Born in 1895, Ford had by now made 125 movies, including many silent films, in a career spanning 47 years and now, though feeling and showing his age and with his sight fading, he was tackling a project dear to his heart, a film about the early life of Irish playwright Sean O'Casey based on his autobiography, *Mirror In My House.* The film was called *Young Cassidy,* and featured ruggedly handsome Australian actor Rod Taylor as O'Casey's alter ego. It covers the period when Cassidy is feeling the first stirrings of the talent that was to elevate him to international renown as one of Ireland's greatest playwrights. Maggie Smith played his first love, who leaves him so that he can achieve more without her, and Julie was cast as Daisy Battles, a prostitute who seduces young Cassidy.

Filming was underway when, sadly for all concerned, John Ford was taken ill and was unable to continue with the movie.

Jack Cardiff, an imaginative cinematographer but a virtual newcomer when it came to directing movies, was hastily drafted in to take Ford's place, the freshman taking over from the experienced old master. Inevitable confusion reigned briefly as Cardiff took the helm. On examining the script and the significance of Julie's role as Daisy, neither she nor Cardiff, according to Julie, were quite sure what she was supposed to do. Julie feared that she would be dropped from the film but gradually her scenes with Rod Taylor were worked through and her fresh-faced beauty and sex appeal on screen eventually sat comfortably with Taylor's good looks. When Julie got a chance to view her scenes on celluloid she thought, 'My god, Christie, you've come out of that very well. You even look beautiful.'

By October 1964 Janni had stitched together a precarious financial deal for *Darling* with the help of Anglo-Amalgamated and the National Film Finance Corporation, but he knew it needed a sizeable contribution from his own pocket to shore up the budget. His faith in *Darling* was unshakeable, however, and he was prepared to invest almost everything he had. Finally, Janni and Schlesinger were able to announce their plans for *Darling* at a launch party held at the Oak Room at Lord's, the famous headquarters of cricket in St John's Wood.

At the party there was no doubting Janni's commitment to *Darling* or his eve-of-filming excitement. 'The world we will see, as Miss Christie weaves her wistful way through it, will shock,' he promised. 'Like other characters in the film she wants something for nothing. Materially she has everything, spiritually she has nothing.'

Julie talked enthusiastically but nervously about a role she felt was a huge step up from the fluffy parts she had started out playing in British film comedies. It was apparent to showbusiness journalists at the party that Diana Scott was one of the longest, most demanding British film roles ever to be entrusted to an actress of such limited experience and some doubted whether Julie was ready for it.

Ahead lay a gruelling three and a half months of filming in a role that was to prove hugely demanding. There was to be little respite for Julie because the screenplay featured her in virtually every scene and even when she wasn't required on set for filming, Schlesinger needed her to be on call. Before the cameras began turning there were dozens of costume fittings. In all, she discovered, there were to be no fewer than fifty-three changes of costume and half a dozen different hairstyles.

When filming began, Julie discovered she could hardly have chosen more generous and sensitive male co-stars than Dirk Bogarde and Laurence Harvey. Both found Julie delightful and, having formed such a favourable opinion of her and established an instantly harmonious rapport, both were also quick to recognize her lack of experience, make allowances for it and give her the help she needed. They understood the pressure their young co-star was under and the enormity of her role.

On set the relationship between Julie and Schlesinger had its uneasy moments. Julie lent heavily on Schlesinger's direction for her performance and he repaid her trust in him by taking the time and trouble to explain everything. At first he found he had to give the young actress very detailed inflectional direction but, as filming progressed, he allowed her a freer rein. Finally he was able to direct Julie with a form of visual and verbal shorthand they had developed between them, indicating what he wanted with a nod, a gesture, a smile or a just a word. At appropriate moments Schlesinger was also not averse to sending Julie up occasionally, which helped to ease the tension. But Schlesinger, a short, stocky man, drove Julie hard to coax the performance he wanted out of her and clashes were inevitable. Harsh words were exchanged, tempers became frayed and Julie found herself regularly fighting fatigue as the fourteen-hour days began to take their toll.

There were moments of heated conflict, Schlesinger recalled, when Julie sorely tried his patience. 'She behaved atrociously at times,' he said. 'She didn't bother with the niceties of being chummy with the cameramen and the whole camera crew were bitching about her like mad to begin with, saying "sour cow" and "what's wrong with madam this morning?" And she was impossible with some of the wardrobe problems.

But by the end the camera crew had come round.' In Julie's defence, her lack of experience in film-making meant she simply had no idea at that stage of her career that it would help if she were chummy with the cameraman and crew. In addition, her natural shyness kicked against it.

Above all, it was the long hours and missed sleep that distressed Julie so desperately. She was up at six o'clock in the morning every day for three and a half months and frequently did not get back to her flat until eight in the evening. Then she'd make herself a meal, tidy up, and settle down to go over her lines for the following day until one o'clock in the morning. 'Trying to do everything, I became bad-tempered and horrible,' she remembered. Without appearing ungrateful for the break *Darling* was giving her, Julie resented the fact that her life did not appear to be her own any more. It wasn't long before the early morning calls after only five hours' sleep began to get her down enough to speak out. 'I need nine hours' sleep,' she complained bitterly. 'I don't bother to get dressed in the mornings now, just slip a coat over my nightie and get into the studio's car. As I've no longer time to be Julie Christie there seems no point in getting into her clothes.'

It was this having no time to be herself which she hated most. 'It was awful being someone else night and day,' she groaned. 'It began to get me. I changed so completely as a person. When I finished work and had dinner with my mates, they could tell I wasn't me. I just began to cry. I was born Julie Christie. I thought, why can't I go on being Julie Christie? I wanted to stop.' The only real break Julie was given was four days over the Christmas holiday period of 1964 when she went to Wales to spend the festive holiday with her mother. But two of those days were spent travelling and she returned to London chiding herself for not using them to catch up on her sleep.

One morning when Julie arrived for filming feeling especially tired Schlesinger asked her what time she had got to bed. It was one o'clock, she said, and Schlesinger told her she had no right to be up that late when she was facing such a demanding day's filming. Julie retorted that she had to cook and clean her flat when she got home at night. To ease the pressure on her, Jo Janni sent round his Italian maid to help with the chores and Schlesinger arranged for his own driver to chauffeur Julie around.

But the consistent lack of sleep often meant she was so exhausted by the time the crew broke for lunch each day that she would retire to a room at the film studio, where a bed had been specially installed, and there she'd curl up like a cat and try to catch up with her rest. That much-cherished hour always seemed to flash by and Julie would be woken in time to eat a few slivers of cold meat before getting back to filming. Perversely, that snatched sleep in itself caused problems for the production's hairdressing department. Any special hair-do they had created would invariably be messed up as she slept and would require further time-consuming attention. Wardrobe also suffered when a yawning Julie would emerge with clothes needing another pressing.

The pace for Julie was relentless. 'I suppose all good directors are merciless,' she said resignedly as Schlesinger tirelessly spurred *Darling* onwards. When she spoke out grumpily about the way Schlesinger was driving her, the director in the end felt bound to justify himself. 'Merciless? I suppose I am in getting what I want,' he countered. 'I don't care if Julie drops as long as I get the right performance out of her. And I am. We're all tired. At least she's tired for the right reason – work. She's young, inexperienced and lacks stamina. But she's learning.'

Julie was mindful, to her chagrin, that her daily pursuit of a few precious minutes of extra sleep contrasted sharply with the energy of everyone she saw around her, especially Laurence Harvey. He was filming by day and appearing in the musical *Camelot* on the West End stage every night and Julie was deeply impressed with his stamina. 'He was leading a very sophisticated life then, very jet-setty, so I didn't have much to do with him. He worked terribly hard, too. During most of the filming of *Darling* he was also working in a play at night and he had to have B-12 injections in his bum to keep him going. I remember being terribly impressed by that because I was knackered just doing the film, whereas he was working on the film all day, then working in a play half the night and probably going off to party after that.'

Harvey, for his part, was fascinated at the frequency and ease with which Julie fell asleep. Although it was partly to catch up with the shut-eye she missed because of the discomfort of bedding down on her lilo, falling asleep was also Julie's way of blotting out all the pressures of *Darling.* 'She was absolutely adorable,' said Harvey. 'She was always asleep, coming to the studio in the morning, going home in the evening. She may even have been asleep while doing the picture,' he joked. 'But she's marvellous, enchanting, sexy, alive, vibrant, astute, clever and knowledgeable.'

Dirk Bogarde also treated with amused tolerance Julie's ability to snatch a snooze at odd moments once he had learned that she was still sleeping each night on her pumped-up lilo. One morning she arrived desperately tired at Paddington Station to film a scene with Bogarde and explained that she'd had very little sleep because her lilo had sprung a puncture and she'd had to sleep on the floor. 'She broke down exhausted, and cried like a mad thing in front of all those people,' he said. 'The laugh here is that Julie is never on guard. She never has a fake moment.'

Bogarde listened sympathetically to the story of Julie's sleepless night and when he suggested it really was time she bought herself a bed Julie replied that she'd seen a very expensive brass bed in a junk shop in the King's Road and she intended to save up for it. A production assistant was dispatched to find the nearest garage to buy a puncture repair kit for Julie's mattress and while Julie herself went off to the ladies to dry her eyes, Bogarde's agent Tony Forwood wrote out a modest cheque for the bed and the actor wrote out another for the mattress with a little in reserve in case she needed to buy some blankets. Then they folded up the cheques and stuffed them deep in Julie's hold-all where she discovered them later in the day while rummaging around for an apple. Julie was deeply touched by their thoughtful generosity.

Julie had much else to be grateful to Dirk Bogarde for. 'Dirk was a darling,' she said. 'He was a very special and dear man and I was very lucky to be working with him. What a treasure for an inexperienced and frightened young girl to have this terribly experienced kind person acting right opposite! And of course he was the most wonderful actor to act with – he gave you everything when you worked with him.'

Bogarde was not only generous with his money and with his time towards Julie but with his praise. He clicked with Julie from the outset. 'Julie was glorious. A gift. We were joined immediately,' he noted  in his memoirs *Snakes and Ladders.* He said he not only found her adorable but that Julie taught him more about ad-libbing than anyone else in the business. During and after the filming of *Darling* he always spoke enthusiastically about her when questioned about his young inexperienced co-star. 'She has more magnetism or, if you like, star quality than any actress I have worked with in all my forty-five pictures,' he said. 'I've never come across anyone quite like Julie. When Julie gives a tender kiss it implies something more, something beyond lipstick.

'Julie has this enormous outpouring of love. She gets bored very quickly. She is mercurial and so in love with just being alive that she even throws herself about in the snow like some small child. She has a wild love affair with the camera but it's a ruthless one. One moment it shows her like a baboon with a rubber face. Five seconds later she is shot into radiance.'

Bogarde also noted: 'She's very much at home visiting a big house with servants. She just worries that her mates might be embarrassed somehow. She lives by the middle-class conservative rules she was brought up with of honour, self-discipline and loyalty. The rules she breaks are the false, snobby ones.' Bogarde also added prophetically: 'Even if she became rich she'd still have mates around and give everything away.'

Despite all these plaudits for Julie Christie long before *Darling'* s release, Pauline Yates, who played Dirk Bogarde's abandoned wife, recalls that when filming of *Darling* began no one could possibly conceive of the heights to which the film was to take Julie. 'I certainly never imagined at the time it was going to produce an Oscar-winning star,' Pauline says now. 'Julie was just another actress really, a nice girl who got lucky. There's an awful lot of luck in our business but with Julie, I think, the key to her success was and is that the camera just loves her. People said the same about Marilyn Monroe and I think it's just as true with Julie.

'She's a very beautiful woman, of course, but you could have an equally beautiful woman who would not come over on screen. Julie does. She has a wonderful, myopic, wide-eyed look. I don't know if she is really short-sighted but that is how she comes across on camera. No amount of clever technical playing with the camera can produce that look if the actress hasn't got it. Julie just had it.'

Like so many others who came into close contact with Julie at that time, Pauline was struck by her apparent indifference to the way she was being propelled to stardom and by her scatty nature. 'She seemed astonished at what was happening to her with *Billy Liar* and then *Darling* but she wasn't fazed by it. She just accepted that she was the lead and got on with it.

'I already knew Julie when we started on *Darling* because we had worked together on the play for Granada TV called *Dangerous Corner* and I remember afterwards on *Darling* she always confused me with my character in the play. I kept having to tell her: "No I'm not Leslie, I'm Pauline." She'd say blankly, "Oh I thought your name was Leslie," and I would explain again, "No, that was my name in the play." Julie was always rather vague. You could never quite pin Julie down on anything.

'She was always late and of course no one got cross with her. She was just not going to be tied down to someone saying "You must be here at 10 o'clock." She was late even before she was a star. In the play she was often late although she was on time on the night. I had been brought up in the theatre where good time-keeping is part of the job but Julie would just wander in as if she had all the time in the world and I would feel like saying to this young actress, "Where have you been?" But I didn't.

'Julie socialized with the rest of us in the Priestley play but because she was new to the business she didn't have much to contribute. She was, and always has been, amazing looking but she was not pursued by hordes of men. She was more of a loner, and I think she always has been. She was an arty person who operated on her own level. Intelligent, very arty, self-contained. She was not affected by the business and I always felt she was very centred. You knew you didn't have to worry about Julie. She didn't seem ambitious or put out when she had no acting parts and when she did get parts she seemed more astonished than anything else.'

Most of Pauline's scenes in *Darling* were shot with Dirk Bogarde at a beautiful house in Hampstead, supposed home of Robert and Estelle Gold. 'Dirk was struck on Julie,' Pauline recalls, 'but he was very good to me as well as Julie. *Darling* was my first big film too and I found Dirk absolutely meticulous about his work. He would tell me what angle to hold my head to get the best shot. He had it all worked out in advance exactly how he was going to play each line. Not many people do that and I'm sure Julie Christie didn't.

'John Schlesinger was an odd man. In *Darling* there was a scene where my character Estelle had to cry because Dirk Bogarde had left me. It was a scene with just me walking along by myself and crying. John was a very brusque sort of director, like camp people often are, and I was waiting to do this scene, trying to get myself psyched up to do it when he said, "Right, go." But I couldn't just cry as quickly as that. So John said "Cut" then, "Right, go on cry." I couldn't do it as the scene before hadn't led up to anything like that at all. But he said, "That's it. It's your fault. We've tried twice. If you don't deliver it I can't film it. Your scene has gone." And I never worked for him again. Now I would say to him, "It's up to you to help me get it, make me able. We're part of a team, aren't we?" I did think he was quite clever but not very understanding. He and the whole unit packed up and went and they just left me. And then I did feel like bursting into tears.'

Pauline was not the only one. As Julie toiled on *Darling* for up to fourteen hours a day for three and a half months, often working Saturdays and Sundays, her commitment, her stamina and her nerves were tested to breaking point. 'When I got tired I became like a very spoiled child stamping and screaming,' Julie admitted. 'It was awful being Diana day and night. For twelve to fourteen hours a day I was living her life and when I went home I had to cook dinner for my mates. They could tell I wasn't me. It made me thoroughly exhausted. I've become very short-tempered and I won't stand for anything that doesn't go my way. I expect everything to be everywhere at the right moment. Otherwise I just can't cope.'

Julie's disposition was not helped by the presence most evenings of one or more of the backers at the screening of the daily rushes. They constantly carped about Julie, and Bogarde recalled an occasion after just one week's work on the film when one of the backers was particularly cruel and disparaging about her looks. Bogarde sat watching the day's rough footage with his agent Tony Forwood in a small projection theatre when this particular backer turned to them both and savaged Julie. 'She's got a face like the back of a bus,' he said. 'She looks just like a feller, look at that jaw. She could play bloody football.' Bogarde and Forwood found themselves confronted by Julie's cigar-smoking critic when the man swivelled round and barked, 'Don't you agree? She's dead ugly.'

Forwood ventured the opinion that Julie was the nearest thing he had seen to Brigitte Bardot. Incredulous that Julie should be likened to the famous French 'sex-kitten', the man asked 'You think she's sexy?' 'Very. She'll be a big, big star,' came the firm reply.

Many years later, in the glorious certainty of hindsight, Bogarde was able to recall with glee how misplaced was the bewilderment on the money-man's face when the discussion about Julie ended with the backer declaring: 'I must be losing my wits. Sexy? It's all going mad.'

Nevertheless, there was a general air of gloom at the time about the backers' view of *Darling* and their realization that they had an unknown female starlet whom they considered lacking sex appeal in the leading role, a male lead who meant little to the general public in America and a director who was also virtually unknown. Another aspect that concerned them was that the film did not have a happy ending and was therefore too downbeat.

From the very first day of filming there was one tricky hurdle which both Julie and Schlesinger knew they would eventually have to surmount – Julie's nude scene. All along Julie knew that the screenplay would require her to strip off for a crucial sequence in which Diana, lonely and bored to distraction by her empty marriage to her Italian prince, rampages in her isolation through six rooms of a Florentine house, shedding jewels and clothes along the way. Finally she reaches her bedroom where she tears off the remainder of her clothes before throwing herself naked and crying on to her bed.

It was a scene which Schlesinger considered central to the theme of the film, revealing the vulnerable, lonely, naked creature beneath the trappings of wealth and splendour that Diana Scott had acquired by marriage. But he was aware it was a scene that had bothered Julie intensely all along. The more she thought about it, the more appalled she became at the prospect of having to take her clothes off in front of the camera. Although from day one she'd been fully conscious of the scene's existence in the script and Schlesinger's intention to shoot it, Julie somehow felt that when it actually came to the crunch he would not seriously insist that she went through with it. She was wrong.

Julie understood its importance and its relevance but as the time approached to film it she became more and more temperamental. 'She would burst into tears at the mention of it,' Schlesinger recalled. 'Whenever the costume had to be fitted she would make some excuse and stand like a sack of potatoes. She behaved like a dreadfully spoiled child putting on a petulant act. I got really angry and decided she needed a bomb and I gave it to her.'

Frederic Raphael was also called upon to try to persuade Julie that the scene was fully justified and must be filmed. Julie listened intently to his gentle but firm reasoning then said finally, 'Oh I don't say the scene isn't necessary. It's just that I don't want to do it. I haven't got the figure for it.' Both Schlesinger and Raphael were incredulous. 'She'd finally explained that she didn't think she had a beautiful enough body,' said Schlesinger. 'I said, "It doesn't matter," and she said, "But it does matter. I will be unattractive to people." '

Coaxed by both Schlesinger and Raphael, Julie finally resolved the whole scene in her mind and went ahead with it. Schlesinger filmed Julie raging through the splendid house before pausing in front of her bedroom mirror to pull her slip over her head and fling herself naked and tearful on the bed. She was professional enough to carry off the scene she had dreaded in one take but the tears she shed in the process were very real. When, later, Julie nervously accepted Schlesinger's invitation to view the rushes she pronounced herself 'not bad' after all.

As producer, Janni had other, more pressing, worries. The purse strings were being pulled ever tighter and financially *Darling* was faltering. There were serious doubts that the film would be completed. When production finally teetered on the very brink of shut-down Janni regretfully appealed to Dirk Bogarde to take a pay cut to keep the film afloat. Janni confided to Bogarde that he had personally mortgaged everything except his wife and now he was also having to ask Bogarde to defer payments.

But as the crisis hovered ever more threateningly over the film, salvation arrived in the unlikely shape of David Lean. The British film-maker was in the process of casting *Doctor Zhivago,* which, so word had it, was planned to be a most lavish screen version of Boris Pasternak's book of a love-affair set against the backdrop of the Russian Revolution. Lean had received encouraging reports about Julie Christie and was impressed that Schlesinger and Janni had been able to mount a major feature film around her. Accordingly he telephoned Julie's agents and asked to look at some film footage from *Darling.* Jo Janni, sensing possible rescue from *Darling'* s dire financial constraints, sent Lean some of Julie's best scenes.

Under his deal with Julie, Janni would, of course, command 50 per cent of Julie's fee if Lean were to sign her for *Doctor Zhivago.*

Understandably Janni was excited by Lean's interest in Julie which was more than could be said for the actress herself. The entire film industry was aware that *Doctor Zhivago* was to be a movie of epic proportions but Julie seemed unconcerned about the interest in her for the leading female role of Lara for which every major actress in Hollywood was vying. As *Darling* continued on its precarious path, Janni was not the only one waiting anxiously to hear from David Lean. So, too, was Dirk Bogarde in whom Lean had also expressed interest, albeit rather more reservedly, for a role in *Doctor Zhivago.*

The call from Lean's office finally came through when Julie was preparing to film a scene in which Diana is visiting her sister in the country to get away temporarily from her hectic London life. It was a pale sunlit morning and Julie was sprawled on the lawns of Skindles in Maidenhead dressed in a tweed suit and pearls reading Karl Marx while awaiting her call. Summoned to the telephone, she returned a few minutes later looking anything but elated and resumed her relaxed position on the grass in wan winter sunshine and buried her head in her book once more. Bogarde, for whom the call from Lean was not to come, assumed Julie had had bad news. Tentatively he asked her what the outcome had been and was ready to offer commiseration but Julie amazed him by informing him she'd got the role of Lara. She said quietly, 'I've got Lara. Rather good.' Bogarde was astounded. Most actresses would have been reaching for the champagne.

The reason for her lukewarm reaction to winning the plum film role of that or possibly any other year soon became clear to Bogarde. Growing visibly angry now, Julie recounted how the *Doctor Zhivago* producers and David Lean had told her they wanted her out in Spain straight away. 'They want me to get out of this little picture,' she fumed. 'Said it wasn't important and I had to get to Madrid as soon as possible and start working on the part. They say I could get an Oscar for it and I should leave John.'

Julie was filled with indignation at the suggestion she should abandon *Darling* right away and leave John Schlesinger in the lurch after all the hard work they had put in together. Naturally, Bogarde was anxious to know the outcome. 'I told them to stuff Lara or wait,' Julie snapped. 'They'll bloody have to wait,' she added loyally.

In view of the faith, patience, not to mention money, invested in Julie for *Darling,* the sentiment was admirable but Janni was quick to intervene. He swiftly arranged a meeting with Julie at which he was at pains to explain the golden opportunity which *Doctor Zhivago* presented for her. He pointed out that stepping into such a markedly different role from Diana Scott in *Darling* would be of immeasurable benefit for her career. Working with a director of such renown as David Lean would be invaluable experience for her and the role of Lara would elevate her to true international status as an actress.

Janni did not shirk, however, from emphasizing to Julie that, quite frankly, he desperately needed the money the role would generate for him. The implications for Julie were that if she didn't take the role of Lara, *Darling* would be in jeopardy. Julie fully understood and agreed to sign up to *Doctor Zhivago.* The opportunity was simply too good to miss but, in effect, Janni was able to sell Julie Christie to David Lean in a deal which paid Julie's salary, gave her a share of the profits and ensured the completion of *Darling.* With the finances now assured, filming progressed with renewed enthusiasm and Julie's remaining scenes were conveniently rescheduled to allow her to travel to Madrid as soon as they were completed.

Gradually the news spread among the British moviemaking community in Wardour Street that something special was emerging with *Darling.* The word was that Schlesinger was on the way to delivering a British film of rare quality and that he was obtaining from Julie Christie a performance to match. The fact that Julie had been selected for *Doctor Zhivago* was proof of it. Now exhibitors and distributors who had previously turned *Darling* down were clamouring for the movie. Joe Levine, having sorted out one John Schlesinger from another, incredibly, went so far as to offer $1 million for the US rights without having seen the film.

With such confidence in the film now being shown by America, *Darling* was shrewdly earmarked for release in the USA first. It was felt that the Americans were likely to cast a less critical eye over a film set in London than the British reviewers and Schlesinger was able to finish editing *Darling* in an optimistic frame of mind before preparing to go off to Stratford to direct *Timon.*

*Darling* was to prove a triumph for Schlesinger and despite its theme of promiscuity, the only cut the censor made was a scene where a man who has had difficulty in finding a parking meter is seen coming into a house already undressing to meet a tart. The fact that the scene, intended to reflect the mundane nature of much of sex, ended on the cutting-room floor, was of no great consequence to the impact of the final film.

Schlesinger's documentary apprenticeship had taught him about risk-taking and decision-making and sharpened his attention to detail and, as a documentary-trained director, he skilfully harnessed his techniques to give depth to *Darling'* s three principal characters, prompted by an intrinsic curiosity about people which was to manifest itself further in future Schlesinger films.

The director established *Darling'* s narcississtic tone and its sense of warped values in the opening seconds of his film. A gigantic poster of Julie

Christie's face is being plastered over an advertising hoarding displaying the emaciated bodies of starving children while, over this image, the husky voice of Julie as Diana Scott is describing her charmed and exciting life to a writer from *Ideal Woman* magazine. From this stinging start *Darling* went on to satirize sixties society, the world of 'Mod' London, high fashion, big business, the pretentious, the idle rich, the Italian riviera, adultery and homosexuality. The film also delivered a scathing satire not just on the morals and manners of contemporary London society but on the wider media: newsreels, BBC TV talk programmes, *vox pop* street interviews, British horror films, women's magazines, TV commercials and advertising campaigns dependent on the exploitation of a pretty face and a fabricated personality. 'It should be so easy to be happy, shouldn't it?' Diana, the Happiness Girl, queries of one lover. 'If I could just feel complete,' she laments.

In Schlesinger's *Darling* there was no escaping the significance of the fact that the three men through whose beds Diana passes in London were all image-makers – TV pundit Robert Gold, Miles Brand, a sleek advertising executive and professional voyeur for whom everything except real feeling comes via his expense account, and photographer Malcolm with whom Diana had to compete for the same lover on her working holiday in Capri.

'A lot of people were frightened by this film,' Schlesinger reflected. 'A bit of our own self-confessions went into it. Everyone knows girls like this. She's a result of affluent society. Although there have always been girls like this, girls in a hurry, there are more of them these days because life is freer. There aren't so many rules. Society as it is now is only too ready to accommodate girls like her.

'It is essentially a study of a milieu. We planned it as an ironic comedy but it's come out more bitter than we expected and ends on a note of despair. I like downbeat endings. We could not have got away with it commercially a few years back.'

When *Darling* was released in America in the summer of 1965 after it had been presented at the Moscow Film Festival at the Kremlin Palace of Congresses on 16 August 1965, the critics were lavish in their praise of Julie. 'At every toss of her blonde mane, every shard of a smile, all else on screen becomes a mere backdrop,' said *Time.* 'Her stunning presence – and Schlesinger's stylish tracking of her playgirl's progress – makes *Darling* irresistible.'

The enthusiasm of the American critics even stretched to the National Catholic Office for Motion Pictures who cited the movie for its 'artistic vision' and 'expression of authentic human values'. Schlesinger was then astonished to be asked to talk about *Darling* to forty Catholic teachers and twelve nuns. 'They loved it,' he said. 'They thought the message was rather old-fashioned morality.' One of the nuns, referring to the scene where Diana and photographer Malcolm court the same man, wanted to know if many Italian men really were ambi-sex-trous.

To Julie's delight, given her Francophile tendencies since her teens, the French also acclaimed *Darling* although some of the popular French newspapers tended to go overboard. 'JC – La BB Anglaise,' blazed one headline, likening Julie's tousled blonde sex appeal to their own liberated screen siren Brigitte Bardot.

'C'est la bombe 1965' screamed another headline. Britain and America were hailing Julie now as 'the Face of 1965' but this particular French newspaper gave the title a typically French tinge and made her the sex bomb of 1965. 'Elle pourrait faire bien plus de ravages encore que Jane Fonda ou Ursula Andress,' it announced which roughly translated as Julie Christie could be even wilder than Jane Fonda or Ursula Andress.

Pressed for her own view of herself Julie said, 'I'm too small and thin to be sexy ... I don't think men see any lusty sexiness in me. The appealing thing is an air of abandonment. Men don't want responsibility and neither do I.'

Was she like Diana Scott? 'I know her, I know lots like her,' said Julie. 'Some of the things in her character I recognize in myself. But the most important thing is that we are, thank heavens, not alike. She's impressionable, easily knocked down by the phoniness of her superficial world. I think I am a lot more intelligent than she is. I'd never make such a mess of my life through being unable to choose. I don't like her very much but I can't hate her because I can see how any girl who is pretty and has a little bit of success can become like her.

'I think Diana was the least swinging person I know. Her friends were all squares as far as I'm concerned. They didn't have style and they had a sort of derived wit. They were just depraved more than anything else. I think it's rather old-fashioned to be depraved.'

A viewing of *Darling* today might prompt the question: what was all the fuss about? Certainly it is a *tour de force* for Julie but, perhaps inevitably, it is a film very much of its time. It sits right in the middle of the Swinging Sixties and the sexual permissiveness indulged in by many of the characters in the movie reflects a time when the Pill had just arrived giving women the opportunity to have sex without risk of pregnancy. As Julie, Schlesinger and Janni all pointed out, Diana Scott was a woman playing it her way, using men to get what she wanted and it was a novel image of women at the time even though she did get punished in the end.

In the fullness of time Julie was able to comment, of her Diana Scott role: 'It wasn't difficult for me, I think it was probably the easiest part I've done! I was pretty silly, selfish and superficial then. I understood a lot of what that silly girl was going through. I did despise that vacuous, empty-headed part of her although one should never despise one's character, but I was reading a lot of highbrow books and being an intellectual snob at the time. But the rest – all that ruthless selfishness and superficiality – I understood very well indeed.'

*Darling* received its European première on 16 September 1965, at the Plaza cinema at Piccadilly Circus, and Julie flew back from the *Doctor Zhivago* set in Spain to be there. She was greeted by hundreds of fans and well-wishers who had turned up to see the girl whom everyone seemed to be talking about. Among the celebrity guests was Ingrid Bergman who said of Julie after seeing the movie, 'I think she has the most forceful personality of all the young actresses in films today.'

Because of *Darling'*s decadent party scene and its examination of the sixties 'sweet life', *The Times* felt that inescapable comparison arose with *La Dolce Vita,* the 1959 movie starring the statuesque Swedish blonde actress Anita Ekberg, which explored the same sort of theme, but in *Darling* there was no compelling empathy for Diana. It added: 'Miss Julie Christie with slender experience and tremendous potential remains magnetically viewable throughout the two hours of the film. She captures the heroine's qualities exactly, the emotional shallowness of the spoiled child and the effortless sensuality of the grown woman.'

The *Daily Mail'*s much respected film critic Cecil Wilson was also full of admiration for Julie's performance: 'With its maelstrom of moods and its marathon length it's a peach of a part for any young actress, however sour the peach may be, and the more you despise the character the more you will admire the electric personality and sheer profession- alism of Julie Christie.'

But not every critic waxed so lyrically. 'The script demands a neurotic,' wrote Kenneth Tynan in the *Observer.* 'Instead it gets a hockey captain with ro- mantic leanings.'

In America Schlesinger was generous in praise of his star, her beauty and her independent streak. 'It's not a traditional face. The jawline is masculine, the lips are full and Bardot-like,' he told *Look* maga- zine. 'The eyes are marvellous, funny little things. This brings about a strange mixture of the hard and the determined, the feminine and the totally carefree – the qualities that dominate in Julie's nature.' He added, 'Julie made no attempt to win audience sympathy or maintain an "image". That's where the rot sets in for an actress. Julie is not a great stage actress or ever will be but she has the intuition, in- telligence and face to become an extraordinary film star.'

That Christmas, after a breathtaking year, Julie showed her appreciation to John Schlesinger for all he had done for her. Having by now spent months working under David Lean's direction she was begin- ning to understand the dedication of film-makers. The run-ins she had encountered with Schlesinger during the filming of *Darling* were now long forgotten and attached to her Christmas present to the director was a tag which read 'To my dear John from his Trilby, with love.'

Julie earned $7,500 for her role in *Darling* and immediately went out and bought a leather jacket she coveted. At last she was able to buy clothes and not have to make her own amateurish copies of Mary Quant. But she was still so wary of the fame now threatening to engulf her. 'Frankly I fear success and all the trappings that go with it,' she said. I'd like to be a more simple person, a truly free soul and for a time I was a vagrant. I used to sleep in attics, even in parks. Now I'm under contract I get £50 a week. I've never known such prosperity and it frightens me. I've had to take an apartment, get my own digs, invite people back to dinner. I'm no hostess. I can't add or subtract. I know nothing about money. I have a flat for which I pay £9 a week. For months I lived in a slum. I couldn't care less. But now it becomes impossible.'

The contract with Jo Janni had enabled Julie to set up her first permanent home in London. Shunning the more trendy area around Chelsea, Julie had taken a two-year lease on an unfurnished flat at number 4 Auriol Mansions, in Edith Road, west Kensington, and the other residents in the imposing four-storey block soon became used to seeing Julie bounding cheerfully up the nine steps to her front door on the raised ground floor. Her un-starry manner gave no clue to her neighbours that she was about to become one of the most famous actresses in the world. 'She was very natural and very friendly,' says Mona Fahmy who still lives next door at number 5.

After the dingy Fulham attic which had provided a roof over her head, Julie now had somewhere fitting to park the ornate brass bed which Dirk Bogarde had so generously helped her to buy. By now she was also sharing her life with Don Bessant, a tall, rangy and good-looking young artist, whom she had met when he delivered a fan letter whilst working temporarily as a postman. He was confident and boldly anti-establishment in his views and they quickly struck up a friendship. Julie was drawn to his relaxed, easygoing attitude to life, which contrasted markedly with the driven and ambitious young men she tended to attract on the set. 'I can't stand extroverted men,' she said. 'I like Don because he's so quiet.' Together they set about making the flat cosy, buying furniture either from junk shops or from the antique shops in Portobello Road. In time, a cat called Doggy and eight budgerigars added a homely element.

For a long while Julie and Don lived with the brown and white lino, the squiggly carpets, beige wallpaper and busily patterned curtains of the previous tenants. But Julie encouraged her arty mates to brighten up the place and the drab kitchen was transformed with a huge red, white and blue bull's-eye painted on one wall and the kitchen units painted red white and blue to match. A marble-topped pub-style table served as a work surface and on the shelves Julie put prominently on display an early American coffee grinder she had brought back from America at the end of her tour with the Royal Shakespeare Company and a selection of old medicine jars and Victorian bottles. The sitting-room was more formal with a chaise longue, a rocking chair, an antique three-legged chess table, an old pine chest of drawers, an old gramophone with a horn and a large ornate mirror over the boarded-up fireplace.

Today the Auriol Mansions flats are highly prized, situated in what is now a sought-after area of London. But back then, as Julie's fame grew over the next two years, she was frequently asked, to her irritation, why she didn't live like a star. Visiting foreign journalists expected the exciting new British star to be residing close to the famous King's Road in Chelsea with its trendy clothes shops and restaurants. What, they wanted to know, was she doing living near un-smart Olympia. 'I like it here because it's friendly,' was always Julie's reply. Besides, she pointed out, she was in easy reach of Baron's Court and West Kensington Tube stations. American media men, used to stars travelling around in limousines and living in the height of luxury, shook their heads in disbelief when Julie would conduct interviews in the kitchen while rolling dough with a milk bottle because she didn't own a rolling pin.

With new-found emotional and financial security on the brink of international stardom, Julie reflected on what the future might bring. 'That's the trouble with success. You become responsible for maintaining it. I want to be the centre of attention, I want to love, I want to achieve, I want to have longer legs. I want men to swoon over me. I want to be totally marvellous in *Doctor Zhivago.* But I don't want success in terms of money or in terms of marriage.'

# 6

# Doctor Zhivago

When she first arrived on set she looked terrified, like a frightened little bird. She had immense courage to face all this, and she emerged from it all with honours.

Rod Steiger

David Lean first read the epic 500-page novel *Doctor Zhivago* on a week-long sea voyage across the Atlantic in April 1963. Russian writer Boris Pasternak had been awarded the Nobel Prize for Literature five years earlier and his most famous work had deeply impressed MGM's ambitious new president, Robert O'Brien, and had the same impact on Lean's agent, Phil Kellogg. But initially, on board the Italian liner *Leonardo da Vinci,* it was hardly a task that lifted Lean's heart. 'I looked at it with its five hundred pages, and I thought, "Oh, God." We were crossing the South Atlantic and I realized I had to get down to this bloody book. So I propped myself up and I read and read the first night and became more interested. The next night I thought, "I'll finish it tonight," and ended up sitting in my bed, with a box of Kleenex, wiping the tears away. I was so touched by it, and I thought that if I can be touched like this, sitting in a liner reading a book, I must be able to make a good, touching film of it. As soon as I landed, I contacted my agent and said, "Yes, I'll do *Doctor Zhivago.* " '

Lean considered it was the best book he had ever read. 'Just a man's life, but somehow it's all our lives.' The book had been banned in the Soviet Union, but an Italian company had used a smuggled manuscript to publish a 1957 translation. The power and simplicity of the story thrilled and enthralled the experienced Lean. Zhivago is a doctor who is also an artist, who loves his wife Tonya, yet has an affair with the breathtakingly beautiful Lara, which makes him feel wretched and guilty, and somehow he manages to remain still strangely honourable. Certainly he is unfaithful, and he walks away from his responsibilities, but he is deeply sensitive and struggles to express his inner anguish through poetry.

The sprawling narrative of the book is set against the bewildering background of four decades of Russian turmoil, which include the Great War and the upheaval of the Revolution. Zhivago is torn between his roots with the Whites and his sympathy with the Reds and attempts to keep out of the civil war, only to be dragged into the conflict when he is captured by partisans and forced to tend to their wounded.

Lean knew that for the film to be a success he required two vital components: a scriptwriter of genius to fashion the brilliant but rambling novel for the screen and a new star of stunning luminescence to carry the crucial central role of Lara. The screen rights to the novel were owned by the Italian producer Carlo Ponti who had already hooked MGM's interest. The giant but ailing film company was then struggling to recover from the disastrous production of *Mutiny on the Bounty* that had lost so much money at the box office that O'Brien had been brought in to replace Joseph Vogel. MGM needed a box-office bonanza simply to be able to stay in business. O'Brien was so keen for Lean to work his magic on the movie, and not be diverted to work for rivals Columbia, that he flew to meet the director in Rome in June 1963 and agreed to pay him a huge salary, reputedly the highest ever paid to a director, as well as a healthy percentage of the profits. O'Brien had complete confidence in Lean's massive ability: 'I could and would trust David Lean under all circumstances we would encounter in making a picture. I regarded him as one of the great jewels of the motion picture industry.'

MGM did not fully realize it at the time but they were pushing against an open door. Lean was already entranced by the idea of the project and his only condition was that Robert Bolt should write the script. The two men had collaborated on *Lawrence of Arabia* with stunning results. Now, as John Simon memorably put it, they would make '*Doctor Zhivago* do for snow what *Lawrence of Arabia* had done for sand.'

After the triumph of *Lawrence of Arabia,* Lean and Bolt began a long and detailed correspondence which reflected a monumental meeting of minds. In his very first letter Lean wrote: 'This film *(Lawrence)* has put me into a fantastic position and a team consisting of you and I would be backed up to the hilt – bigger than anyone in this so-called industry. We could really call the tune and if money is of interest to you, you wouldn't have to worry about it for the rest of your life if we hit the jackpot. The more I see the reactions to *Lawrence* the more I realize we have something very out of the ordinary as a joint team. I won't say why. I know it's so. I'm just mad keen to work with you again.'

Other projects were considered and dismissed. At one point Bolt suggested an adaptation of Joseph Conrad's *Nostromo* and then a film based on the Charge of the Light Brigade but Lean dismissed them as backward steps and seemed obsessed by a rambling science fiction idea reflecting the development of man from prehistoric freedom to the pointless grind of modern society. But they both kept coming back to *Doctor Zhivago.*

Robert Bolt was the media darling of the moment. He expounded his racily fashionable left-wing views on the BBC's long-running discussion show *The Brains Trust* and argued about the Profumo Affair on ITV's rival programme *Dinner Party* with Malcolm Muggeridge. But behind the scenes his marriage was creaking as his long-suffering wife Jo was sidelined by her husband's success. She was finding it hard to cope with a house full of parties for the leading lights of the film world like Leslie Caron, Michael Caine and

Vanessa Redgrave. At one gathering an excited Peter O'Toole was seen to hurl Bolt's son's soundtrack recording of *Lawrence of Arabia* into the fire. When Sean Connery and his wife Diane Cilento joined the guests Jo was shocked by the revealing shortness of Cilento's skirt and declared to her husband, 'I'm not having someone dressed like that in my house.' Unfortunately Connery overheard and the master dramatist had to provide instant words of soothing eloquence.

Bolt grasped the offer to write the screenplay of *Doctor Zhivago* with great enthusiasm. He already knew the book and told Lean he was 'perfectly mesmerized' by the project. Following the dismal box-office disaster of his stage play *Gentle Jack,* he was also in serious need of the money. He asked Lean how much he could expect and also impressed the director with his vision of how the great novel could be brought to the screen.

Money was certainly not a problem. MGM was counting on Lean to provide a desperately needed box-office winner so he was able to negotiate a then world-record directing fee of $500,000 plus 33 per cent of the net profits, while Bolt settled for a still impressive $200,000, sadly, as it turned out for him, without any add-on percentage bonus from possible profits. That settled, the two men hurled themselves into the creative process. At first their ideas diverged. Bolt's biographer Adrian Turner says: 'To begin with, and to put it crudely, Robert wanted to make a film about humanity in the grip of the Russian Revolution, while David wanted to make a film about fucking. Robert thought the central thread of the story – that of the woman falling for the artist, the poet Zhivago, not the man – rather clichéd. This provoked an extraordinary response from Lean whose earlier love-stories *Brief Encounter* and *The Passionate Friends* had been about sexual repression.'

Bolt talked about the 'old story' of the woman falling not for the man but the artist, not realizing that only the man and not the artist can return her love. But Lean was determined that the film should not be cold and hard to comprehend for the mass audience and wrote to Bolt in colourfully earthy language stressing the potency of human emotions unleashed by the artist expressing himself in love-making. 'I won't accept that only the man and not the artist can return a woman's love. The artist's woman also takes his hatches off. Don't tell me that Anne Hathaway didn't experience a full Cape Canaveral countdown (forgive the vulgarity) which she could never have experienced with an uncreative Mr Jones ... Isn't love-making one of the greatest forms of self-expression known to man. It certainly is to a woman. The imaginative lover must surely take her further up the scale than Mr Jones ... A woman who has been an orchestra is in a perilous emotional situation if he should leave her.' Bolt got the point.

Screenwriter and director became totally absorbed in their massive task of bringing Boris Pasternak's masterpiece to the screen. The more they worked the more convinced they became that the character of Lara was crucial to the success of the whole enterprise. At that early creative stage she became a subject of near-obsessive fascination for both men.

Letters between them reveal that Lean was hugely impressed by Bolt's handling of Tonya, yet deeply concerned about his treatment of the all-important Lara and suggested the writer take advice from his wise and experienced agent Peggy Ramsay. Lean cautiously prefaced his thoughts with a desperate plea for Bolt not to take offence. It is an indication of how involved both men were when he went on to say that he knew he was being personal and critical about a woman Bolt was in love with.

Bolt was not remotely offended. Indeed he thought the letter was marvellous and noted that he was totally enthralled by his task. 'I am sure what I meant Lara to be like is what you and I both want her to be like ... I have never done anything so difficult. That bugger Pasternak! It's like trying to straighten cobwebs.'

Both men were struggling with difficult marriages while they strove to create their dream woman, Lara. Bolt's wife, Jo, was becoming closer to a local carpenter in a friendship that was to develop into an affair. Friends who visited their home began to notice that an inordinate number of shelves were being put up and doors replaced as the covert romance flourished. And Lean's fourth marriage, to Leila, was falling apart in a flurry of rows in their Venice hotel suite. Leila had a history of mental illness and her fragile emotional state was not helped by Lean's total absorption in his films. Unable to bring himself to break with Leila, Lean had already embarked on a long-lasting affair with Barbara Cole, his continuity girl on *Lawrence of Arabia* and *Doctor Zhivago.*

Like a shining beacon of femininity the image of Lara focused their energies and diverted them from their own domestic difficulties. And the harder they worked on *Doctor Zhivago* the more they realized that a very great deal rested on the elegant shoulders of whoever landed the role. MGM had an awful lot riding on the success of the massive movie and, as costs and estimates started to mount, both Bolt and Lean recognized that it was going to take an exceptional performance from a stunning new star to convince the international audience to warm to a woman who betrays her own caring husband and launches a passionate affair that splits up another loving husband and wife.

In an intuitive description of Lara – before Julie Christie had even been considered for the role – Bolt said he saw her as 'rather heavy and sweet, like a pot of fermenting honey. I see her a shade on the sulky side.' Bolt continued his vision of Lara: 'She is devastatingly attractive and at a glance a physical magnet. What's more she has to be a going concern sexually, on good terms with her glands yet not at all loose. Indeed there has got to be a modesty about her and no conflict between the sexuality which radiates from her, and the modesty – shyness almost – which shines upon her surface.'

The range of actresses considered to play the key role was certainly impressive. In 1964 Greta Garbo gravely announced that she might possibly make another film, but only if David Lean directed her. Lean had indeed been dreaming of discovering a new young Garbo to play Lara. But as he enveloped himself in his subject more completely he realized he needed someone rather less spiritual. Lean's other problem was that producer Carlo Ponti who owned the film rights had precisely the actress in mind: his spectacularly glamorous wife Sophia Loren.

Lean was frightened that Ponti might insist that Loren, who was then traffic-stoppingly beautiful but thirty years old, should become Lara, who is just seventeen when we first see her in the film. Indeed as the casting crisis developed the producer invited David Lean and his lover, Barbara Cole, for dinner and Loren appeared in a little plain dress with a demure lace collar looking the picture of innocence. When they returned home David Lean said to Barbara Cole that if anyone could convince him Sophia Loren was a virgin he would let her play the part.

He sympathized with the producer's ambitions for his wife. But he felt so threatened by the possibility of having Loren foisted on to him that he made his feelings plain to O'Brien at MGM. Lean wrote that while Ponti had behaved with the utmost correctness it was impossible not to imagine what was in his mind. Lean explained this was an embarrassment and spelled out that the whole credibility of the film hung on the audience sympathizing with a young virginal Lara being swept away by the depth of her first passions. 'This is why I want a young actress. Innocence cannot be acted except on a superficial level. I would not believe this was Miss Loren's first encounter with sex and if I don't believe it I would think she's a bitch. This is why I want young people (as Pasternak wrote them for good reason) in these parts.' Lean knew that for the film to work the audiences had to see a youthful Lara bloom into a young woman, who was patently good and innocent yet endowed with a screen sexuality of Cape Canaveral power.

The vitally important discussions on casting went on and on. Once Loren was politely positioned out of the running, MGM proposed Yvette Mimieux, who was firmly rejected, and then Jane Fonda was considered. But although Lean was impressed with her as an actress he was concerned about her accent. He knew a Russian heroine with an American accent would have the critics sharpening their sarcasm. Fonda was eased out of the frame and Lean suggested Sarah Miles, who had scored a major hit in *The Servant.* But Robert Bolt was horrified: 'No, no, no. She's just a North Country slut.' Which seems a shade churlish considering he was later to marry the very same Miss Miles. David defended Sarah Miles insisting that Bolt was guilty of believing the publicity but the seed of doubt was sewn and the search continued.

The two men were stumped. They knew that they had a magical love-story to unfold which had the potential to entrance the world. They had the backing to create the wonderfully romantic Russian backdrop, to recruit the world's finest actors and film craftsmen. They knew their own lofty reputations and the very solvency and existence of MGM could well depend on their decision. Most of all, they knew that whoever played Lara had to be capable of making the world love her even though she was to steal another woman's wife. Somewhere from the back of his masterful mind Lean dredged the memory of a glimpse of Julie Christie he had seen in *Billy Liar.* There was something about that haunting smile, that provocative pout, that youthful earnest innocence that told him that she, not Sophia Loren, not Yvette Mimieux, not Jane Fonda, not Sarah Miles, was the one woman who could carry this whole intricate enterprise to success. He remembered the free-spirited handbag-swinging girl who boldly turns her back on the North to take the train to London. 'I have never met her but she has extraordinary screen presence,' he wrote. But even the ultra-confident David Lean needed to check out his most important potential signing. He contacted the legendary John Ford who had begun the direction of *Young Cassidy* before being taken ill. Ford responded unequivocally: 'She's great, the best young actress that has ever come into the business. No one in the past has shown such talent at such an early age.'

It was then that David Lean telephoned Jo Janni and asked to see the clips from *Darling* that persuaded him that he might, finally, have found his Lara. Notwithstanding the approval of figures like John Ford and David Lean Julie herself was less than confident. Her reaction was: 'I thought they must be off their nuts,' and she went out to Madrid not so much for the screen test as for a free holiday. But she passed the test with flying colours. Lean was staggered when he met her in the flesh and told friends she was the answer to all his prayers because he had been wondering if it was going to be possible to find anyone with the perfect combination of innocence and sex appeal. 'She has both in spades,' he told a colleague. 'She's perfect.'

Julie Christie was astonished. 'I wouldn't even have rated myself as an actress at the time,' she said. 'My tendency was to put myself in the position of a child, and David was paternalistic. He behaved like an authoritarian but kindly father. He must have had some expectations after what Ford said, but it doesn't seem to me I did very much. After the rape scene, for instance, he was not getting what he wanted, and he and Freddie Young [director of photography] had a long talk, they put more sweat on me and then suggested I breathe more deeply and look into the camera. He was obviously used to power and authority and he understood his position. I wasn't scheduled to work for weeks and we were based in Soria. This was a wonderfully beautiful part of the countryside. My boyfriend Don Bessant had flown over and I was longing to travel round it with him. I asked permission and was forbidden to go. David wanted us all to be there. I was as furious as a little girl – with a certain amount of justification. I suppose this wasn't a very democratic time in film-making, was it? But I did trust him. He was an old-fashioned gentleman. Whatever he asked you to do professionally, you knew it would be okay. I never got to know him very well, but I liked him. He seemed distraught about his personal life a lot of the time. That was one of the reasons I liked him. He was a human being who couldn't quite sort things out. I found this rather touching, considering how hugely powerful he was. Like many people who are insecure, he didn't realize how autocratically he acted. And he could easily be hurt by people not realizing his vulnerability.'

To play Yuri Zhivago himself, Lean and Bolt were desperately searching for an actor who could follow his heart and betray the wife that loved him and still emerge as a hero, with the added difficulty of not being given any traditionally heroic scenes. To make matters more difficult for Lean, MGM wanted Paul Newman. He was quickly written off by the director as too down to earth and practical ever to be convincing as the dreamer, Zhivago. Bolt and Lean wanted Peter O'Toole, although the director had reservations after O'Toole's colourful celebrations when  in New

York for the opening of *Lawrence of Arabia*. 'O'Toole is much too extrovert for ideal casting,' wrote Lean, 'but I would rather suppress his exhibitionism than attempt to coax strength out of a lily. Unfortunately Zhivagos do not become actors.' But in any case O'Toole saw an early script and was highly critical, which caused a rift which put him out of the frame. It was Barbara Cole who suggested Omar Sharif and Lean seized the idea instantly. 'I rang him up and offered him the part,' said Lean. 'His agent called to find out how much I was willing to pay. I said, "I'll pay what Omar asks." And that's what we did. I've been friends with Omar ever since. I wish I'd offered him more parts. The trouble with Omar is that he suffers from that awful thing of being too good looking, and almost too expert, and people smile when they mention his name. It's something to do with jealousy, particularly with men. A kind of scathing put down.'

Certainly the idea of Sharif landing the starring role, of an Egyptian playing a Russian did attract criticism. But Lean was not to be diverted. In any case Sharif had just played an Armenian in *The Fall of the Roman Empire* and was playing the Mongol warrior Genghis Khan. So it did not seem too much of a leap and Lean used tape to pull his eyes back to 'take the orbs out of it' and straightened his hair. 'David was the only one who believed that I should play Zhivago,' said Sharif. 'It was against the opinion of Carlo Ponti, the producer, MGM and everyone. They did not think that somebody who was Egyptian, last seen on a camel, should play a Russian poet. But Lean knew me well. We had worked together for two years on *Lawrence of Arabia.* He knew I had it in me to play that part.

'The Slavs are very melodramatic people. They like to cry and hear violins which is exactly what Orientals like me enjoy as well. That has been my problem. On *Zhivago* David Lean would always tell me: 'Omar, you use too many violins, you have to keep your violins down.' So when we did a scene over and over he would tell me to take out some violins and tone it down. But no matter what I've done I've never managed to take out all the violins.'

For the role of Pasha, Lara's idealistic young Bolshevik husband who gradually metamorphoses into the cruel tyrant Strelnikov, Robert Bolt was very keen on Albert Finney, and he wrote to the actor stressing the dramatic quality of the role. But Lean could not forgive Finney for having turned down *Lawrence of Arabia* so Tom Courtenay was cast, possibly because Lean had seen him with Julie Christie in *Billy Liar.*

As the sinister and evil Komarovsky, who seduces both Lara and her mother, Lean wanted Marlon Brando, but the actor did not reply to his letter. Lean next approached James Mason who was delighted to accept the key role of the dapper grasping lawyer whom Lara attempts to kill in a fury of revenge. Lean noted that he needed an actor who had enough 'dexterity and personality to convince an audience that he could not only weather a revolution, changing sides as he does, but that he could end up as Minister of Justice. He must be old enough to make his seduction of the schoolgirl Lara shocking and not attractive enough to be in any logical sense a rival to Zhivago.' Mason wrote back by return of post, signing his letter of acceptance 'Elatedly, James,' but later dropped out, to be replaced by Rod Steiger.

It was producer Carlo Ponti who suggested Geraldine Chaplin as Zhivago's tragic wife Tonya, but Lean was unimpressed initially. He wanted Audrey Hepburn for the role, but Chaplin, daughter of the legendary Charlie, gave such a brilliant screen test she stole the part.

Lean's old friend Alec Guinness came on board to play Yevgraf Zhivago and Ralph Richardson and Siobhan McKenna completed the line-up of major roles. MGM's O'Brien had given Lean *carte blanche* to pick his team, but there was much muttering from the 'American money' about the scarcity of proven glamour. Who is Julie Christie? was the cry at one meeting. O'Brien wisely refrained from passing on the doubts to Lean, who insisted, 'I picked her because of that scene she had in *Billy Liar.* In that small amount of footage she gave every evidence of being an outstanding actress.'

*Doctor Zhivago* was the next big production in the fashionable new style of supermovies. Lean's own *Lawrence of Arabia* had been the critical hit of 1962 while Elizabeth Taylor as Cleopatra had provided the memorable movie spectacle of the following year. It was on 3 August 1964 on a rubbish dump at Canillejas outside Madrid that David Lean and his MGM army began to construct Tsarist Russia and start to bring a dream to the screen.

The cost of filming *Doctor Zhivago* in Hollywood was explored but it proved too astronomic to consider seriously. Producer Ponti would have preferred Yugoslavia and reckoned filming there would have brought the budget down from seven million to five million dollars. But when Lean drove into the then firmly Communist state in his Rolls-Royce he found a degree of unco-operation that he could not abide at any price. The authorities in Moscow were keen on the foreign currency that a production in *Zhivago'*s authentic setting would have brought, but less enthusiastic about the subject matter. Boris Pasternak had been told in October 1958 that if he flew to Sweden to accept his Nobel Prize he would not be permitted to return to his homeland. He died two years later in Peredelkino, just outside Moscow, and his great novel remained banned in his own country for another twenty years.

At the CEA studios, conveniently close to Madrid airport, local inmates in the nearby prison were amazed to see a vision of pre-Revolution Moscow taking shape. Lean's 800strong crew constructed a giant exterior set which included a remarkably realistic copy of the Kremlin and a half-mile-long paved city street complete with shops and businesses created with astonishing attention to detail. That excellent English actor Mark Eden, who shares the opening scene of the film with Alec Guinness, was astonished. 'It looked totally convincing. There were streets and side streets, factories and homes and there was a tramline with real trams running along. I've never seen anything like it.'

The new Moscow set also featured a viaduct which carried railway engines, and more than fifty business premises. And a study of weather patterns convinced Lean that the snow he needed to re-create his bitter Russian winters would be found just 150 miles to the north east in Soria which was 4,000 feet above sea level and looked similar to the steppes of Russia. Here, miles of railway tracks were laid and the course of a river was altered. Lean and his faithful production designer John Box had a formidable force of operatives which included 120 plasterers, 210 carpenters, 60 masons, 25 tubular steel specialists, 30 painters, 20 electricians and more than 350 assorted technicians to get ready for shooting the epic.

When Julie Christie arrived in Madrid she was simply overwhelmed by the scale of *Doctor Zhivago*. It was her first real experience of Hollywood-style film-making at its most formidable. With her background in smaller and much cosier movies with a vastly smaller crew she was shocked by the prospect of spending a year as a tiny cog in this huge moviemaking machine. Rod Steiger arrived in Spain and quickly came to regard Christie as 'a frightened little bird' struggling to come to terms with the scale of it all.

In fact she was heartened by Steiger's presence and by his firm refusal to be awed by the towering reputation of director Lean. When the actor first arrived in Madrid he went to the caravan where Lean was holding court and instantly detected a tense and troubled atmosphere. Never one to shy away from an awkward situation, Steiger snorted, 'What's the matter? Somebody's father just died?' The chill in the air was unmistakable and Lean was less than amused.

Nevertheless the two cinematic giants did manage slowly to establish a genuine respect for each other. When Steiger later had dinner with Lean, the director told him, 'I'm glad you're here. You know, they told me to watch out Monday morning "because Mr Steiger is coming".' Steiger replied, 'They told me to watch out on Monday because "you're going to meet David Lean".'

Christie realized that she was not the only one who felt ill at ease and was able to relax a shade. The director was an extremely slow worker and Steiger found himself in Madrid for six months. He reflected, 'I don't like bullfighting. I can't stand flamenco and I can't eat fish: Madrid is a lot like Chicago – awful.' But the actor found solace in his character, whom he refused to regard as the villain. 'People say Komarovsky was such a mean man. I say, what did he do? He slept with the mother and the daughter. Most of the men in the world would give their right arm to sleep with two women – the mother and the daughter. He came back and tried to save them both. His mistake was that he thought Lara was another one-night stand and he fell in love with her. He wasn't a bad person.'

Of his young co-star Steiger says: 'Julie seemed partially paralysed. She looked as if she had tripped over a brick in the King's Road and come up with the part of Lara. She was still so much a slave to her freedom that at first she wouldn't easily submit to what she thought was Lean's regimentation. All the "powers that be" shook their heads and asked, "What do you think of her?" When she first arrived on set she looked terrified, like a frightened little bird. She had immense courage to face all this, and she emerged from it all with honours.'

In the early days, when the pressure of the massive responsibility became too much for her Julie reacted badly and even threw tantrums: 'You wouldn't say that if I was Elizabeth Taylor.' She resented having to dress up completely one hour before she was due on set to play her scenes and to parade in boiling heat to try the lighting. Instead, at first, she'd turn up in a grey sweater. 'I'd do it on purpose because I thought the idea was a bit daft. By the end I wouldn't have dreamed of doing it. Towards the end of the film when we got to my most difficult and lovely stuff I was so potty about the film I would have done anything.'

154

The staid older members of the *Doctor Zhivago* company at first thought David Lean had made some kind of mistake in casting this mod girl in his expensive film. Nobody had yet seen *Darling,* which Christie had only just completed. The 'new girl' looked as though she cut her stringy hair with a knife. She moped about moodily because her 'mates' weren't with her, would speak only to the young members of the company, flopped into chairs in newly pressed costumes and dozed off to sleep like a baby at any time of the day.

Christie used her newly acquired star status to fly out friends to keep her company on the months of location work in Spain but still had long periods of loneliness. Her boyfriend Don Bessant had by now found a teaching post in Maidstone that meant they were forcibly separated. But after one passionate visit  the couple announced their engagement. 'We don't know when we will get married,' she was quoted as saying. 'Probably not for two years. Don is very shy. He would simply hate any publicity. It would be awful for him ... He isn't just an art teacher. He's a painter, a good painter. The most important thing in any man–woman relationship is for the man to be the dominant one. This is what Don and I have and I can't imagine our ever letting it change. Marriage sort of frightens me though. We've talked about it, of course, and we've talked about having children. I don't think I'll ever want anyone else except Don.' But the marriage was quietly forgotten as, although Julie was still very much in love, she was terrified of commitment.

Initially, when she threw her tantrums David Lean sent her home for a few days and she returned cheerful and complaisant. But she was often lonely on set. In the evenings she sat in her Hilton hotel room, and Tom Courtenay sat in his 'like a couple of lonely cows', she said on the phone to Don Bessant. But she perked up dramatically when she got the first US reviews of *Darling* while on the set of *Zhivago.* A friend send her a three-page telegram from Manhattan with the glowing notices.

Omar Sharif enjoyed a somewhat variable relationship with his co-star. On some days they would be close and easygoing and on others there would be a stormy atmosphere between them. He hated the way she binged on up to eleven fried egg sandwiches a day and was somewhat piqued at all the attention she received on set. 'David Lean's direction to me was to do nothing,' recalled Sharif. 'He said, "Every scene you are in is the scene of the other person." It took us thirteen months to make the movie altogether, and after three months no one says I'm good. They would say, "Did you see Julie Christie today?" I was having a nervous breakdown.'

However, Sharif grew to respect Christie and commented, perceptively: 'She loves having her own life as a woman before anything. She is a new-generation person who is indifferent to the formalities of life. She is instinctive, very physical, very sensitive to smells, to everything that is the emotional part of a human being.'

The temperaments of the actors were not helped by the temperatures they had to work in, from blistering heat in Madrid to well below freezing in Finland. 'When we filmed *Doctor Zhivago,* it was supposed to be St Petersburg in midwinter. In fact it was Madrid in a freak heatwave,' Julie recalled. 'There we were, waiting for this multi-million dollar epic to be made while sweating away in our furs in 100 degrees heat. Finally we were saved by the props and set dressers who covered the whole of the set in mountains of marble dust – for the long shots, the fields were covered in miles and miles of bed sheets. I think the villagers were a little perplexed.' Lean had been assured that the mountainous area north of Madrid would be snow-covered for four months but the snow was light that year. As director of photography Freddie Young explained: 'Soria was about four hours north of Madrid and it was reputed to be the coldest place in Spain. When we went there to do it, it had been snowing, but you could still see the furrows in the field.' Hence the marble dust and sheets.

For authentic snow a few scenes were shot in Finland, as Omar Sharif recalled: 'The only real cold was when we shot for two months in Finland close to the Russian border. It was very, very cold, about 40 degrees below. We were on a frozen lake. One day we were filming on the lake and the lunch wagon arrived. Everyone was standing around and we suddenly discovered that we were slowly sinking. The heat in the lunch wagon was melting the ice. We got out of there in a hurry. For the cast and crew, trucks were there to make tea and coffee and serve food. But they had forgotten to measure the thickness of the ice.'

Julie had no idea that *Doctor Zhivago* would look so beautiful when it eventually reached the screen. 'I was so removed from all that stuff and so much more interested in something else all the time. You know, "The grass is always greener in some French film or Italian film..."' And the scale of the Lean epic impressed her not at all. Julie said: 'I was annoyed by all the money, the cost and the grandiosity of it all, although I'm an admirer of David Lean's earlier work.

'He really was very paternalistic as a director, that's for sure. If at that time I had developed any feminist ideas, there would have been a lot of problems. Fortunately, I hadn't. I loved his paternalism, just loved it. It reassured me because once again I was so scared. He was very reassuring. He had the power, he knew what he wanted and I have always been delighted to deliver to people what they want me to deliver. I suppose you could call me a bit passive in that way, though I'm not so much like that now. My joy was in trying to do what the director wanted me to do, and if he was going to tell me exactly what that was then it was fine by me. So David fathered and mothered me through that role. He is a good director of actors – he had to be. What people didn't like, I think, was that he perhaps imposed his will on them too much because he was extremely authoritarian and some people dislike that. Fortunately, I didn't mind it at all.'

During filming Julie said: 'I know I have a very funny face and I've suffered a great deal from some of the things I've seen in newspapers and magazines. I have a trick of pulling in my lower lip and David Lean reminded me of this before every take.'

But Lara was one of the most coveted women's parts since Scarlett O'Hara. And Julie conceded: 'I acted more in *Zhivago* than in *Darling.* Lara is strong, womanly, brave, pure, passionate – all she is is adjectives. Her emotions are deep. I learned to constrain myself in a downbeat role and was criticized. But how could I be upbeat playing a girl who was raped, whose mother tried to commit suicide, who stole a woman's husband, whose own husband got murdered?

'Sweat was pouring down underneath. You could feel it crawling down inside your clothes. I don't know how people act in hot situations. It fried the brain. "Lara's theme!" It makes me laugh. It's connected with me and it has absolutely nothing to do with me whatsoever. It is a very successful tune which is for many people actually moving, but it's not my sort of music. Languorous, lingering, the old wavery balalaika, you know, that sort of Hawaiian effect. David Lean? He controlled every single aspect of film-making including actors, which suited me just fine because I hadn't got a clue what I was doing. At that point I needed a patriarch to take care of me. More skilful and knowledgeable actors didn't like that at all. Understandably.'

For Omar Sharif, Lean's greatest asset as a director was a phenomenal sense of rhythm and a mastery at editing. 'David thought the most difficult thing for a director was to know how quickly actors should speak. On *Zhivago* we would rehearse scenes and get them wonderfully well. Then he would say at the last minute, "I want it done exactly the same but in half the time" or double the time. Always he wanted to conserve for other scenes in the film.'

Julie's relationship with Lean followed a similar pattern to the one with Schlesinger. Initially she resented and rejected his instructions but gradually he became just the kind of strong father figure she had missed out on in real life. In this period Christie started to try to draw the curtains on the endless enquiries about her private life.

'David is tremendously disciplined,' recalled Julie. 'He couldn't stand me fooling around. I didn't intend to change my ways for anyone. But as the part became more difficult, I submitted myself to David completely. I had learned discipline. My biggest problem in playing Lara was the stillness, the serenity of the character.' By the end of the production she surprised herself and became every bit as serene as her director demanded and Lean admired her greatly. He observed thoughtfully: 'She is an independent creature with strong views of her own. She doesn't want to be turned into something that arrives on a conveyor belt. She won't either.' Her co-stars joined in the chorus. 'She's a woman that other women like,' says Geraldine Chaplin, who was starting her own big-time film career in *Doctor Zhivago.*

Many close observers are convinced that Julie Christie stole director David Lean's heart during production. There was something in the great man's eyes that conveyed devotion to something more than simple duty. Barbara Cole certainly believed Lean was smitten by the shimmering beauty: 'I noticed it during the scenes where she's having a mixed-up relationship with Komarovsky. I thought to myself, "He's really attracted to this woman." But I was there.' Julie herself seemed to remain blissfully unaware of the nature of the feelings she provoked in the aged and distinguished director.

Lean's mammoth movie took the 800-strong crew two years to make in three countries and doubled its original budget. Julie's generosity took care of much of her £40,000 earnings from *Zhivago* which were already halved by Janni's cut. Julie's army of friends and followers had always shared everything and just because she was now making real money she was not about to change that. She was proud of her attitude: 'People help you when you're down. You should help them when you can.' But she had to do an advert for hair conditioner to balance the books. She regretted her early success: 'I stopped working at acting. My development was arrested because I suddenly got these great parts in films. I couldn't do workshops because I was so famous. I just used to shut my eyes and hope it would be all right.'

Years later Julie could hardly recall what all the fuss was about. She said her chief memory of the production was nothing to do with the haunting Russian drama but of bullfighters. When *Zhivago* was screened on television at Christmas 1990 she saw it on a friend's television in Wales and thought how long and slow the film seemed. She could scarcely recall what all the fuss was about. 'Yet when I went into the village afterwards,' she said, 'everyone was crying. It touches people's emotions, but it doesn't touch mine.'

Shooting on *Doctor Zhivago* ended on 7 October 1965 and the action transferred to Hollywood where the editing was done at a tremendous pace because MGM insisted the picture be ready for Christmas release so that it would qualify for the Academy Awards and take advantage of increased cinema audiences over the holiday. Lean's verdict on Julie Christie's work became more and more laudatory as he carefully spliced the epic into shape.

His friend Bolt wrote from England with a note of warning: 'Marvellous that you find Julie so good. If you're right in thinking she'll soon be where Peter [O'Toole] was after *Lawrence of Arabia* I hope she isn't exploited, or doesn't exploit herself, so hard. He seems to be in a bit of a pickle. Why do films destroy so much young talent?'

Sharif recalled the director's heroic efforts in the cutting-room: He worked with thirteen editors for two months and made the deadline. 'The critics didn't like the picture, nor did the audiences. David took another look at it in theatres and said: "I cut it all wrong." MGM gave him permission to re-edit it and change the music and the new version was sent to theatres. It caught on immediately and became a big hit.'

*Doctor Zhivago* opened in America at the Capitol Theater in New York on 22 December 1965. Writer Bolt was unable to be there because the United States immigration service refused to grant him a visa. He had a criminal record thanks to his activities on behalf of CND and had just completed a trip to communist China, which the US authorities viewed with great suspicion.

Predictably it was regarded sniffily by the upmarket critics but the popular papers were more enthusiastic and the public simply loved it. For this artfully conceived piece of movie merchandizing, MGM planned a massive campaign, trumpeting the $11 million production as the greatest thing since *Gone with the Wind*. Although the *Los Angeles Herald-Examiner* cried yes, indeed it was, most reviews were mixed and a few critics were downright hostile. *Newsweek* shed tears, not for the film's highly emotional moments, but for what it decried as bad drama. 'It is all too bad to be true: that so much has come to so little, that tears must be prompted by dashed hopes instead of enduring drama.'

Not what MGM wanted to hear, but the *Hollywood Reporter* praised the movie as a 'majestic, magnificent picture of war and peace, on a national scale and scaled down to the personal. It has every element that makes a smash, long-run box-office hit.'

Other reviewers took a stand somewhere between the two, leaving MGM wondering if it had a hit or a costly turkey on its hands. Fortunately, audience word-of-mouth fulfilled the *Reporter'* s predictions. Movie-goers bought their advance tickets, eager to sit through the 3-hour 17-minute panorama of love and human drama played against the backdrop of the Russian Revolution and World War I. The excellent production values – exquisitely photographed scenery, a gripping narrative, striking sets, a moving score (Maurice Jarre's 'Lara's Theme' helped push the *Doctor Zhivago* soundtrack album to number three for the year) and fine performances all helped to make this MGM's second biggest moneymaker ... after *Gone with the Wind.* It was 1965's most successful film, grossing $47,116,811.

Omar Sharif and Julie Christie both found their reputations soaring, even if it was hard to tell which of them was the more beautiful. And on both sides of the Atlantic the fashionable folk of the sixties rushed to dress in *Zhivago* style – heavy long skirts, leather boots and fur hats. And the haunting 'Lara's Theme' suddenly seemed to be playing in every hotel lobby and lift in the land. Not that Julie Christie was too interested in becoming a fashion icon. 'I hate long dresses. I hate them. They're such a problem. I hope after the *Zhivago* première I won't ever have to wear a long dress again. Right now I have to comply. But later on...'

As Julie prepared to fly to the all-important New York première and what she dreaded would be the hell of 'total exposure ... for dear David's film', *Women's Wear Daily* covered her departure with a breathless bulletin: 'Julie Christie – the hottest property in the movies – discovered in *Billy Liar* – smashing in *Darling* – and about to enchant the United States in *Doctor Zhivago.* Julie the new bombshell wings in stealthily from London late Friday night to Kennedy airport – just a few hours after granting an exclusive interview to *WWD* while in the hands of her Mayfair hairdresser.'

In a graphic example of precisely the sort of attention which was to drive her to loathe the media, the magazine went ungrammatically on: 'Julie Christie's last hours in London – before flying to New York ... rush ... panic ... rain ... solid traffic jams. Half an hour late she swept into André Bernard's hairdressing salon on Old Bond Street. Short, belted, brown broadtail over lilac check chemise. Deep red shoes. Natural make-up. Straight blonde hair in a ponytail. She slumps into a chair –"This rush, it's ghastly, ghastly. Don't know how I'm going to make the plane." '

Coiffeur Edward evidently calmed Miss Christie down as she was able to observe that she 'enjoyed making *Zhivago.* Don't know how it's going to work out but it's been the most enjoyable role yet ... Geraldine Chaplin was an absolute dear. We got on very well, but we're different types.'

In New York Julie insisted on staying at the Bohemian Algonquin while Omar Sharif and Geraldine Chapman were at the Waldorf Astoria. But she could not escape the publicity round. 'At parties after the premières in New York and Hollywood, we would be sitting there, mouths full, when we'd hear our names being rolled out in alphabetical order beginning with Chaplin, Geraldine. We would all have to get up one by one, like a bunch of bananas.'

MGM's first British screening was in London on 11 February 1966 but writer Bolt was not in attendance. When he finally got to see the finished product, Bolt wrote approvingly of Lean's genius in the editing studios. 'It is a tremendously good film and anyone who doesn't like it condemns himself. It's moving, powerful, beautiful, serious and continuously held my rapt attention. Peggy [Ramsay, Bolt's agent] and I sat like a pair of housemaids and ended with sodden handkerchiefs. I can't tell you how proud I am to be your lieutenant in the enterprise. It's in a different street from *Lawrence* and that is saying a lot. If I have to select any one thing to congratulate you on, it's Omar. I believed in him utterly. It is, or looks like, a performance of great depth and stunning restraint. He almost never seemed in the slightest degree inadequate. Not so Julie, I thought. It's a lovely performance, that goes without saying, and sometimes remarkable, but once or twice I thought the King's Road Chelsea nearer than the Nevsky Prospect. That's a criticism of perfection, mind you. She's lovely.

At the Academy Awards ceremony on 14 April 1966, *Doctor Zhivago* was to collect five Oscars. Julie Christie was nominated as Best Actress, not for *Zhivago* but for *Darling.* Contemplating her career at this exciting time, Christie was clear-headed about her ambition. 'I want to be considered the top actress in the country. Being on top right now is a fluke. If I'm a passing fad, I hope it will be over fast – voom ... Acting is very self-indulgent. The important thing is that I get a walloping satisfaction out of it.'

She had no illusions about the nature of fame. Returning to her flat after shooting on *Zhivago* was completed, Julie found the hall awash with flowers. 'They have no meaning,' she told a friend. 'They were probably ordered over the phone or picked by a secretary. It's like a funeral – enough to make you cry.'

Interviewed shortly after completing *Zhivago,* Julie Christie revealed the quality that gave her performance some of its emotional intensity: 'I enjoy almost any sensation. When a toothache or a chilblain is gone I miss it. I live as though I'm going to die tomorrow. All the time I see how short life is. It is today – now – that counts for me.'

# 7

# 'And the winner is...'

The promotion tour for the American première of *Doctor Zhivago* – ten days of non-stop rushing about from one taxi to another, endless interviews, photographs, 'Pose this way, Miss Christie.. a smile please, Miss Christie' – finally wore me out. I could think of nothing but wanting to go to bed and sleep for ever. I've never been so drained in my life.

Julie Christie

Julie Christie collapsed with nervous exhaustion after the *Zhivago* launch and was ordered to enter a hospital for a prolonged rest before she could even consider beginning work on her next project, François Truffaut's *Fahrenheit 451.*

'When I returned to London the doctor assigned to my new film said he would not insure me for it. I was suffering from nervous exhaustion. I had lost much more weight than I could afford. I was tensed up and taut to breaking point. I also had a badly infected wisdom tooth, and I believe the poison entered my bloodstream. I had the tooth out – and if anything it made me feel even worse. When pressures like that are exerted on me, well I just break down and cry. The worst of the pressure was, "Oh God, why can't I lead my own life?" I want to be me. I know I've become a "name", but that shouldn't mean I've got to say Yes to everyone who wants to latch on to that name for their own purposes.'

What Julie found most difficult to cope with were 'the unending demands on the private time that I cherish so much. I can no longer indulge in the things I really like doing. Things that have nothing at all to do with acting. I just find myself getting more and more rude just to preserve my sanity. I love my work, the actual acting, and I wouldn't want to do anything else. But when I'm off I just want to forget the whole business.'

Julie insisted that she had not set out to be famous. 'I never wanted to be a film star, I just wanted to act. I never even imagined I would be successful. And I never even thought of the screen until I was sent by my agent to audition for a film part. Films were something other people did. Sometimes I feel that my life is just a dream that is hurtling along much too fast, and that this dreadful fame thing will all end as quickly as it began. Before it all became so big, when I was making *Young Cassidy,* I thought it would all probably end before I got this far. I still feel without a doubt it will all decay. But now it will be a public decay, whereas before it would have been a quiet little decay, acted out in private. But a dream or not, it is of no importance ... the public acclaim is meaningless to me ... the image one gets from that is not real at all.'

Julie Christie's struggle with nervous exhaustion after the long ordeal of *Doctor Zhivago* was one of the most difficult times in her young life. Returning to London and the waiting arms of her devoted boyfriend Don Bessant after almost a year in Spain, Julie realized she should have been thrilled and happy. But she was knocked for six by her ailments, and struck by doubts and anxieties about her future, she began to question whether she really wanted to continue with her career and life as a film star. She loved the work itself, and she knew that after the difficult start she had recovered well enough to satisfy even a director as demanding as David Lean. But she was finding it hard to live her life in the spotlight of an intrusive press.

'Why do they have to ask me all those endless questions,' she moaned to a friend. 'And the photographers. They seem to come up out of holes in the ground. How many more pictures of me can they want? If only I could just do the job and then go home and get on with my life. Fame is like a prison and I feel as if it carries on like this I am facing a life sentence.'

But she was already contracted to play two roles in François Truffaut's prestigious new film *Fahrenheit 451.* The film, which gets its title from the temperature at which paper burns, was based on a story by science fiction writer Ray Bradbury set in a totalitarian world of the future where the authorities curb all freedom of expression and knowledge is carefully restricted by having all books burned. Until, in the words of Truffaut, 'one day one of the firemen begins reading a book and wonders why he has to burn it. The whole film is there...' Austrian actor Oskar Werner was to play Montag, the fireman whose job it is to search for books and incinerate them. He is married to the faithful believer of the given way Linda, but falls for her 'double' Clarisse, who encourages him to rebel against the repressive system. When Linda denounces his deviation from his orders Montag turns his flame-thrower on his fellow workers and escapes to join Clarisse in the secret hiding place of the Book People.

The film's American producer, Lewis Allen, came up with the idea of using a single actress to play Linda and Clarisse. Truffaut was enthusiastic: 'It's a brilliant idea. We can have two different hair-dos, and different clothes. This solves all the problems that have been plaguing me for so long about their figures, their ages, their looks and so on. And it is wonderful that we have secured Julie Christie for the role.' However, as the film's start date, 10 January 1966, approached, the gifted French director was nervously studying the disturbing health reports on his beautiful leading lady. The doctor decreed that Julie was not ready to work yet and Truffaut was concerned that Universal might cancel the £1 million movie. He told himself that the company had already spent hundreds of thousands of pounds on exotic, futuristic sets at Pinewood studios and would surely not want to write off such an investment without giving Julie Christie time to recover. Production actually began on 17 January, with the star still confined to bed, sleeping almost round the clock and eating as much as she could bear to try to put back lost weight.

She said she was 'terrified, almost paralysed' at the prospect of yet again facing the daunting task of 'discovering' her director. But this time her fluency in French helped and Truffaut, whose English was less than perfect, was surprised and impressed that an English actress could speak easily to him in his own language. On 31 January she arrived on set and Truffaut noted approvingly: 'Julie was jittery but she came through well.' As work on the gloom-laden tale proceeded, director and star became very close. Truffaut admired Julie Christie's beauty and unusual lack of vanity, and was delighted when her quirky friends came visiting. However, his relationship with Oskar Werner deteriorated almost as quickly as the one with Julie Christie improved, as Truffaut noted in his meticulously kept diary. 'Everyone on the unit likes Julie, as opposed to her co-partner. She has many friends who often come to watch her shooting and every time she first asked my permission. The last time I told her it was marvellous to have so many friends and I added, "It's a funny thing – one never sees any of Oskar's friends on the set." She replied with a sweet smile, "That's because we're not shooting in Austria." '

In fact, relations between Truffaut and Werner plummeted even further until, by the end, they were hardly speaking. 'We used to speak but not any more,' said Werner angrily after the filming had finished. 'During the making of *Jules et Jim* I gave him advice, and I tried to teach him something, and he listened. Whole pages of dialogue, whole scenes came from me. But when I went to England to make *Fahrenheit 451* he thought he had learned it all, he destroyed that film. It was a 70mm film with an 8mm print. It had nothing left of Ray Bradbury in it. It was ridiculous to cast Julie Christie in two parts. He only did that to save paying an extra salary. Nothing was worked out. The dramatic plot was completely lost, he refused to accept any of my suggestions. I was fifteen when Hitler came to power and I saw the real book burnings. Truffaut's film was child's play compared to that. Every time I had to register an emotion that was true to my character, Truffaut cut away with his camera. That's the trouble with these *nouvelle vague* directors. They care nothing about actors. Antonioni is like a man masturbating. He does it all by himself.'

By the end of the film Truffaut was completely smitten with Christie and drooled into his diary: 'You have two kinds of actors, the poetic and the psychological. Julie is the latter and a pure joy to work with. On top of that her French is so good I may even have to dub her in the film!' However, Julie failed to generate very much screen chemistry with the unhappy Oskar, either as his wife or his lover. Things might have been very different if another, rather better-known actor had gained the role he keenly desired and so come into her life a year earlier. For, before production began, the actress Leslie Caron had been persuaded by her lover to arrange a lunch in Paris to introduce him to Truffaut because he wanted to star opposite Julie Christie in *Fahrenheit 451.* His name was Warren Beatty, and, instead of giving him a part in his film, Truffaut gave him a screenplay about two young American outlaws called Bonnie Parker and Clyde Barrow.

Julie attempted to keep her head down and stay out of the fiery feud between Werner and Truffaut but when filming finished on 14 April, her birthday, she was not unhappy to be jetting off to Los Angeles to exchange Oskar for the Oscars.

Ever since America's Academy of Motion Picture Arts and Sciences handed out its first statuettes in 1929 in recognition of outstanding talent, the Oscar has come to be recognized in the cinema industry as the supreme prize. No matter how frivolous, meaningless, trivial, even humiliating these awards have been regarded in some circles down the years, there is and always has been an irresistible aura of fantasy surrounding the annual opening of the Oscars envelopes accompanied by the tantalizing words 'And the winner is...'

It was no different in 1966 but when that year's Oscar nominations were announced in Los Angeles on

21 February, unusually for the Best Actress category, not one but three British actresses were named by the Academy – Julie Christie, Julie Andrews and Samantha Eggar. Julie Christie was quietly pleased but genuinely astonished and not a little alarmed to have been nominated for an Oscar. Because of her limited screen experience, she did not believe for one moment that she was going to win but her mates began telling her she stood a real chance especially when, the following month, the British Film Academy named her Best Actress for *Darling* and another major accolade arrived with the New York Critics Circle also pronouncing her Best Actress for the same film.

Still Julie refused to get carried away with any thoughts of actually winning the Oscar. She pointed out to everyone that she would be vying for the award with distinguished French actress Simone Signoret and American newcomer Elizabeth Hartman as well as Britain's Samantha Eggar and Julie Andrews, who was returning to defend the Best Actress Oscar she had won the year before for *Mary Poppins.* Julie Andrews was nominated this time around for her role as the governess in *The Sound of Music,* the $8-million adaptation of the Rodgers and Hammerstein Broadway musical which was well on the way to digging Twentieth Century Fox single-handedly out of the hole it had dug for itself by making the hugely expensive Elizabeth Taylor – Richard Burton epic *Cleopatra.*

Hollywood was divided as to Julie Andrews's Oscar chances. One obvious opinion was that the Academy was unlikely to vote her Best Actress two years in a row but there was still undeniable support for her. Film critics everywhere had agreed unanimously on the brilliance of her performance in *The Sound of Music* as the postulant at Nonnburg Abbey in Saltzburg who becomes governess to widower Captain Von Trapp and his seven children and brings music, gaiety and romance into a household that had until then been run on a strict naval office regimen with no frivolity permitted.

The magic and charm of the 1959 stage hit had transferred vibrantly to the screen in a magnificently mounted production and Julie Andrews had massive Oscar support from a public who had given *The Sound of Music* as warm a reception as the critics. As Oscar-time drew near and film companies began to beat the drum for their respective nominations, in city after city across America, cinema managers were able to round up people who claimed to have seen *The Sound of Music* as many as thirty times. One typist in Los Angeles announced she had seen it 300 times and a little old lady in Wales said she went to see the film every day. A man in Oregon saw it so frequently that he sent Twentieth Century Fox a copy of the script declaring he had been able to write it down just from memory. Each one was a publicist's dream.

Samantha Eggar, like Julie Christie a beautiful English actress in her twenties, was thought to provide less formidable opposition than Julie Andrews although she had a degree of Oscar backing for her role in *The*

*Collector,* William Wyler's adaptation of John Fowles's novel. The film, starring Terence Stamp as a young, sex-obsessed English butterfly-collector who abducts a young art student, played by Samantha, and holds her prisoner in the cellar of his secluded farmhouse, had won honours for both its stars at the Cannes Film Festival earlier in the year. In the run-up to the Oscars, America's prestigious *Time* magazine described Samatha as 'a rare combination of acting talent and physical beauty', which did her Oscar chances no harm at all.

Also in the running against Julie Christie were Simone Signoret in *Ship of Fools,* and Elizabeth Hartman, a twenty-two-year-old newcomer, in *A Patch of Blue* starring Shelley Winters as the villainess and Sidney Poitier as the hero in a fable about racial intolerance. Elizabeth had won glowing notices for her role as Winters's daughter who is accidentally blinded by her mother. When it came to assessing her as a potential Oscar-winner, Elizabeth was assured of getting the sympathy vote and MGM campaigned vigorously on behalf of Elizabeth and the film with a pair of sunglasses in a Price Waterhouse envelope, to remind Academy members that Elizabeth had played a blind girl.

Against all the campaigning for her rivals, Julie was winning plenty of support herself from within the cinema industry. America had taken to her ever since *Darling* had opened in New York on 3 August 1965 to superlatives from the American critics for her performance as Diana Scott. 'Julie Christie is just great,' enthused Robert Salmaggi in the *New York Herald Tribune,* before predicting that *Darling* would 'put Julie Christie right up there among the celluloid goddesses. This girl is a delight with her mobile child and sorceress face that registers rage, helpless misery or innocent joy.' *Life Magazine* said the movie contained '...a performance by Julie Christie which is pure gold. By turns wilful and willing, greedy and contrite, intelligent and self-deceiving, innocent and teasing – it is a characterization such as one rarely sees.' There was fulsome praise, too, from the *New York Journal* which reported: 'It is the first major role for the glistening beauty and sensuousness of Julie Christie and she handles it with the ease of a veteran.' The *New York World Telegram* echoed that acclaim. 'Julie Christie is brilliant. The character feels or fakes every emotion known to women. Miss Christie manages them all. She has sexy good looks, an electric personality and great skill as an actress.'

On 28 March 1966, just nineteen days before the Oscars, *Darling'* s American distributors took out a full-page advertisement in the showbiz bible *Variety* which featured an alluring photo of Julie from the film, accompanied by Robert Salmaggi's *Tribune* piece and a reminder that Julie was Winner of the Best Actress Award from both the New York Film Critics Circle, and British Film Academy.

It was a feverish pre-Oscar Los Angeles climate into which Julie prepared to fly with Don Bessant after completing work on *Fahrenheit 451.* Truffaut had thrown a birthday-cum-sendoff party for his star at which many a glass was raised to toast Julie on her way.

Julie confessed that when she was initially told that she might have to fly over to Hollywood for the Oscars she was consumed with terror. She said she would look and feel completely out of place among the Hollywood élite and it took a great deal of persuasion to make her go. 'It was the last thing I even thought of,' she reflected thirty years later. 'Especially being in England where people don't exactly crowd round, although it's getting more that way. But I don't think I'd ever watched an Oscar presentation at that point. It was something to do with another country. I remember the only reason I went is because I wanted to go to the desert and the producers promised to pay for a holiday there afterwards.'

When she and Don arrived in America, Julie Andrews hospitably invited the couple to come and stay at her home but *Darling'*s American publicists persuaded them to book in to the Beverly Hills Hotel. They felt it would make their job easier and they also argued that it wouldn't help the cause of either Julie if the two Best Actress nominees were seen to be mingling quite so cordially. Hollywood liked to encourage competition between its nominees and they were playing up the Andrews – Christie competition as the Battle of the Julies. 'Our schedules were both so hectic,' was how Julie explained her choice of accommodation and both Julies played down any suggestion of rivalry. 'Of course I'd love to win the Oscar,' Julie Christie elaborated, 'but, believe me, being nominated is praise enough.'

In the build-up to the awards, gossip columnists wield a powerful influence on the Oscar campaign and Julie had dutifully subjected herself to a number of interviews, including one with the much respected Sidney Skolsky of the *Hollywood Reporter.* He did Julie's Oscar chances some good by saying, 'She looks a bit like Brigitte Bardot, like Joanne Woodward, like Juliet Prowse yet she retains her own individual look and personality.' Asked about her overnight success, Julie replied: 'Success is a trap. I don't know if I am prepared for it.'

Much was made by the American media of what Julie intended to wear to the ceremony since *Darling* had ushered in a new look in fashion but she told them just to wait and see. 'I remember when Mary Quant introduced the miniskirt,' said costume designer Anthony Powell. 'It got a lot of press but it wasn't really accepted much beyond the mods in London. Then *Darling* came out and the public saw beautiful Julie Christie walking around in miniskirts. Suddenly we saw miniskirts everywhere.'

There was added enthusiasm generally about the run-up to the Oscars in 1966 because for the very first time the event was to be broadcast on TV in colour. The giant American network ABC, which held the TV rights, whipped up interest for weeks beforehand with a series of trailers in movie theatres in which comedian Bob Hope, the chosen MC for the Oscars ceremony, enticed the audience with: 'Just think, for the first time you can actually see the losers turn green.'

The Oscars night itself, 18 April 1966, turned out to be one of the coldest Hollywood could remember. Instead of the normal balmy ocean breezes, the glamorous celebrity audience arriving  at the Santa Monica Civic Auditorium had to contend with strong, chilly winds whipping around their finery when they stepped out of their limousines to walk the gauntlet of fans and photographers. The icy gusts didn't dissuade the usual crop of starlets from posing, goose-pimpled and shivering, for the flashbulb frenzy in their off-the-shoulder gowns. When Julie Christie arrived, she not only looked beautiful in a gold pyjama-style outfit made by a girlfriend but, significantly, she won the admiration of everyone for clearly having assessed the inclement weather to perfection.

Clutching Don's arm to steady her nerves, Julie made her way to her seat among the 3,000 showbusiness luminaries packed into the vast, tiered auditorium. Moments after the couple had sat down, Hollywood's annual jamboree was under way with pictures of the nominees flashed up on a screen as a chorus off-screen sang: 'Which new face, which new name, will rush down the aisle to claim that golden statuette.' Don gave Julie's hand a squeeze of encouragement.

The lavish set of forty-two splashing water fountains drew gasps from the audience and before long Julie was seen by millions of TV viewers across America smiling and clapping as *Darling* won the Oscar for Black and White Costume Design. *Doctor Zhivago* made it a double by winning the Colour Costume Design Oscar. When Debbie Reynolds and Warren Beatty announced that *Zhivago* had won Colour Art Direction Award, the TV cameras picked out another shot of Julie smiling broadly and applauding enthusiastically.

Again the TV cameras were on Julie, this time bursting out laughing, when Bob Hope segued into a Cyd Charisse dance number, saying, 'Today's ballroom dances like the Swim, the Frug, the Chicken and the Monkey are really nervous disorders set to music.'

There was further joy for Julie and the *Doctor Zhivago* contingent when Maurice Jarre won the Orginal Score Award and the orchestra played 'Lara's Theme'. As the evening progressed it was turning into a good night for Britain and by the time Rex Harrison stepped up to announce the Oscar for Best Actress, the two films showcasing Julie Christie had garnered seven Oscars between them. There were five for *Doctor Zhivago* and two for *Darling,* Frederic Raphael having been awarded the Oscar for Best Original Story and Screenplay. Robert Bolt also won an award for his screen adaptation but, once again, the US authorities prevented him from attending, so it was David Lean who strode up to collect the award on the writer's behalf, struggling hard to disguise his disappointment at losing out as best director to Robert Wise for *The Sound of Music.*

Now Julie Christie's big moment had arrived and as the nominations were read out the cameras showed Julie, Samantha Eggar and Elizabeth Hartman in the audience, all nervously awaiting the winning name and Julie Andrews, who had just presented the Best Actor Oscar to Lee Marvin for *Cat Ballou,* waiting calmly backstage. At that instant, Julie Christie was a jumble of emotions, half of her wanting to win, half not caring at all, and somewhere inside her was a voice telling her that she shouldn't be there at all, that she simply did not belong in such illustrious company.

'And the winner is', said the suave Rex Harrison tearing open the envelope, '...Julie Christie.' At the mention of her name Julie clapped her hand to her mouth then leaped out of her seat, ran to the stage amid deafening applause from the audience and ploughed excitedly into Rex Harrison embracing him warmly. 'I heard my name called and that was worse than anything,' Julie later recounted. 'I kept wondering, why me? I stood up and I didn't know where to go or what to do. I only felt a great wish to laugh, no, to cry. No, both.'

Rex Harrison for once seemed nonplussed as Julie shed tears while he too applauded her warmly. Never seriously able to believe that she was going to win, Julie had not prepared a proper acceptance speech and she was trembling as she choked out: 'I don't think I can say anything except thank everyone concerned especially my darling John Schlesinger for this great honour.' Then she fled the limelight for the sanctuary of the wings as the applause rang round the theatre once more.

Backstage there was pandemonium when Rex Harrison escorted Julie into the room reserved for the winners. She was greeted with whoops of excitement from the triumphant British contingent and all eyes were on her, except for those of Shelley Winters. In the excitement of winning her Best Supporting Actress Oscar, Shelley had somehow contrived to lose the diamond necklace she had rented for the evening and was in a rare panic scrabbling around on the floor and entreating everyone to search for it. The missing necklace soon turned up and Julie once again found herself the focus of attention. Naturally she was flushed with excitement, all the pent-up emotion of the past few days now running free. But she could barely take in the impact of her victory and the real significance of the statuette she clutched in her hand.

Eventually finding a spare few seconds to inspect her Oscar statuette more closely, Julie asked Rex Harrison naïvely, 'Why isn't my name on it?'

'They didn't know you were going to win, dear,' Rex explained to her gently. 'They'll take it from you and put your name on it and then you may put it on your mantelpiece.'

'But I haven't got a mantelpiece,' said Julie dissolving into tears once again and being comforted by Don Bessant who must have realized at the very moment of his girlfriend's triumph that Hollywood had now irrevocably claimed her and that he would lose her to its glittering grasp.

When she had gathered some composure, Julie was able to recall more clearly her big moment when Rex had called out her name in front of the star-studded audience and many millions more tuning in on TV. 'I just sat there and I saw the TV cameras moving all around and I thought, "Oh well, that's it. It's not me, maybe some other time." I even stopped being nervous for a time ... and then they called my name. All I can remember is that I wanted to cry and cry and cry ... I was hoping for me,' she went on. 'I wanted to win.' Did she think she deserved it, she was asked. 'Of course, I deserve it,' she laughed.

Later Julie revealed that for a split second she had frozen in absolute terror the moment Rex Harrison had called out her name, a legacy of her schooldays when she dreaded hearing her name announced in public because it meant that, once again, she was being hauled up in front of school assembly for some heinous schoolgirl crime and humiliated in front of all the other girls and her teachers. 'That was the feeling when I got the Oscar,' she said. 'It was "I've got to get up there, what am I going to do?" I burst into tears, to my shame.'

But on that gusty April night in California Julie Christie was the toast of Hollywood, drawing praise even from Edith Head, fashion consultant for the

Oscars TV show, for the originality of her gold lamé pyjama suit. Some observers churlishly interpreted Julie's outfit as an attempt to dress up like a gold Oscar statuette, as if she had the arrogance to think she was definitely going to win. But Edith, herself a seven-times Oscar-winning designer, dismissed that as jealousy of Julie's independent approach.

Edith was grateful for Julie's streak of individuality. She was furious that so many of the female presenters at the Oscars ceremony had worn white dresses simply in order to look tanned on colour television. 'I looked at all those white dresses and thought we were doing a reprise of *White Christmas,*' she hissed. 'But Julie Christie, how did I know she was going to get dressed up as an Oscar until she got up on stage? Some people are just so independent that you expect them to dress differently and if she had come out in some proper little black dress and a string of pearls, we'd all have been disappointed.'

The following year Julie Christie was to return to Los Angeles for the Oscars and caused a sensation by wearing a polka-dot miniskirt as she presented the Best Actor award to Paul Scofield, with whom she had toured with the RSC, for *A Man For All Seasons.* It was typically Julie but glamour was too valuable a Hollywood asset to surrender to the latest fashions and the next year a dress code was sent out to participants in the 1967 Oscars. Piquantly women were asked to forget what a stir Julie had created the previous year in her miniskirt and to dress in long gowns.

Inevitably the press began stalking Julie and Don Bessant the moment they left the Santa Monica Civic Auditorium and headed off for the Governor's Ball. 'I can't say I'm sorry that Julie Andrews lost, she won it last year after all,' the winner remarked without malice as she went off to celebrate with champagne long into the night. Julie Andrews, who was to prove herself a gracious also-ran, had the consolation of *The Sound of Music* winning the Best Picture Oscar.

At the post-Oscars ball Julie was at her sparkling best, almost giddy with excitement. The scale of her achievement had yet to sink in and she was in a daze as a succession of well-wishers came up and grabbed her hand, kissed her, hugged her and offered their congratulations. Everyone, it seemed, wanted to dance with her, and Don politely stepped aside from time to time. At one point she was on the dance floor oblivious to the fact that she was rubbing shoulders, literally, with President Johnson's daughter Lynda who had arrived escorted by actor George Hamilton.

Early next morning, inevitably, the world's press was congregating at the Beverly Hills Hotel desperate for pictures and interviews with the British actress who suddenly had the whole world at her feet. But Julie was happy to let them all wait. It had been a momentous night and she wanted time for a little quiet reflection. Of one thing she was sure, life would never be the same again and throughout the night of celebration there had been no shortage of people telling her precisely that. Now, apart from Don, there was only one person Julie Christie was seeing that morning and that was Earl Blackwell, the designer responsible for drawing up an annual list of the world's worst-dressed women.

For two and a half hours while the press waited at her door Julie had a leisurely breakfast with the man who had made a name for himself decrying the lack of dress-sense of the famous. On the face of it, Earl Blackwell seemed an unlikely choice of breakfast guest for Julie but she had been curious to meet up with him and they had in fact met before in London. They had been introduced when Julie had by chance popped into an antique shop he was visiting during a trip to England. Earl's recollection of that meeting one summer was that Julie looked, in his opinion, like no girl ever should. She was barefoot, her hair was unkempt and she was wearing a baggy old sweater, and yet he immediately adored her. 'I loved her though she was very whimsical,' he recalled. 'We talked about food and where to eat in London, without getting hung up on snobbery. I was curious to meet her when she came to Los Angeles for the Academy Awards and she was curious to meet the man who could compile a list of the worst-dressed women.

'When I went to her hotel for breakfast the morning after the Oscars she was drinking tons of coffee and watching old movies on TV. Mostly I was curious about how she would react to this great thing that had happened to her. It was almost like making a queen out of a child. The crown was very heavy. It was too heavy for the child to carry with the supposed dignity that we, the American public, expected of her. It was a shame because we wanted more of her, visually, than she was able to give. She only owed us the performance – the performance in *Darling* – nothing else.'

Earl noted that Julie was enchanted with the Oscar she had won and recognized that it was indeed a great triumph. But she wanted to escape. 'She was like a little wild animal that wanted to run away,' he said. 'She was pleased she had won but more concerned with going back to just being Julie Christie.' He noted, too, that Julie was more pleased with the huge paper rose Julie Andrews had sent her than with the dozens of ever more extravagant bouquets of flowers which kept being delivered to her hotel room throughout the morning. Typically, Julie Andrews's personal thought had impressed her far more than the obligatory floral tributes pouring in from movie executives she had never met.

Earl was so struck by Julie's determination to get away from all the fuss over her that he offered the couple his little three-bedroom house in Palm Springs as a refuge. Gamely Julie faced up to the press for a day and then, tiring of all the attention, she and Don headed off to Earl's home in Palm Springs for a week which was largely undisturbed. Appreciating her desire to get her feet back on the ground as quickly as possible, even Earl left them entirely alone except for two brief phone calls simply checking that everything was to their liking.

But as they sped off to their retreat, Julie wasn't totally fed up with Hollywood's adulation. Following behind her limousine was a car containing all the flowers she had received from well-wishers, including Julie Andrews's much cherished paper rose.

Back in England, as the news was relayed that Julie had won the Best Actress Oscar, Michael Winner picked up the telephone to make a call he knew he was going to enjoy. He rang Daniel Angel, the producer of *West 11* who had dismissed Julie as a B-picture actress and said with justifiable satisfaction, 'There has been a terrible mistake. A B-picture actress has just won the Academy Award. I think you should write a letter of complaint.'

That Oscar night and throughout the following day Julie Christie was the most talked-about, most sought-after actress in the world and she was not at all sure she liked it. Many years later she was able to look back and explain: 'I didn't feel I merited all that success. I was rather ashamed of it, rather embarrassed. I rather saw my success as a sort of scruffy dog, a little mangy dog that's following you around and you just can't get rid of it. It was a kind of fear that everywhere you went this little thing was always at your heels. I was very frightened. Very shy. I felt so damned inadequate about everybody, everything.'

When Julie Christie returned to Britain after the Oscar ceremony, John Schlesinger was at Heathrow Airport to meet her, along with a large division of Her Majesty's press. The director was keen to divert some of this particular blast of the oxygen of publicity towards the next project, a star-studded production of Thomas Hardy's classic novel *Far from the Madding Crowd.* Smarting at all the superlatives surrounding *Doctor Zhivago,* Schlesinger had announced that his new film was to be the most expensive British production of the year. And Christie was looking forward to a reunion with Schlesinger. Although she had been thrilled to work with Truffaut, *Fahrenheit 451* proved nowhere near hot enough to charm the critics or even attract large audiences. She said it was her best film yet, but sadly no one seemed to agree.

Fortunately, *Far from the Madding Crowd* was not due to start filming for a couple of months, so Julie was able to enjoy an idyllic summer with Don Bessant. After the traumas of *Doctor Zhivago* and the excitement of the Oscars, Julie was entranced to take time out to relax and spend time with friends at her Kensington flat. Julie was horrified when a leading American columnist suggested during an interview that now she had made it she would obviously be moving out to somewhere much grander. 'Moving out,' she shrieked in echo. 'I'm only just moving in. Besides my flat has the sort of unpretentious atmosphere I like and lots of little shops all around where I can dash out and buy stuff for a meal at the last minute.

Still, if I go on making money on this scale, I'd like to have something to show for it eventually. I'm appalled by the amount of money I've frittered away on nothings since I've had some to spend.'

But Julie did confide that she planned to buy a house in time. 'I want to buy a house for about £35,000 with a garden in the right part of London. A marvellous mystery house, all nostalgic and full of memories of the past, with a garden like *The Secret Garden.* ' She thoughtfully paid off debts for assorted old friends and relished her freedom after her punishing schedule. The Oscar was plonked carelessly on a shelf above her old magazine collection just on the right of the boarded-up fireplace. She and Don Bessant were so close that this was perhaps the time she might have followed up on her frequently quoted references to marriage. Journalists certainly kept asking and with increasing irritation Julie Christie turned them away.

A friend said: 'Julie had changed an enormous amount in the first half of the sixties. She had been through so much. She never wanted to be famous in the first place and now she was suddenly this amazing icon of the sixties. She hated that word and the whole celebrity business. In the beginning she was so open and honest she would have talked all day to reporters and told them everything they wanted to know. But she hated the way they hounded Don. She didn't mind for herself but she thought it was so unfair that he should be pestered. 'He's an artist, for God's sake.

Leave him alone,' she yelled at one photographer who followed them shopping in High Street Kensington. She really loved Don and they were so good together. If ever they were going to get married then I suppose it would have been then, but they were starting to move in different worlds. Julie knew films and success would change her and she fought hard to stop it. When she changed it was not in a nasty way. She was so kind and generous with her money. But you cannot become public property like that and not build up some form of defence, some way of dealing with the endless recognition and requests.'

It was a wonderful summer and Julie Christie enjoyed it to the full. She was so relaxed she could easily sleep for fourteen hours at a time and she frequently prepared exotic meals and then somehow never got round to eating them. One brainwave was to take driving lessons but the anguish on the face of the instructor convinced her she was not somehow born to be a motorist. She and Don Bessant slipped away from London and holidayed in Holland and then in Greece before filming began on *Far from the Madding Crowd.* But she was saddened to realize that her recognition factor had increased massively: 'I specially chose some remote little island,' she complained afterwards, 'where no one could possibly recognize me. But no such luck. I was gaped and ogled at by every man I saw and, while women naturally like men to go dotty over them, there was something terribly off-putting about their stares. It brought the worst out in me. I wanted to shout at them, and all the time my anger made me feel guilty. It was awful.' But when she returned to London her spirits lifted. 'This sort of heroine worship doesn't happen so much in London. I am accepted as part of the scenery. Dozens of girls look like me, dress like me and think like me. I have no novelty value at home. If I'm supposed to typify 1966, as some people have claimed, then I'm only one of many who do.'

After her mostly joyous and relaxing summer, Julie had a heavy heart as she was swept by taxi to the Royal Hotel in Weymouth to start what would be almost six months of filming as surely the most beautiful of all the assorted Bathsheba Everdenes to grace the screen. She was heartened to recognize some old friends, like cinematographer Nicolas Roeg whom she had first met in Spain and who had also handled the photography on *Fahrenheit 451,* and Bubbles Elliott, her friendly stand-in. Her old drama-school friend, actress Fiona Walker, was in the cast playing the faithful Liddy, and they later moved into a rented house together. Bessant was busy scuttling between jobs in London and Kent, but promised to visit as often as possible. Julie had enjoyed reading Hardy's novel and was sure the leading role as the tempestuous Bathsheba would be her best yet. But she did confess later, when asked if it had been helpful to go back to the original text, 'Well, at the time I was not only selfish and superficial but also lazy, I think. I don't remember doing proper work on those things. I think I just walked in and assumed I would be directed through them. I wish I had done more preparation because I don't think I was very good in that. Later I played a small part in a medieval thing and I simply immersed myself in medieval history, none of which was of the slightest use and nobody knew any of the stuff except me, but it was essential to get a backing for my character. I didn't do that then and I should have studied the Hardy book with a fine-tooth comb. I have done since and I understand it so much better than I did then, I'm afraid. I certainly read it at the time but not with attention. I didn't explore it or investigate its detail like a historian, which I should have done. I now know that the original book is the best thing you could possibly have because you are being led, told what you feel by the author. It's marvellous – you can't make those mistakes, you have beautiful stage direction. Screenplays don't tell you what you feel or why you feel it; all that is extra work, whereas if you have a book with all the signposts up, it is an enormous help.

'*Far from the Madding Crowd* was shot in a most beautiful place and was very important to my life. I lived in a little cottage and I remember driving to work very early each morning, seeing the dew in the trees and lots of dead animals on the roads too because it was early and they hadn't been cleaned up yet. How fast motorists travel on country lanes!

Apart from that it was a wonderful experience after which I decided I was going to live in the country.'

Julie was delighted to be working with John Schlesinger again. She said: 'It was not so much that we had a good working relationship as that John was so terribly kind and a very dear person. I have a great fondness for him and we understand each other. After *Darling* I think we both understood a lot about each other's weaknesses and faults and that bound us together.'

*Far from the Madding Crowd* was certainly a high-quality production. Frederic Raphael's excellent screenplay drew fine performances from Julie Christie and the three distinguished leading men who played her rival suitors – Terence Stamp as Sergeant Troy, Alan Bates as Gabriel Oak, and especially from Peter Finch as the machiavellian William Boldwood. Julie Christie was entranced by working with Peter Finch and several years afterwards she paid him a warm and significantly worded tribute: 'Peter Finch was the most wonderful actor I've worked with, almost. What an actor! First of all I admired Peter on screen, I just couldn't keep my eyes off him. It wasn't that he was the most wonderful person to work with but that he was one of the best actors I've ever worked with. I think his work is so complex, dense, original and heartfelt. I could watch him for ever. The other quality Peter possessed as a screen actor was his charisma and that is sometimes missing in such a good actor. It was a privilege to work with him, thrilling. And in the part of that awful man, the pain – oh, he was lovely.'

In spite of her severe self-criticism Julie Christie appeared to work hard at her role in the location village of Bloxworth in deepest Dorset. She was well liked by the crew, who sometimes teased her about her cigarette consumption. Although her caravan became a popular open-house meeting place during some of the long delays, the clouds of smoke from her mentholated fags certainly prevented one or two visitors from outstaying their welcome.

But as the end of the year approached the film seemed to be developing problems. Both producer Janni and director Schlesinger believed Julie Christie was the nearest thing to Bathsheba to be found in real life. In Christie's own words, Bathsheba was 'illogical, vain, proud, but she cares to be good. She has high values and a violent temper. She's vulnerable and eager, but privately resourceful.' It's a fabulous story and the three male leads were excellent but somewhere in the mix wise heads detected trouble. By Christmas of 1966 even the normally ebullient Schlesinger sounded wary and cautious instead of confident: 'Its problem has always been not to make it come out as a sort of *Reader's Digest* of a very long, gigantic novel, instead of doing it the justice it deserves. I think we've done it as well as we can.'

So with an unspoken understanding of impending doom all around her Julie Christie was receptive to the offer, from Beatles films director Richard Lester, of a script bizarrely entitled *Me and the Arch Kook Petulia,* a half-baked modern romance which was to be his introduction to Hollywood. In London Julie had just settled the deal on buying a new home, a highly desirable two-storey terraced house at No.1, Selwood Terrace, South Kensington, and the faithful Bessant was happily supervising the move.

When *Far from the Madding Crowd* finally emerged into the cinema it was immediately clear that the early love affair between Julie Christie and the critics was well and truly over. The film flopped badly in America where it was written off as slow and boring after being badly over-hyped as the big follow-up to *Doctor Zhivago* and in Britain it was also badly savaged.

But before then Julie Christie was settling into her houseboat in San Francisco working hard for Dick Lester with George C. Scott and Richard Chamberlain in the film which had by now been very sensibly renamed simply *Petulia.* And she had attracted an admirer in the internationally admired shape of Mr Henry Warren Beatty. He had seen her winning her Oscar. He had spotted her at several showbiz parties. He had seen her lips quivering with passion as Doctor Zhivago's beloved Lara. And he very much liked what he saw.

# 8

# Warren Beatty

Seduction was his greatest asset. Once he was interested in a woman, he would never let go.

Leslie Caron on Warren Beatty

Leslie Caron was married to Royal Shakespeare Company director Peter Hall when she first met Warren Beatty at a showbusiness party in Beverly Hills in 1963. The function was to promote her Oscar chances – she had been nominated for an Academy Award for her role in *The L-Shaped Room.* She was instantly bowled over by the charm and sex appeal of Hollywood's most famous multiple lover: 'I was struck by his appearance and his personality. He had star quality: very good looks, a great smile, he was tall and athletic. Seduction was his greatest asset. Once he was interested in a woman, he would never let go. He enveloped her with his every thought. He wanted total control of her, her clothes, her make-up, her work. He took notice of everything.' The attraction was mutual and overwhelming. 'We practically did not leave each other for the next two years,' said Caron. At the Oscar ceremony the following year, on 13 April 1964, Caron arrived on Beatty's arm at the Santa Monica Civic Auditorium. But for the most part the couple tried to keep their liaison out of the public eye.

Until early in 1964 Peter Hall's marriage to the famous French film star had seemed idyllic. They had two children – Christopher, who was six and Jennifer, four – and lived in two large and stylish family homes, one in London and one in Stratford-upon-Avon. Leslie Caron was six years older than Warren Beatty and in those days much more famous than he was. She had become an overnight star back in 1950 when she was surprisingly chosen to star alongside Gene Kelly in his Oscar-winning film *An American in Paris.* She had gone on to star with Fred Astaire in the 1955 hit *Daddy Longlegs* but remains best known for her stunning performance with Maurice Chevalier and Louis Jourdan in the multi-Oscar winning 1958 film musical *Gigi.* Peter Hall had directed her in the stage version of *Gigi.* In early 1964 Hall was overwhelmed with work masterminding the celebrations of the 400th anniversary of the birth of Shakespeare and Leslie Caron, by now totally besotted with Warren Beatty, announced that she would be working in America for the next six months. She said that she could not find suitable work in England: 'It's very tough on my husband, I know. But I am an actress and I cannot change. I have never intended to stop work. I have been working since I was fourteen years old. Peter knows that. For the sake of my marriage and family I never wanted to make another picture outside of England. But now I realize I must, if I am to continue working.' She acknowledged that working on opposite sides of the Atlantic would involve 'pressure', but she and Peter Hall had talked it through and decided it was the only solution. The children would fly to see their mother in America in the school holidays.

But on 4 April 1964, Peter Hall and Leslie Caron admitted the painful truth of the end of their marriage to the world in a joint statement: 'We have found that the demands made upon us by our very different careers, often in different parts of the world, make it no longer possible for us to remain together. We are both deeply sad.' When the news of Leslie Caron's affair with Warren Beatty hit the newspapers, the couple prepared themselves for a media blitz. They were not disappointed. Beatty was dismissed as a philandering playboy who wrecked marriages without regret or compunction.

Peter Hall filed for divorce in June 1964 and named Warren Beatty as the co-respondent. In the ensuing custody battle for the children, fought in a blaze of publicity, Warren Beatty's colourful amorous history, provocatively sprinkled with names like Jane Fonda, Natalie Wood and Joan Collins, was widely written and rewritten in a flood of sensational stories, many of them inaccurate, but all of them damaging.

The divorce finally came to court in February 1965. In spite of Peter Hall's own admitted adultery with an unnamed woman, Warren Beatty was portrayed as very much the ruthless, wife-stealing villain of the piece. He and Leslie Caron tried to throw themselves into work, but the film they made together, *Promise Her Anything,* was a dismal flop. Warren Beatty's reputation was now based on his performances in the bedroom rather than on the screen and he was becoming increasingly frustrated as his lightweight career spluttered. So when Leslie Caron and Warren Beatty arrived in Paris to see the famed film-maker François Truffaut to plead for a role alongside Julie Christie, he was much more desperate than he sounded.

Truffaut quickly ended the discussion by saying that he had already contracted Oskar Werner but he provided Warren Beatty with perhaps the most important offer of his life, the script that was to resurrect his floundering career and focus attention back on the screen – *Bonnie and Clyde.* Truffaut suggested that if Beatty was looking for a movie that could unite him and Leslie Caron, it could well be this strange story of a couple of outlaws, a hoodlum named Clyde Barrow and his girlfriend Bonnie Parker. In the early 1930s the violent couple had acquired a brief notoriety by robbing banks and killing people across Texas and Oklahoma before they were blasted to death in an ambush by Texas Rangers on 23 May 1934. Neither Bonnie nor Clyde lived past their twenty-fifth birthday and, intriguingly, Clyde Barrow was said to have been either homosexual or impotent while the exotic Bonnie Parker was hooked on the excitement of breaking the law.

There had already been a flimsy 1958 B-movie version of the tale, called *The Bonnie Parker Story,* but Truffaut clearly thought there was potential in a new script sent to him by two young unknown American writers on *Esquire* magazine, David Newman and Robert Benton. Beatty had never heard of them, and Bonnie and Clyde registered only vaguely, but if the great François Truffaut made a suggestion, he was certainly bright enough to take the time to examine it properly. Beatty wondered why two unknown American writers would send an American story about American gangsters to a French director and Truffaut explained that they had been impressed by his film *Jules et Jim,* with its acclaimed treatment of a *ménage à trois* of two men and a woman, because they felt the peculiar sexual background of Bonnie and Clyde made this much more than just another action movie. Also, no one in America seemed remotely interested.

Beatty was hooked. Beatty and Caron already felt vilified and under siege, so they could easily identify with life on the run. Truffaut advised them that after having the script translated into French he now realized the film needed to be made by an American. In the event, Leslie Caron's unmistakably French accent was always going to be an insuperable problem playing an all-American gangster, but she still sparked Beatty's enthusiasm for the idea. He decided this could be the powerful project to launch his long-awaited move from simply acting for a living to producing movies as well. Beatty flew back to America and contacted Robert Benton direct. The writer was elated to get a response from a real live film star rather than the more usual subtle expressions of interest from agents or managers. But he was also keen to know if the great macho lover of women was really prepared to play a homosexual. Beatty replied that he really loved the script and offered the writers a $10,000 deal on the understanding that he wanted to bring in a more experienced screenwriter to help them.

Beatty's enthusiasm to play Clyde Barrow was enough to produce some development money, but after Leslie Caron accepted her inevitable unsuitability for the role he needed a Bonnie Parker. He asked his former lover Natalie Wood, who declined, apparently on the grounds that she was not prepared to be separated from her analyst for the three months of location filming in Texas. The search widened to include such names as Carol Lynley, Tuesday Weld, Sue Lyon and even Beatty's sister Shirley MacLaine. But Arthur Penn who had been brought on board as the director, had been impressed by the little-known Faye Dunaway in *Hogan's Goat* and she landed the role that made her an international star.

Beatty's battle to get *Bonnie and Clyde* made is the stuff of Hollywood legend. In those days actors were not often taken seriously as producers and Beatty had to literally get down on his knees and beg Jack Warner for support. He eventually got it, but his troubles were just beginning. Beatty was forced to make his film on a very limited budget and even to bail out the project with his own money more than once. Shrewdly, as it turned out, each time he invested he increased his share of any profits. Jack Warner by then was not expecting much in the way of success. And when Beatty had completed the ultimate gangster movie, and struggled with unenthusiastic studio bosses for a helpful release schedule only to find his movie pushed out on a strictly limited release in the summer in August 1967, he found the critics lining up to lambaste him. They attacked the movie on grounds of taste, rushing to point out that the sensational gun-blasting orgy of violence was filmed in Texas just three years after President Kennedy was shot there. The *New York Times* slammed the 'hideous depredation of that sleazy moronic pair'. *Films in Review* said the movie displayed incompetence at every level. *Newsweek* attacked 'the most gruesome carnage since Verdun, and for those who find killing less than hilarious the effect is stomach-turning.' *Time* magazine called it claptrap and said: 'Like Bonnie and Clyde themselves, the film rides off in all directions and ends up full of holes.'

But the public loved every raucous, highly charged minute. Fans were quickly queuing round the block in New York and their enthusiasm was repeated across the country. The public perception of Warren Beatty changed almost instantly from thoughtless lightweight playboy to visionary producer and inspirational star who had his finger firmly on the pulse of the popular mood. There was something irresistible about Bonnie and Clyde, something in their energy and their humour and their hatred of authority that captured the very spirit of the sixties. Beatty assaulted Warner Brothers with fistfuls of figures from early box-office results and, by sheer force of personality and clever use of publicity, he made the giant film company throw its weight much more seriously behind the surprise success. His insistence made him many enemies as he argued and argued with Warners that they arrange an instant unheard-of re-release. He threatened to sue Warners, an astonishing, unprecedented act for a lone maverick actor – producer. Then in January 1968 *Bonnie and*

*Clyde,* the orgy of escapism that had been rubbished by the learned critics, received no fewer than ten Oscar nominations. Warners eventually bowed to Beatty's endless pressure and at the end of its first year of release the film had grossed $30 million in the United States alone which had earned Warren Beatty more than $6 million.

His attention to detail amazed all close observers. In the making of the film he had copied the ear-splitting emotional force of the gunfire of the classic western, *Shane.* His own sound man, Francis Stahl, was instructed to give the audience shots that 'jump out at you' and so heighten the viewer's involvement. But when he was at the London critics' screening at the Warner Theatre in Leicester Square he realized that the sound of the shots was tame. 'I ran up to the projectionist,' recalled Beatty, 'and I walked into the booth, and he was a little surprised to see me, because I was in the movie. He didn't know I'd produced it. And he said, "You're the producer of this picture?" and I said, "Yeah." And he said, "Well, I've really helped you out in the sound here. I've made a chart, and I turn it up here and down here, and so on. It's the worst mixed picture, I haven't had a picture so badly mixed since *Shane.* "'

This was the charismatic, brilliant, egocentric, ruthless, movie genius that Julie Christie was to shock herself by falling head over heels in love with. Someone who would stand up for what he believed in against a powerful studio and the entire Hollywood hierarchy was exactly the sort of man who could capture her heart.

Beatty was busy winning his *Bonnie and Clyde* battles, and he was still entangled with Leslie Caron, who had left her husband and children for him. But there was something about the haunting English beauty of the young Academy Award-winning actress that made the legendary Hollywood lover desperate to add Julie Christie to his long list of conquests.

Warren Beatty was obsessed by Julie Christie for a long time before she would agree to go out with him. An ex-girlfriend said: 'Warren told me how he first met Julie. He said he was in a restaurant with her and a crowd of other people. He said he was trying to make it with her and she was being very cold towards him. When he tried to get her to go to bed with him she turned him down flat. He has been crazy about her ever since.' Julie turned down many requests to go out with Beatty before she was finally intrigued enough to agree. She was attracted by the handsome millionaire, who wouldn't be, but she has a strong code of fidelity and had no wish to deceive her lover of three years, Don Bessant.

Julie had made no secret of the fact that she was attracted to strong men. Warren Beatty was in the process of proving his worth at taking on the very industry that at times terrorized her. He made several approaches but the one that worked was the 'casual' visit he made to the set of *Petulia.* The attraction was mutual, and quickly overwhelming. Observers at the time noted that Julie Christie and Warren Beatty 'detonated like a match in cordite' and a passionate love-affair, between arguably two of the film world's most attractive stars, was under way.

Beatty's name had been linked with some of the most beautiful women in the world, but it seemed that Julie was different. He said she reminded him of an unmade bed while she struggled to keep to herself what she really thought of him. But it was the start of a stormy seven-year relationship that made them the natural successors to Richard Burton and Elizabeth Taylor as Hollywood's most glamorous couple. In many ways Julie Christie was the mirror image of Warren Beatty, especially in her steadily developing, uncompromising and antagonistic attitude to the movie business. She was inspired by Beatty's bold stand against Warner Brothers over *Bonnie and Clyde,* because she had a growing feeling that she no longer wanted her life to be controlled by a few powerful movie moguls in Los Angeles. Beatty adored Christie's peculiar mixture of shattering self-doubt and rigid integrity. 'She is almost pathologically honest,' he said. 'She is beautiful by all your conventional standards and I admire her work, so it is no surprise that I love her.' The headlines about the new love hurtled around the world and Julie Christie was desperately concerned about their effect on her long-term boyfriend Don Bessant, waiting patiently back in London for her to return.

Dick Lester filmed *Petulia* on location all around San Francisco and Julie found herself followed not only by Beatty, but by an enthusiastic British press corps in hot pursuit of a juicy scandal. Julie told the reporters only that she was 'loving every minute of being in San Francisco. It is a wonderful city and everyone here seems so friendly and easy going.' But she firmly refused to discuss her private life. The truth is that Christie and Beatty were so bowled over by each other that they did not quite know what to think. The mutual attraction was powerful and even all-consuming at times but both stars were cautious. Julie still planned to return to Bessant and spoke about how homesick she was and of her plans for the house they shared. And Beatty's relationship with Leslie Caron still hung in the air. Meanwhile the peculiar *Petulia* demanded much of Christie's concentration. In the title role, she played a former flower-child who was married to the hard-driving David, played by

Richard Chamberlain, yet was attracted to unsuitable men like Archie, played by George C. Scott, a doctor struggling to bring up children after a divorce. Lester called it a 'sad love story', which seemed to suit Christie's mood of the moment perfectly. When it was completed, the *New Statesman* pronounced: 'Miss Christie is in her element which is discotheque rather than Dorset. The freshness of *Petulia,* and the force of it, come rather from a series of extraordinary performances. Julie Christie and George C. Scott are very good.'

When *Petulia* finished shooting in the autumn of 1967 Julie flew home ... alone. Back at Selwood Terrace she tried hard to show that nothing had changed. But a widely reported affair with the world's most infamous lady-killer is a hard thing to ignore. She still spent evenings at the Queen's Elm but underneath the good humour no one was drinking to a long future for Julie's relationship with Don Bessant. In the event he quietly and sadly moved out of Julie Christie's life and the couple remained good friends. He knew that however firmly his lover tried to keep her feet on the ground it was impossible for her not to be whisked off them at some point.

Julie Christie's next film was *In Search of Gregory* to be shot in Geneva and Milan with John Hurt. It was the first to be directed by theatre director Peter Wood and had been set up especially for her by Jo Janni. It was a forgettable story about the desperate pursuit of a mystery man called Gregory – played by a largely baffled-looking Michael Sarrazin – by an evidently deranged nymphomaniac called Catherine Morelli, played by Christie. The *Daily Telegraph'* s verdict was that it was essentially an extremely silly film but Julie Christie did everything possible with her part.

Her concentration was hardly helped by her flourishing relationship with Beatty. He pursued her to Europe and even took over the Frank Sinatra role in *The Only Game in Town* which was being filmed in Paris and where he found himself playing opposite Elizabeth Taylor. Darryl F. Zanuck was so desperate to get Beatty to step in when Sinatra dropped out that he agreed to pay him a cool $1 million. In the end, that was only a little less than the picture took at the box-office. It is instructive to record that even while in the early passionate throes of his new love-affair with Julie Christie, Beatty found the time and inclination to flirt outrageously with an older woman locked with Richard Burton in one of the world's most celebrated romances.

On the first day on the set in Paris he approached Taylor, and studied her with a slight smile on his face. She knew she was being assessed, and he was just seven years younger with a well-publicized enthusiasm for brunettes and English origins, and she asked: 'What is it?' 'Oh nothing,' said Beatty, who then laughed out loud, and walked away. The following day he said nothing so Taylor asked: 'Why did you laugh, Warren?' He paused for maximum effect and then said, 'I laughed because nobody can be that beautiful.' For once he declined to make a pass, but he could never resist making an impact. Burton, however, who was filming *Staircase* in another part of Paris, took the threat of superstud Beatty seriously enough to warn him off even thinking about falling in love with his wife.

Warren implored Julie to use a short break from *In Search of Gregory* to come to visit him in Paris. She flew over in a trice and seemed completely smitten. An observer noticed that she bought a roll of Indian silk for a dress and instantly had it altered when Warren didn't find it to his taste. In the event both films were flops but the love-affair was really full-on now. Julie Christie and Warren Beatty finally had time they could spend together and they used much of it to travel to exotic places like India and the Far East.

For varying periods of time Julie moved into Warren Beatty's suite, the Escondido, at the Beverly Wilshire Hotel, which makes a convenient base but is hardly a lavish home. Elvis Presley used the same suite as a rehearsal room when he stayed at the hotel. But the couple travelled widely, often to Europe, where Polanski and Victor Lownes, the British Playboy boss, were close friends. Beatty spent days going through mountains of scripts, anxiously keen to find the next big hit to follow *Bonnie and Clyde.* His own acting career seemed strangely neglected at this time when he and Julie Christie were vying to be the more unavailable for hire. He turned down *Butch Cassidy and the Sundance Kid* and passed on *The Godfather.* But with the popularity of *Bonnie and Clyde* and the arrival of more exciting and innovative films like *Easy Rider* and *Midnight Cowboy,* Warren Beatty and Julie Christie were suddenly being seen as the new most glamorous movie couple, rivalling Richard Burton and Elizabeth Taylor. They both called a halt to media interviews and travelled the world at their leisure. For a period of almost two years they took time to spend some of the vast fortunes they had earned. It became clear that they were searching for a film they could make together, but they were in no hurry at all to find it.

Julie was lifted by her lover's passion and drive, and she supported him to the hilt when he moved into unfamiliar political areas, not always too successfully. Beatty refused to take the safe no-comment route on major issues. He insisted: 'There is no reason why the artist is not part of his times. The artist simply says in an uncompromising way what the truth is. People were dying in Vietnam and the racial problems at home were very immediate things. And you had the sexual revolution on the 1960s. This was a very immediate thing.' Beatty simply refused to be uninvolved. He became close to Robert Kennedy and was an articulate spokesman for him across the USA. And after Robert Kennedy was assassinated in June 1968 he spoke up firmly in support of gun control. Of course filmgoers who had recently watched

*Bonnie and Clyde* unleash their indiscriminate firepower considered Beatty's position somewhat ironic. But he did not back down. When critics blamed him for glamorizing violence he insisted *Bonnie and Clyde* had showed the bloody reality and consequence of violence and there was no double standard about his position. The right to bear arms is close to the heart of many Americans and Beatty's position did not increase his popularity. He worked on the John Glenn Emergency Gun Controls Committee and went out to face the public with his passionately held views.

Famously, he went with a wide-eyed Julie Christie to Candlestick Park, San Francisco, on 6 July 1968, just one month after Bobby Kennedy was killed, and before the game between the San Francisco Giants and the St Louis Cardinals, he spoke to the impatient and unsympathetic crowd. 'A sound and reasonable gun control law will only help curb violence in our society,' he said, but the crowd booed, and chanted for the game to start. Beatty ploughed on: 'Now is the time to act and Americans should wire or write to their congressman to approve a law that will impose reason and good sense on possession of firearms.' The boos got louder as the crowd demonstrated that it was more interested in a football game than in Warren Beatty's opinions on gun control. But Beatty was not dissuaded from his cause. He and the faithful Christie moved on to Cow Palace to make a similar powerful plea before the start of Sonny Liston's heavyweight fight with Henry Clark. This time the crowd's reaction was even more forceful. As well as the boos and jeers Beatty was pelted with bottles and beer cans.

Because of Christie's love of London the couple spent a lot of time in England where controversial Polish director Roman Polanski became a great friend. Polanski asked Beatty to play the husband, the evil agent of the devil in his upcoming film, *Rosemary's Baby.* But Beatty delayed making a decision for too long, as usual, and finally rejected the role as not important enough. His parting shot to Polanski was: 'Hey, can I play Rosemary?' Christie and Beatty were in London on 10 August 1969 when the terrible news came through of the murder of Roman Polanski's beautiful wife Sharon Tate and other members of her household by the Charles Manson gang in the house on Cielo Drive. Victor Lownes and Warren Beatty helped to cut through the red tape and escorted Polanski in his darkest hour to Los Angeles.

Beatty was now searching in earnest for the perfect film to share with his lover and it had to be something exactly right for both of them. After almost two years of travelling, Julie decided that she did not want to spend the rest of her life living in a hotel, albeit a luxury hotel, and she rented a beach house owned by actress Gayle Hunnicutt in Malibu. That way they could be together or apart as the mood took them.

Towards the end of 1969 Beatty found what he had been tirelessly searching for – a script he and

Julie Christie could turn into a fine film together. *McCabe and Mrs Miller,* based on a 1959 novel by Edmund Naughton called simply *McCabe,* was to be made by quirky but brilliant Hollywood director Robert Altman. Originally Altman had wanted Elliott Gould but the financiers were a good deal happier with the more bankable Warren Beatty, especially when he came with Julie Christie.

The story had Beatty as professional gambler and alleged gunfighter John Q. McCabe riding into a small town as a man of mystery and getting involved with Christie's character, Constance Miller, a high-class madam with an expensive drugs habit. The two start a successful brothel, but when big business tries to take them over she wants to do a deal and he wants to fight.

All the planning and the urgent phone calls seemed to whet Julie's appetite for work. She decided she was ready to face a camera again and when it transpired that *McCabe* would not be ready to roll until the end of 1970, there was time to consider something else. In the growing mound of submitted scripts she found a gem, Harold Pinter's brilliant screenplay based upon L. P. Hartley's classic novel *The Go-Between.* Julie was just a few pages into the haunting story of how a young boy was drawn into taking messages between a pair of secret lovers when she decided she simply must play the part.

In Britain, acclaimed director Joseph Losey had been trying for eight years to get this wonderful tale on to the screen. But long and bitter arguments about the rights and the adaptation had caused endless delays and his search for a leading lady to play beautiful young aristocrat Marian had been long and fruitless. She was supposed to be eighteen or nineteen and Losey had attempted to recruit Julie Christie back in 1964. He had always wanted an 'unknown girl' for his beloved project, which surely now ruled out Julie. But producer John Heyman and writer Harold Pinter pushed Losey to reconsider her. He agreed and Losey recorded: 'I conceded Julie Christie, whom I had tried to get initially, at which point she would have been almost the right age. And I must say, to her very great credit, she insisted she was too old.' His memory was that Julie was hard to convince to take the role and her services had to be sought through Warren Beatty. In any case they agreed and Julie's fee was $50,000 plus a percentage of the profits.

By the summer of 1970 she was thirty years old, but director of photography Gerry Fisher insisted he could make her look eighteen. In the event she looks much younger than her real age – hardly still in her teens, but radiantly beautiful all the same.

Hartley had based his story on a real visit he made as a boy to Bradenham Hall in Norfolk, which belonged to the Rider Haggard family. His own youthful experiences as an unofficial postman for two illicit lovers inspired the novel which is set in 1900, and has twelve-year-old Leo Colston being invited to spend three weeks of a very hot summer with schoolfriend

Marcus Maudsley in his family's large house in the country. Leo is entranced by the elegant lifestyle, the elaborate picnics, the croquet on the lawn and, most of all, by Marcus's beautiful older sister Marian. She quickly makes a friend of shy young Leo, but there is an ulterior motive. Although she is engaged to be married to the gallant Viscount Trimingham, a scarred hero of the Boer War, she is conducting a passionate secret affair with lusty tenant farmer Ted Burgess. Leo finds himself drawn into their plotting as he becomes their messenger. But the responsibility of sharing their secret weighs heavily upon his young shoulders and it all ends in tragedy when Marian's mother drags Leo to the outhouses where Ted and Marian are in the throes of noisy passion. Ted shoots himself and Leo becomes a bachelor for life. Half a century later he is brought back to the large house for a dramatic postscript – hence the eerie line of introduction: 'The past is a foreign country. They do things differently there.'

Losey felt that the important thing was what became of the boy, what kind of man he became, and why and how he was destroyed. In the early sixties, when first pressed by Losey, Harold Pinter said the book was so fine that it had reduced him to tears but he did not feel that he could write the screenplay: 'It's wonderful. But I can't write a film script of it. I can't touch it. It's too painful, too perfect, if you know what I mean.' Fortunately, Losey persuaded him to change his mind.

Filming took place in stylish Melton Constable, some twenty-five miles north of Norwich, where Losey discovered a magnificent 1660s house, in a state of neglect and decay but highly suitable. Joseph Losey and Julie Christie had an enormous mutual respect for each other's talents and corresponded long after the film was finished but it was not always an easy relationship. Christie felt humiliated after she arrived late on set one day and Losey roared: 'I would accept that from a star like Elizabeth Taylor but not from you.' Not even Losey's closest friends would say he was an easy man to work with. 'I found him very much anti-female,' Glenda Jackson has said. 'There was something very misogynistic about him.'

Leo was played by fourteen-year-old Dominic Guard who was excellent in the demanding role, although Christie reflected afterwards that acting with children was difficult: 'You feed in, but you don't get feedback. You have to make the best of what you have.' Ted Burgess was played by Julie's old friend Alan Bates, and Edward Fox was the scarred war hero Viscount Trimingham, although Losey pulled back from making his facial wounds anything like as horrific as described in the book.

Deborah Kerr had been offered the part of Mrs Maudsley but after she had been left for several hours in a hotel waiting for Losey to call she turned the part down and Margaret Leighton was brought in. Julie Christie and Alan Bates were comfortably the best-paid of the talented cast. Edward Fox, who was about to intrigue cinema audiences across the world with his role of the assassin in *The Day of the Jackal,* was paid £1,750. Margaret Leighton was paid £2,500, and Dominic Guard, £1,000.

All the cast were astonished to see the press entourage that followed Julie Christie, and Warren Beatty when he also arrived in Norfolk. The relationship that neither of them wanted to talk about was big news. Christie tried to keep her life as low-key as always. She rented a small house not far from the sea and bought a bicycle to ride to the set each day. But the location was under siege from photographers and reporters. Large lenses poked over every available gate and the intrusive presence of the journalists routinely raised the blood pressure of perfectionist director Losey.

Christie and Beatty were asked thousands of times whether they would marry and they resolutely kept their plans to themselves. Her long-forgotten early quote that she wanted to have a baby by the time she was thirty was frequently thrown back at her, but failed to provoke a reaction. There was even speculation that they were already secretly married, to which Christie snorted unhelpfully: 'If we are, we are, if we are not, we're not.'

Whilst refusing to discuss her private life, Christie did talk about her visit to a local intensive pig farm, where the privations of the animals sparked a furious reaction. 'It was so appalling,' she said. 'I couldn't believe that that was what was meant by "factory farming". Animals were being kept in a concentration camp.' Warren Beatty supported his lover and loyally announced that he, too, would never eat meat again.

Long afterwards she reflected that Marian Maudsley in *The Go-Between* had much in common with Diana Scott in *Darling.* They were both charming and beautiful on the surface but capable of real selfishness and cruelty: 'I think Marian is a bit smarter than Diana and she would probably have handled her life a bit better. Marian was quite ruthless and incapable of thinking of anyone but herself. She would have been like her mother. The location in Norfolk was brilliant and I have very happy memories of it because it was a very happy time for me in my private life.'

The film was a success. It made a comfortable profit and won the prestigious Palme d'Or for best film at the Cannes Film Festival, dramatically beating *Death in Venice* by a single vote. Julie Christie did not attend, as she had rushed back to America to start work on *McCabe and Mrs Miller,* but with Warren Beatty she did help to promote the New York launch.

Warren Beatty's strong liberal political views were part of his appeal for Julie Christe. He threw himself into George McGovern's campaign to reach the White House and although the senator lost by a landslide, he gratefully acknowledged Beatty's contribution: 'Warren Beatty took a year out of his life. He travelled around the country making speeches, debating issues, interpreting me to the public, and he personally was responsible for raising more than a million dollars.'

With Christie in enthusiastic attendance Beatty orchestrated political concerts where major performers would give their time and their talent to boost campaign funds. Carole King came out of her temporary retirement for Beatty and popular stars like James Taylor, Barbra Streisand, Joni Mitchell and Paul Simon joined this heady mix of showbiz and politics. At Beatty's side throughout stood Julie Christie: serene, concerned and involved.

At this time many thought that the great womanizer would marry the shimmering beauty he had courted so long and so assiduously. But Christie resisted the proposals. Having worked hard to achieve financial independence and overcome the insecurities that still haunted her, she was not about to plunge into wedlock with Warren Beatty, however much she loved him. He was in many ways the strong man she had longed for, but she could hardly fail to realize that men with Beatty's track record of infidelity are not exactly ideal husband material, even if they do sweep you off your feet, satisfy your every whim, and relentlessly tell you how much they love you. They had some furious rows because Julie refused to compromise. She told friends: 'Warren doesn't drink, doesn't smoke, doesn't swear. That makes it a bit hard on me, because I can't do any of those things with him either!'

She didn't cheat on him either. Julie Christie hates any form of lying or duplicity so while Warren Beatty was sharing her life she was never inclined to sleep with anyone else. Unfortunately the same cannot be said of Beatty. Britt Ekland described Julie Christie as 'foolishly absent' when she encountered Beatty at a London dinner party for Roman Polanski. They had met years before when she had been with Peter Sellers and he with Leslie Caron. At that time she had been so besotted with Sellers she failed to respond to Beatty's charm and sex appeal. This time was different. As she put it, 'Warren's gaze descended on me, and the moment our eyes met I knew we were committed physically.'

She was happy to have a fling with Beatty. It provided a welcome diversion to dodging the relentless pursuit of a certain photographic aristocrat who was proposing marriage. But what Britt did not realize was that she was falling in love with Beatty. For a time she thought her love was reciprocated but she overheard too many 'whispered phone calls' to Julie to believe that.

Britt paid glowing tribute to Beatty's skills as a lover. No man had made her happier and when she flew to Los Angeles to appear on the *Dean Martin Show,* Beatty followed, and she joined him in his suite at the Beverly Wilshire hotel. Beatty told her that he wanted to keep their relationship a secret from Julie, saying, 'She'd hit the roof if she knew. But I guess that is one of the gambles we're going to have to take.'

The inflamed couple even slipped into a sleazy porn theatre and Britt joked afterwards: 'How can cinema audiences be turned on by simulated sex? I will never make a porno film unless it's for real and only with you!' Beatty laughed: 'In that case we had better get a camera crew to film our activities in the penthouse.' But when she flew back to London the affair ended leaving Britt wishing she had had the courage to bid a final farewell to Hollywood's great lover saying it had been great while it lasted.

On location for *McCabe* in Vancouver, Warren Beatty and Julie Christie blessed the distance from Fleet Street, as they were so much freer and un-pestered. Director Robert Altman wanted his western to look different, with snowy forests in the background instead of the usual rocky and rugged cowboy back-drop. Some critics said Julie struggled with the accent, and that traces of Cockney were mixed in the vowels but her portrayal of the resourceful Constance Miller remains one of her finest roles. McCabe shared her bed but he still had to pay his $5.

Julie remembers it best 'because it was made at such an extraordinarily happy time of my life'. Typical Altman violence and realism lifted this already superior script. Beatty was excellent too, playing McCabe full of wise-guy philosophy: 'You know how to square a circle? You shove a four by four up a mule's ass.'

In many ways this was their happiest time togeth-er. Warren Beatty tried hard then to persuade Julie Christie to become his wife. But she was happy as she was. Friends said that Julie did not need any more commitment, preferring things the way they were.

She knew that other women came into her lover's life and although his infidelity sparked rows and threats about the future, theirs was still a stimulating and loving relationship. But Julie had no wish to be a wife whose husband played around. So she declined the chance to get married.

After completing *McCabe and Mrs Miller* Warren Beatty flew to Europe to star in *The Heist,* with Goldie Hawn. Julie Christie flew back too, but she holed up in Selwood Terrace, where, it is said, there were many serious disagreements between them. Warren said that Christie was 'one of the great actresses in the history of films ... if we ever split up, I'll pay her alimony ... that's if she wants it or needs it.' Mind you, on another occasion he also said that the best time for a wedding was noon. Then, if things don't work out, you haven't blown the whole day.

The cooling of the relationship gradually became obvious to a growing circle of friends. Robert Altman had noticed during filming *McCabe and Mrs Miller* how Julie Christie would prefer to sit on the edge of movie parties, becoming animated only when conversations moved off the popular subject of movie gossip to more political topics. Meanwhile Beatty would be busy being the life and soul of the event.

Certainly Julie placed great importance on faithfulness. She said forcefully: 'Infidelity destroys love. If you love someone and it's good, you've got to have the sense to stick with it. This doesn't mean you will never be attracted to another living soul. But if you give in to that attraction, then you risk losing the person you're in love with. You can't just go swanning off with everyone who attracts you. It's greedy and selfish. It sounds great to do whatever you want at a given time. But it never works out in real life – only in the movies.'

# 9

# Don't Look Now

Making love on camera is such hard work that there is no time for the libido to take over.

Julie Christie

Daphne du Maurier's strange, simple and haunting story about a couple who move from their home in England to a new life in Venice – to try to recover from the tragic loss of a child – was transformed by the genius of director Nicolas Roeg and towering performances by Julie Christie and Donald Sutherland into one of the most justifiably famous films of all time. *The Times* rated *Don't Look Now,* the classic 1973 movie, at number five in its top 100 list of the best cult films ever made.

Yet it could so easily have been very different. When the charismatic Roeg was struggling to nurse the idea towards production in the early seventies both of his chosen leading players looked seriously unavailable. Roeg's reputation as one of cinema's most imaginative yet at times darkest talents was firmly established. He had served a long and rewarding apprenticeship as camera operator for the legendary cinematographer Freddie Young, which gave him invaluable experience working on George Cukor's 1956 film *Bhowani Junction* and David Lean's *Lawrence of Arabia* in 1962. By the mid-sixties he had risen to the level of director of photography, working with accomplished directors like François Truffaut on *Fahrenheit 451,* John Schlesinger on *Far from the Madding Crowd* and Roger Corman on *The Masque of the Red Death.* His ability for setting the most astonishingly atmospheric scenes for movie-goers was second to none and the strength of his friendship with and his admiration for Julie Christie was high indeed.

Julie Christie, with whom Roeg had already successfully worked on *Doctor Zhivago, Fahrenheit 451* and *Far from the Madding Crowd,* was enthusiastically involved not only with Warren Beatty but also with her lover's support for the United States Presidential campaign of outspoken Democrat senator George McGovern. Christie was fully committed even if she did note frankly afterwards: 'I didn't know what I was doing then. I knew that McGovern was an extremely decent man, but I was not an independent agent in that: I was organized into it by Warren.'

With Donald Sutherland embarked on another film there was talk of hiring husband and wife stars Robert Wagner and Natalie Wood to play the tragic couple. But Roeg was not a man to be easily diverted from his aims. And within a few weeks Richard Nixon politically overwhelmed his rival in the race for the White House, while Sutherland's film expired in acrimony and both stars were, at a stroke, free. Roeg was delighted. His initial instinct that a married couple made up of an American husband and an English wife would provide exactly the right slightly misfitting partnership to the central characters was correct.

It proved to be a decisive time in the life of Julie Christie. Her long romance with Warren Beatty looked over as she flew back to Europe, this time without her famous lover in pursuit. In fact he was quickly spotted following Norwegian actress Liv Ullmann around the California night spots and Christie was delighted to join old friend Roeg and throw herself into an extraordinary and demanding new role.

Roeg was an energetic and determined director with a very clear idea of what he wanted. While Christie was happy to be moulded by a strong-willed film-maker whom she trusted and respected, Donald Sutherland, still basking in the wealth of international popularity his role as Hawkeye, in Robert Altman's smash hit *M\*A\*S\*H,* had provided, was more cautious. The record of his reaction to Roeg's original approach is revealing: 'I phoned Nic Roeg from Florida after I had read the script of *Don't Look Now* and said that I wanted to sit down and talk to him about it. He said, "What do you want to talk about?" I replied with this long speech about how I felt that extra-sensory perception was a positive part of our lives and therefore we should make *Don't Look Now* a more educative sort of film, that the characters should in some way benefit from ESP and not just be destroyed by it. Nic said, "That's not how I feel." I said, "What do you feel?" and he just said, "What's in the script, do you want to do it or not?" I asked if we could talk about it and he said, "No." So I said, "Well, if you want to put it that way, yes I do." And I just went ahead and obeyed orders and had a wonderful time.'

The conversation demonstrates how resolute Roeg was that *Don't Look Now* would have only the one director. Sutherland accepted Roeg's authority wholeheartedly and was tremendous in the role. One creative suggestion from the actor was accepted, however. Sutherland arrived with a curious curly wig, which he felt was appropriate for his character. Roeg who instinctively disliked wigs agreed because the fake hair looked peculiarly authentic and also made his leading man less initially identifiable as a famous Hollywood star. With typical modesty, Christie wondered why on earth Roeg had wanted her for the role. But she was thrilled by the script and she trusted his judgement implicitly. 'Nic has an unusual eye and an unusual mind,' she said. 'As a director he is quite secretive, not enormously collaborative, but this is the way he succeeds. The whole film could have gone completely haywire. It was a bit of a risk, but I don't like run-of-the-mill stuff. In the event the risk paid off. Whatever else may be said about it, it is certainly technically interesting.'

On location Julie noted: 'Venice and the whole atmosphere of the film is very eerie, but I think it's exciting, too. Although it is not intended to, it may make a lot of people question whether there really is a life after death.' But when asked if she herself really believed in the supernatural she deftly brushed aside the unwanted personal enquiry. 'It's not really within my realm of interest. The reason I'm doing *Don't Look Now* – my first film since *The Go-Between* – is because I like the script and I have great respect for Nicolas Roeg. He's one of the best men I've ever worked with. I've only done six films in about ten years, mainly because I haven't found many films that truly interest me. Sure, I could have done films for the money, but as an actress that is not the primary consideration.' When pressed on her feelings for the supernatural Christie smiled and said, 'I'm not one to believe in not walking under ladders and avoiding the number thirteen. However, I do feel that other worlds, other things can exist apart from those we know, those we take for granted. I think one should hold an open mind to all sorts of phenomena. One should be ready to observe, not to judge. The universe is complex and there are many things in it to which logical explanations cannot be attributed.'

*Don't Look Now* begins with the harrowing scenes of a child drowning. In a flurry of astonishing images we see a beautiful little girl meet a grisly end in a pond, an incident which clearly devastates her parents John and Laura Baxter, played by Sutherland and Christie. In an emotional attempt somehow to cope with their overwhelming grief, architect Baxter and his wife move to Venice, and, while leaving their other child in boarding school in England, they find the city in the throes of being terrorized by a ruthless and mysterious murderer. John throws himself into his work on the renovation of a beautiful but decrepit church; Laura meets a pair of sinister Scottish sisters, Heather and Wendy.

The Baxters are lunching in a Venice restaurant when Wendy is in some distress with a tiny particle in her eye. Her blind sister Heather is unable to help, so, in the restaurant toilets, Laura kindly goes to the elderly woman's aid. Heather, who is brilliantly portrayed in the film by veteran British actress Hilary Mason, is a blind clairvoyante who apparently makes a sudden and disturbing contact with Christine, the dead daughter. She tells Laura that she can 'see' the little girl and tries to reassure her that she is happy. Laura is deeply shocked by the chilling encounter and, returning to her table, she faints and is rushed to hospital.

John is reluctant to accept that Heather has any ability to contact the dead and is delighted when his wife recovers. But, gradually, Heather's astonishing gift draws the traumatized couple into a bizarre horror story. As they are returning to the hotel by launch, Laura insists on visiting a church to pray and they are forced to take a detour to avoid a disturbing murder scene on the maze of canals. All the time Roeg uses the eerily empty ancient city as an increasingly chilly backdrop to his tense tale.

On returning to the banal reassurance of their hotel, the couple make passionate love in scenes that created headlines around the world because of their stunningly erotic realism, but when they go out for dinner they find themselves lost and panicking in a maze of threatening alleyways. John sees what he believes is a small child wearing the same sort of shiny red mackintosh Christine had on when she drowned and the tension mounts inexorably.

Laura attends a seance with the sisters and returns with a stark warning from Heather that John is in grave danger of his life as long as he remains in Venice. He is much more concerned that Laura seems to be falling under the spell of the sisters than he is about any imagined threat to his life. Next morning comes a call from their son Johnny's English boarding school where he has been hurt in an accident. Laura flies back to England but, in Venice, John almost falls to his death from high in the church after a working platform becomes dramatically dislodged.

The police become involved and the sisters are arrested. As the barriers of reality are delicately nudged open, John becomes involved in a final heart-stopping chase along a deserted canal, which ends with him being savagely hacked to death by a cackling evil dwarf wearing the red mackintosh that his daughter drowned in.

The film works on many levels: there are elements of black comedy; it is a haunting examination of grief, as well as an intriguing exploration into the powers of the paranormal. The brutal forces acting on a couple following the death of a child, are stunningly conveyed. And, of course, it is a classic Gothic thriller.

As production got under way Roeg himself said, somewhat mystically, 'Superficially you could say it is a thriller, but for me, it's about the nature of reality, in fact what one perceives through one's mind, or is it the universe as one is obliged to accept it?'

Certainly it is an enormously moving and unsettling film and one of the reasons it provokes such powerful feelings in its audiences is that they see it all coming. In a remarkable seven-minute opening sequence containing no fewer than 102 separate shots, including the drowning, Roeg flashes at lightning speed through everything that is to follow, right up to John Baxter's dreadful death. The bright red coat provides the colour that is used throughout the film to suggest extreme danger and the fusion of paranoid and paranormal builds steadily to almost unbearable levels.

Consequently there is an awful inevitability about the grisly ending which has fascinated film fans ever since *Don't Look Now* was first released in October 1973. Roeg said, 'People imagine they are psychic or whatever and some try to have it more than they have got it. But with Donald's character, I wanted him to not want it but still have it there, something strange. Maybe his moment at the beginning is nothing – but all knowledge is connected. Amid the chaos, we are all part of an incredible scheme. It may not be our business to understand all the threads, but suddenly understanding the connection is what happened to him, quite naturally. I quite like the inevitability of things, and the way we're out of control, hanging by a thread, and we're so cavalier about it. And we have to be, otherwise, as seems to be happening today, we become too cautious about everything.'

The spiritual aspect of the film was crucial to director Roeg. In search of authenticity he took Julie Christie to a seance before they started filming. They went to a gathering in Notting Hill held by direct voice medium Leslie Flint and sat in a circle to try to experience the ultimate powers of the mind. At one point Flint ordered Roeg to: 'Uncross your legs' and the line found its way into the film.

Over the years the spookier elements of the movie have given it a haunting reputation of immense magnitude. Certainly there are many grim coincidences associated with the film. Natalie Wood, who was an earlier suggestion to play Laura Baxter, was drowned while making the film *Brainstorm* in 1981. Julie Christie's friend's young son drowned in a pond on her farm in Wales in 1979. Nicholas Salter, who played the Baxters' accident-prone son Johnny, was later to die in Brixton prison. Clelia Matania, who played Wendy, was soon to die of breast cancer.

To her large and faithful army of admirers, Julie Christie has hardly ever looked so breathtakingly beautiful. Her black mourning clothes and the sombre elegance of Venice proved a memorable combination for millions of movie-goers around the world. During the filming she stayed in a villa owned by friends in Giudecca: 'It had an amazing formal garden – even the vegetables were laid out formally. You would open these magnificent Venetian wrought-iron gates at the bottom of it and there, suddenly, would be not earth but water. It was quite surreal. I remember walking through Venice at night with Nic and Tony (Richmond) the photographer. We were half-cut and wandered through all these mysterious, damp alleyways looking at the reflection of the water on the wet stone and the reflection of the buildings in the canals. I loved it, but I have never been back.

'Many years before, I came to Venice to present *Billy Liar,* which was the first important film I did, at the Film Festival on the Lido. I only stayed for a day or so. It was my first trip to Venice, but I didn't have time to see St Mark's, or any of the historical part of the city. I didn't know what I missed until now. Best of all I simply loved working with Donald Sutherland. He is a fine actor. The only problem I had with him was that it was very hard to appear romantic when he was making me laugh all the time.'

Some critics seized upon Roeg's familiar dependence upon scenery and carped that Venice itself was the star, at the expense of narrative and characterization. But the director was sure of his ground. 'It is like an image of Venice,' he said, 'a memory. It's an extraordinary place, a testament to human endeavour and folly. It's venal, it was a refuge. It's romantic. Everyone has a different image of it – gondolas and canals and Cornettos. Going there I hoped to capture it – St Mark's Square and all that. But as a photographer, you realize that it's all alleyways, you burst out on to things – to a doll in the water, to birds flying away. You're always looking up, there's no view. And that was fine because it is a strange story, and the strangeness of Venice lies in the alleyways. You're lost, as if in an Eschler drawing – you think you're going down but you're going up. It is like a curious dream.'

For many practical reasons Venice was not at all an easy place to film. The perpetual rise and fall of the tides played havoc with the continuity and some of the equipment was too large to float under bridges at high tide so the crew found themselves constantly measuring the headroom.

The film seemed to have a profound effect upon almost everyone involved in it. For actress Hilary Mason, who played the crucial, haunting role of Heather, it remains one of the most memorable highlights of a long and distinguished career. 'It started with my then agent saying it was time I did some theatre,' said Hilary. 'They wanted me for an audition for a play called *The Big Romance,* on at the Royal Court for two Sundays, just for the profession, a most daunting audience comprised just of actors and directors. It was very frightening, we had to go and see the director Roger Williams and audition and I got the part, which was the wonderful part of a woman who had had a child forty years before. She thought he had gone for good and suddenly he turns up. I was playing opposite Brian Cox, and there was a scene in it where I had to just break down after he has gone. I simply had to very slowly sink on to my knees and go hysterical. We only did this for two Sundays and I got two guineas per performance. I had no idea who was watching but in the audience was a casting director called Miriam Brickman. Literally two years went by and my husband Roger and I went down to see my mother who lived on her own then in Paignton in Devon. We drove on into Cornwall and we were looking in a second-hand bookshop in Truro and Roger picked up this book and said, "I'll buy this for you, Hilly. I know you love Daphne du Maurier."

'In those days it was a collection called *Not After Midnight,* and the very first short story in it was *Don't Look Now.* I was riveted by it and I said to Roger, "This would make a really good film." When we got home a couple of days later my agent left a message to say there was a Mr Nicolas Roeg who would like to see me because he was doing a film of *Don't Look Now.* I went in to London to meet him and he said, "I'll tell you the plot." I said, "You don't need to tell me the plot Mr Roeg, I have just read it."

'I came to realize later that Nicolas Roeg is an extremely superstitious man, and of course he thought this was a very good omen. Somehow I knew then that I had got the part. It was about four months later when they came back and said I was to play Heather.

'Originally Daphne Heard was going to play my sister Wendy. But the film company discovered she had a heart condition, so she had to drop out. Instead it was Clelia Matania, who was Italian and a very wonderful actress. Nic said, "I want to come out to your house and choose all your own clothes from your own wardrobe. Because your sister does not care what you wear, you match all the wrong colours together – you can feel things but you can't see them.

'I wondered what on earth we were going to do with this great director coming to our house and Roger said, "Just buy a bottle of whisky," which turned out to be exactly the right thing to do. Roger had a book on Eschler on the table and when Nic arrived he had a fit when he saw it. He said, 'Whose book is that? I have just been reading that to try to use that style in *Don't Look Now.* What an extraordinary coincidence.' He wanted all my brightest most vividly clashing clothes.

'Then it all started and odd things happened all the way through. There was a very strange and sometimes claustrophobic feel to the film set throughout. At one time the whole crew went mad because they said they felt so isolated in quiet motor-vehicle-free Venice they wanted to see a car. I remember production man Steve Previn, brother of the conductor André, screaming, "I gotta see a car, a motor," and they all went to Mestre had a look round and they were all right again. Venice is quite a strange place; you can actually hear people talking to each other.'

Hilary Mason joined the cast on location in Brox-bourne in Hertfordshire, during the filming of the first scene, where the little girl is drowned. The house belonged to the actor David Tree, who played the headmaster Anthony Babbage in the film. He was a descendant of the famous actor-manager Sir Herbert Beerbohm Tree, and the highly individual house be-came the home of the Baxters in the film. But that key first scene proved immensely difficult to capture. Nicolas Roeg recalled: 'The girl who played Christine was very pretty – exactly the sort of child John and Laura would have had – and she was a good swim-mer, too. Her mother and I took her to the swimming pool to practise going under the water and she was perfectly happy but as soon as she saw the pond she would just not go under. She screamed and screamed. The farmer on a neighbouring farm had a daughter of similar age and said that she was a lovely swimmer so we tried her out and she was fine but as soon as she got the red mac on she refused to go under the water. In the end we rigged it in a water tank with a double: there are actually three children in that sequence. All three, when they saw the pond and the weeds, must have felt the terrible truth: "I'm drowning, I'm drowning." '

Hilary Mason recalled: 'It is not easy to play a blind person and I wanted it to look totally convinc-ing. In the end I had to have two pairs of contact lenses for the film. At first I said to Nic, "I shall be able to look as though I am blind without contact lenses," and he looked at me and said, "Not when you see how near the camera is going to get to you, you won't." So I was dispatched to the opticians to be fitted with not one set but two. One was to shield my eyes against the blind solid ones that went on top. The only trouble was that when the two pairs were in place it was extremely painful and after a time my eyes started to run. I went on that very first visit to Broxbourne to show Nic what they looked like. I met Julie there and was introduced to her. My first impression was that she was very pretty and not much else. But gradually I learned that you don't get to know Julie very quickly. She is very difficult to talk to, particularly for strangers. I realized she was very nervy, and highly strung.

'But, of course, she was preparing to work when I first met her and I later learned she found it very hard, if not impossible, to pop in and out of character. I soon became a great admirer of her acting talent. Certainly she was beautiful but also she had the most remarkable screen presence. It is just a natural thing for her, I don't think she realized how special she was. I have seen all her films and I am a great admirer of her work but I think *Don't Look Now,* and *The Return of the Soldier,* which I was also in years later, are very difficult parts. And I believe they are the best performances she has ever given.'

Hilary watched with amazement as Nicolas Roeg ruthlessly toiled to get the very best out of his cast: 'I believe a lot of Julie's amazing performance in *Don't*

*Look Now* was down to Nic. He is a very hard taskmaster. I was a bit in awe of both of them at the time. It was my first big film, although I had done a lot of little bits and pieces. Julie doesn't do small talk a lot, she concentrates, she couldn't switch off in between takes and talk to me like some actors and actresses would. I understand that, she was like that all the way through the film.

'And often Nic had to coax her performance out of her. He seemed to know just how to handle her. There is one scene in the park, when Julie and I were to have a conversation as we walked along. She suddenly said, "Nic, you know very well I can't walk and talk at the same time. I can't do it." Nic took a very deep breath and had to take her away and reassure her that of course she could walk and talk at the same time. It took a little time but whatever he said worked. And of course she did the scene brilliantly. Julie is always very conscious of the fact that she doesn't think she can do it but she can and she does.

'She is not just pretty, she has something else about her – an amazing and very English attractiveness. Her hair caused a good deal of trouble. It is usually very straight but it was very curly for *Don't Look Now.* But the curls fell out at the slightest provocation and we all had to wait around for half an hour for her hair to be curled again. Julie could appear standoffish but she is not. She is just so far into the part. Her brother and mother came out to see her in

Venice and I realized she was really quite posh. My most abiding memory is that she always seemed very detached.

'Gradually we got closer and when I was talking to her one day I really got to know a bit more about her. I asked what she was doing next, and she said she was going to America to do some theatre, to play in *Uncle Vanya* with Nicol Williamson and George C. Scott. If you can think of two more frightening actors I can't, and she knew their reputations as well as I did, but once she had decided what she wanted to do nothing would deflect her. She was very brave in that way. Nic adored her. He loved her, and after we had finished filming he went off to America to see her.

'By the end, Julie and I talked about the part quite a lot, but there was always a distinct gap between Julie and Donald and myself and Clelia. The pecking order certainly had them as the stars well above everyone else. Donald and Julie got along like a house on fire. But then I think there are very few people who can't get along with Donald in some way or other. He is such a lovely man. In contrast Julie appeared very cold to start with but I think that is just concentration really. She can do it but it requires enormous concentration and sometimes we had to do things over and over again.

'It's difficult to talk to Julie at all except about the part. We had some very very close scenes with each other. The sobbing scene between the two of us took more than two hours to film with Nic going on and on at us until we were sobbing for real. He kept saying, "Again and again and again," until we were shaking and crying and just about hysterical, which was exactly what he wanted. Even at the time I was conscious of that, but I couldn't do anything about it except go on with it.

'Julie resists doing anything and has to be pushed and persuaded but when an understanding director coaxes her properly she is brilliant, she is quite remarkable. In Venice in the beginning they all used to go out for enormous meals at nine o'clock at night to eat in a big party and Julie would come in around half past nine, looking absolutely gorgeous, and everybody would crowd round her because she was the leading lady. Clelia and I would creep off and eat in our rooms. Donald was very good because at first we used to have lunch brought to us in a bucket, but Donald insisted we were taken out for lunch in a restaurant every day. Julie would always make her entrance and just become the centre of attention because she was so beautiful. She blossoms when she's finished but it is her concentration keeps her quiet. In the evenings she was more relaxed and enjoying herself.

'I can't say I ever got to know her very well. I did talk to her when we were off waiting for a scene but she was obviously thinking about the work. I believe she believed very much in the theme of the story, that a medium like my character might very well be able to convey a message from a dead child. *Don't*

*Look Now* is an astonishing film. Just after it was finished I found a lot of middle-aged men used to doff their hats to me and ask very respectfully if I had been in *Don't Look Now.* That had never happened to me before.

'Nic was a remarkable man. He would do anything to make a scene look more real. When Donald is in the church and the rope slips and he is swinging desperately to save his life, he did a lot of that himself because the stunt man had vertigo. Donald volunteered and Nic said okay. But he hurt his knee doing it, and there is a moment when he is swinging when if you look very carefully you can see a stick come out to push him further out into the church to make a more dramatic shot. That was Nic Roeg with the stick and he was saying, "Get out, get out." I was amazed. Think of the insurance claim if he'd fallen.

'When you're working on a long day you've got to have somewhere to spend a penny occasionally. And there only seemed to be one convenience in Venice and that was shut at lunch-time so when we were working in that ladies loo I thought to myself, "Wonderful, my little problem won't arise here." We got there early one morning to use the loo before we started but I had both my pairs of contact lenses in and I suddenly realized there was a cameraman in there as well. Fortunately he had his back to me! He and his assistant were shaking with laughter. I just said, "Don't look now," which seemed appropriate at the time. Those eyes had to come out after every take, but I had a very dishy make-up man who worked with his brother, so Roberto and Giovanni looked after me and bathed my eyes. They were very painful, it is a great intrusion on the eyes. But the brothers almost made up for it.

'Nic took me out to lunch at Harry's Bar for one important briefing. He was a sweet man who always seemed to find the time to take the trouble to do the job properly. He said, "I want to talk about your second scene right at the end, where you know that Donald is out there and you must find him." I suggested I wanted to play it as if I was going to have an epileptic fit and he thought that was a good idea. We agreed that over the *osso bucco,* which he introduced me to. Nic always goes for "over the top", he wanted "over the top" all the time.'

'The crew were half Italian and half English, and they were always falling out and we had a strike in the middle of the night, because Tony Richmond was talking very loudly about how bad they were all not providing me with a stand-in. I didn't mind in the least, I've never had a stand-in, but the Italians understood English far better than we understand Italian so it caused a strike. It was soon sorted out and we carried on and I went as far over the top as I could, which made Nic happy as he liked to have the extremes on film so he could calm things down in the editing.'

The director's relentless determination to tell his story with the maximum amount of power and realism was, of course, famously to plunge him into controversy with the sensationally graphic love scene. Hilary Mason remembers: 'That love scene, oh dear, oh dear. Clelia came to me one morning and said, "Hilary, I am in a blue film! Do you know what they are doing?" She told me that Nic had sent everybody out, told them what he wanted and just let them get on with it. I think it is the most beautiful scene. It is so clever, cutting from the love-making to them getting dressed, it was super. But Clelia was horrified. She was wonderful to me because although she couldn't understand all of the Venetian dialect she knew what the crew was saying. And this time the crew was astonished that Nic had sent them all out and taken the camera himself.

'Evidently Donald and Julie were both, oddly enough, very timid about doing it. Although I suppose they would be. I mean, it is a very difficult thing to physically simulate "the act" for the cameras. So Nic sent everybody out except him and Tony Richmond and shot it all himself. He has got a very, very strong sexual streak, that side of things always intrigues him. And so after they had finished doing the love scene he and Tony simply went out, shut the door and left them to it. And, said Clelia, "We do not know whether they performed the act or not!" She was shocked and horrified by the whole thing. But I should think they probably did carry on and become lovers for real. Nobody knew for sure but that was what the crew certainly thought.'

Donald Sutherland insisted the powerful sequence was the work of the director. He said, 'I shouldn't get any credit for one of the sexiest film scenes ever. That's all Nic Roeg's work. He kept cutting away from the sex to shots of us getting dressed. That allowed the audience to think of themselves. They weren't just voyeurs as in most erotic films. There was a time to remember one's own love-making.

'When we shot it we had no idea that was what Nic was going to do. It was just Julie and me naked on a bed with cameraman Tony Richmond and Nic calling out to us, "Put your hand on his thigh, grab her breast, lift your knee..."'

Julie Christie said afterwards, 'People didn't do scenes like that in those days. There were no available examples, no role models, and I did find it very difficult. I just went blank and Nic shouted instructions. I hardly knew Donald then but, apart from being a bloody good actor, he is a responsible one and he took responsibility for the scene, helping me through it.

'Making love on camera is such hard work that there is no time for the libido to take over,' said Julie, insisting that such sex scenes were not a turn-on. Although she did add with a provocative twinkle: 'Well, not particularly a turn-on for me. I mean, they might be afterwards. That sometimes happens. The reality of what you've been doing with someone can be quite stimulating.'

Nicolas Roeg said that he had never planned the famous and for its time very daring love scene between Julie Christie and Donald Sutherland. He reflected later: 'I didn't consciously set out to make it that way. It came out of the fact that their performances were so wonderful. I gradually realized as we were shooting that they were a young married couple with children and that in every scene they were rowing or something, and they were two rather grumpy people. But in their private time they would have moments of intimacy. They are dressing to go out and she is lying on the bed looking at a magazine. 'Look at this,' she says to him. He flops on the bed beside her and looks at the magazine, stroking her back as he does so. By that you know they are a married couple and they are in love. Sexual intimacy is part of love and marriage, closeness and oneness, and it was very innocently shot. The scene stemmed from their performances and because the moment was right. I pondered about putting the scene in or leaving it out, but whenever I ran the film without that scene there was obviously something it didn't have. Once you knew they were in love it had a different dimension. It is sexy but it is not prurient.

'When the BBC first screened *Don't Look Now* they cut out the sex scene which had an odd effect on the film because it meant the couple could do nothing but row all the time. The next time they showed it they reinstated it because there had been so many complaints.'

Julie Christie recognized from the beginning that Donald Sutherland was a very fine actor and as work progressed on the film a real affinity developed between the two leading players. Roeg was delighted because he knew the relationship between John and Laura Baxter was one of the keys to the film's success. He explained: 'The loss of a child is a terrible thing, maybe the very worst. And to see the one you love in grief is dreadful also. It splits many couples up because it is an impossible situation to deal with. One grief compounds the other. Someone has to step back and try to make everything move forward. Maybe that is Baxter's problem: it's his love for his wife and his desperation to have the relationship survive that stops him understanding. Maybe that is why at the end she has a triumphant look. She understands and she has survived. And that is why as she has her arms through the railings as he's going to his death, she says, "Darlings" not "Darling", because she knows they will all be together in the end.'

The screaming headlines which were inspired by the love scenes certainly upset the director. As Roeg strove to ensure that the fullest and fairest picture of the Baxters' marriage was reflected in his film the American film censors insisted firmly: 'We cannot see humping. We cannot see the rise and fall between thighs.' Roeg said: 'I honestly couldn't remember if there was any rise and fall. I went away and examined the sequence very carefully, took out just nine frames and sent it back. They scrutinized it and found absolutely nothing they could object to. If someone goes up, you cut and then next time you see them and they're in a different position, you obviously fill  in the gaps for yourself. But, technically speaking,  there was no "humping" in that scene.'

All concerned threw their hands up in horror when coverage of the love scene hit the headlines just as the film was opening, though it hardly hindered business at the box office. As it became clear that the American censors were being much more strict than the British, the papers reported with glee that 'one of the frankest sex scenes ever  to be filmed' was about to plunge Julie Christie into the biggest censorship row 'since *Last Tango in Paris'*.

British film censor Stephen Murphy ignored considerable pressure from the clean-up-the-screen campaigners of the day and passed the entire six-minute sex scene without cuts. Secretary of the British Festival of Light Stewart Stevens was quickly  up in arms: 'If it's too hot for America, where almost  anything gets shown, it's not difficult to imagine how explicit it is.'

Donald Sutherland weighed into the argument and defended Mr Murphy's decision: 'The censorship in Britain is terrific. They thought the scene was one of the most beautiful they had seen. They're going  to cut that scene in the United States because they  are frightened of risking legal action. But the scene  is fundamental to the film and takes it from something else into a love story. Take the scene out and the film loses a whole dimension.'

As Roeg and the actors writhed with irritation, Jack Worrow, spokesman for the film's distributors, British Lion, made his own contribution to the growing argument: 'Julie Christie and Donald Sutherland are both unclothed during the scene. They are making love and their bodies are entwined, so you see some bottoms and bosoms but no full frontals. The scene is done with sincerity and skill. It was not injected for the sake of the box office. British Lion does not consider it near the knuckle, and clearly, neither does the film censor. The love scene goes on for several minutes, but there are cuts away from it to show the couple dressing for dinner. The scene shows how the couple resume their normal life together after the shock and depression caused by the loss of their child.'

Censor Stephen Murphy himself later observed, 'My decision to pass the scene was one of the easiest of my career. Certainly the scene was erotic and highly charged but it was so beautifully filmed and so essential to the story that in spite of all the hullabaloo, I never for a moment considered it should be cut. And the fact that it was one of the finest films ever made and one of my personal favourites had nothing to do with it, of course.'

Hilary Mason thought: 'The sex scene is so explicit and so beautiful. Nic's whole technique was to get the actors worked into whatever emotion the characters were experiencing so I can imagine how Donald and Julie felt. We always suspected Julie and Nic were an item. Nic said to me once when he took me out to Harry's Bar, "I worship her little behind." And he said it with such great feeling I knew that Nic was really very passionately in love with Julie at the time.

'After we had finished he went over to America to see her in *Uncle Vanya*. It is pretty usual in our business in the highly charged relationship between director and leading lady for them to become incredibly close and get involved and I think that is what happened in this case. It is very difficult to work with somebody that you don't like.'

Julie said enigmatically: 'If you ever grow to love a director it is very nice to work for them,' including John Schlesinger as well as Nic Roeg in her small group of favourites. 'Nic and I have very different ideas about things so we're too busy challenging each other and arguing ever to listen to each other much. He is a nihilist, isn't he? We get off on arguing.' But *Don't Look Now* remains one of her favourite films.

By the end of filming Christie had grown tired of Venice and had decided the sophisticated locals were not the friendliest of folk. In a room in the Atlantico, an old student pensione used by the film company, she reflected: 'Perhaps it is depressing here. But I find that almost every room I've seen in Venice has a mood to it, and a lovely view. Here, if you glance out of the window you can see a charming courtyard.' And as her hard-working hairdresser poured a glass of champagne for the star, she said, 'I'm glad we're leaving Venice soon. Can't wait to be back in lovely London. You've got to admit that the people in Venice simply aren't friendly – not like other places in Italy. Just look at the history of the city and you'll understand why. Way back to the time of the Doges, Venice was always a terribly independent, insular city. These characteristics have persisted into successive generations.' But she concluded her outburst with a familiar Christie plea: 'I hate talking about myself. I'm totally and thoroughly unpublic and I dislike speaking about other people too. I reject forming words into solids because I believe what is true for one person at one moment can be completely different at another time. Do you understand?'

The film version of *Don't Look Now* contained many changes from Daphne du Maurier's original short story. For instance the Baxters' daughter had died from meningitis in du Maurier's story and the couple are holidaying in Venice rather than the husband working. As production concluded, one of the producers warned Nicolas Roeg: 'We're going to have to show it to Daphne du Maurier but don't be there because she doesn't know what you've done to it and we need her support.' But the director was delighted to discover that 'Daphne du Maurier was a true writer and understood about translating a story into another medium. She wrote to me, "I saw your film of my story and your John and Laura reminded me so much of the young couple I saw in Torcello having lunch together. They looked so handsome and beautiful and yet they seemed to have a terrible problem and I watched them with sadness. The young man tried to cheer his wife up but to no avail and it struck me that perhaps their child had died of meningitis."

'It was a wonderful letter. I know the place she meant, too. That couple were the authors of the story. Du Maurier was not obsessed with the big I. She didn't cry, "But it was my idea!" The ideas are all around us.'

The author was particularly captivated by Julie Christie's shining performance as Laura Baxter. She said, 'Miss Christie appears to possess an extraordinary presence on screen. She gave Laura a wonderfully self-possessed calmness in the midst of all her traumas. If only I could have her for all my lady heroines...'

Although the love-affair between Julie Christie and Warren Beatty was over, the friendship remained. He was still one of the most stimulating men she had met and after *Don't Look Now* she returned to America. She had another lover, who was a successful businessman, but she was still in touch with Beatty.

When Christie had appeared in William Wycherley's Restoration comedy *The Country Wife* at the Birmingham Repertory Theatre there was something about the way Horner, the vain seducer, pretended to be homosexual to prevent his lovers' husbands from becoming suspicious that struck a chord. The play is one of Wycherley's more vulgar efforts and even though it was written in 1675, Julie Christie knew the plot was still relevant today.

She suggested it to Warren Beatty when he and writer Robert Towne were working on an idea for a film about an inveterate seducer. The central theme was an energetic lover troubled because there were 'so many pretty girls and so little time'. They went along to the Chichester Festival Theatre and saw a production of *The Country Wife* starring Maggie Smith, and realized that the concept of a Casanova hiding behind a gay persona still had potential. Julie was delighted when the 300-year-old theme found new relevance in the present day. Even though her love-affair with Warren Beatty had cooled to a warm friendship by 1974, when *Shampoo* lurched into life, she was delighted to play opposite her former long-term partner. He was the apparently camp hairdresser George Roundy, a sex-crazed star of a top Beverly Hills salon who was trying to find time in between busily seducing his gorgeous pouting female clients to start a business of his own.

Beatty's casting of co-stars like Julie Christie, Goldie Hawn, Lee Grant and Carrie Fisher was inspirational. Not only did they all give fine and feisty performances but they guaranteed a constant flow of speculation, gossip and publicity which meant the movie generated maximum controversy which was great for the box-office.

Jack Warden played the big-time Republican who foolishly trusted his wife, Lee Grant, with George because he was sure he was gay. George also found time to squire Jack's mistress, Julie Christie, and his own girlfriend, Goldie Hawn. Most of the action was set on election night 1968 and at the big party George gets his come-uppance when all the women leave him and he realizes they have been using him rather than the other way round. Julie Christie was sensational in the film, and believed in the project enough to utter the film's single most memorable line: that she would like to suck George's ****.

The critics were divided over whether it was delightful or disgusting. The *Los Angeles Times* said: '*Shampoo* will be worth studying a century from now to know what part of our times was like.' While *New Republic* raged: 'It is disgusting! Fake porno of the most revolting kind.' The United States Catholic Conference was similarly outraged and gave the film a C rating, ruling it morally objectionable to Catholic society.

All of which was great news for cinema owners who saw long queues for the sexy and intelligent movie. It showed that Warren Beatty's finger was still on the pulse of what moviegoers wanted. He made more than $8 million, more than any other actor had ever made from a single film.

Throughout the making of *Shampoo* it was hard for gossips to detect whether or not the big romance was back on again. After filming finished, Christie was reported to have finally dumped Beatty for an unnamed American industrialist. He quickly took up with Michelle Phillips, once a member of the chart-topping Mamas and Papas. Michelle at least got to move into the house Beatty had bought for Julie Christie, a Mulholland Drive mansion which formerly belonged to opera singer Lauritz Melchior, with grounds comprising of four and a half acres of pinewoods looking down on Beverly Hills.

But within months he and Russian actress Viktoria Fyodorova were said to be an item. Meanwhile Julie Christie was keeping her own counsel at Malibu. But there were frequent sightings of Beatty and Christie together and the truth was they stayed friends after they stopped being lovers. In August 1975 as *Shampoo* hit London, Warren Beatty and Julie Christie were together enjoying dinner for two at Leith's restaurant in Notting Hill. Less than a year later Beatty was in love with Diane Keaton, yet another Oscar-winner to add to his collection.

In 1977 Christie surprised her fans by agreeing to star in *Demon Seed,* as a scientist's wife who is raped by a super computer. Based on a Dean Koontz novel and directed by the off-beat Donald Cammell, who co-directed *Performance,* with Nicolas Roeg, this was not a success. Publicity concentrated on the ludicrous and deeply unbelievable mechanical assault on Julie Christie and the film was received like a bad joke.

Christie's disillusion with Hollywood grew and she was delighted to wind down her life in America and retreat temporarily to her Welsh hideaway. After *Shampoo* she had been irritated and offended by the string of dismal sex movies she had been offered. The call from Warren Beatty offering another film lifted her spirits, but she would not agree straight away. Beatty had to coax, cajole, almost beg and offer her a far from small fortune to play the part. He could afford it. It is an illustration of how Beatty's star had continued to rise that he had already negotiated himself a magnificent deal to bring *Heaven Can Wait* to the screen – an upfront fee of $3.5 million, plus a percentage of profits and total creative control. All he had to do was write, star in, direct and produce the strange story of a football player who is killed in a traffic accident then given another chance at life in the body of an aged millionaire. It had already been a hit play called *Halfway to Heaven* which turned into a successful 1941 film called *Here Comes Mr Jordan.*

Beatty had considered turning his good friend Muhammad Ali into a movie star. The original play had featured a boxer. But Ali was unavailable and even then possibly not up to the role. Now approaching forty, Beatty decided instead to make the central character a footballer and play it – including many of the sporting sequences – himself.

It's a fun comedy and Beatty cleverly negotiated the fine line between light-hearted and ludicrous, but there is also great poignancy in the closing scenes between himself and Julie Christie, which serve as a final screen farewell between two of the movie world's great lovers. She plays fervent conservationist Betty Logan who gets the chance to bang on at length about some of the actress's actual causes. The amazing thing was that it worked as a public goodbye and it worked as a popular movie as well. Beatty hit his biggest jackpot yet, earning an astonishing $15 million dollars from his time playing one of the least likely angels ever.

Beatty was desperate for Christie to play this last role with him and some of his script surely echoes his real-life feelings for the one lover to dump him, rather than the other way round. When Beatty's character Joe Pendleton first meets Betty Logan, Beatty's original screenplay says: 'Joe learned in one split second the difference between a pretty girl and a beautiful woman. In one split second his brain registered an image so intense as to leave its imprint there for ever.' Betty is described as 'what nature must have intended woman to look like when time first dawned on Earth. She was the living reason Adam ate the apple. Her hair was a golden mass, clouds, yellow clouds. Her mouth was full. Where had lips like that ever been before?'

But it was over between them. The truth was that he had wanted to marry her but she had not wanted to marry him.

Certainly at that time his family hoped Warren would marry Julie. In a rare interview Warren's father, Ira Beaty (who retained just the original single 't' spelling of his name), a retired schoolteacher from

Arlington, Virginia, declared he would have been delighted to welcome Julie Christie as a daughter-in-law: 'Julie used to visit us with Warren many times. Of all his girlfriends she was our favourite. We used to love her coming to visit. She is such a little lady ... A real lady, with those lovely English manners. I always used to tease her about her accent. We really love her, Mrs Beaty and me, and it would be just fine if Warren married her. I can't think of anyone else I'd rather he married.

'But sometimes I wonder if Warren will ever really settle down. He's a real nomad, like Shirley [MacLaine]. I thought he might with Julie and it would make us really happy if he did marry her. She has changed her hair now, made it all curly. I don't like the style, don't approve of it really. But she still looks beautiful to me.' Warren Beatty flew his parents to Los Angeles for a private screening of *Heaven Can Wait,* and his father said, 'I'm so glad she was with him in that film. I loved it. I thought it was the best thing he's done so far. But you know, I'm not weeping because he never married. It would be nice, but I don't want him to settle down if he doesn't want to. It's his life and I don't want to try to influence him or push him. So I don't mind what he does if he's happy, and if he doesn't get married, well that's fine.

'But we will always have a soft spot for Julie, his mother and me, and she will always be welcome in our house.'

But Julie had finally had enough of Hollywood. She wanted to go home to Wales: 'Suddenly one day I was forced to make a decision, America or Britain. I had some very dear friends there and I was in love with an American. No, it wasn't Warren Beatty. By then he had become one of my very dear friends. There were months of unhappiness when I couldn't make up my mind whether to leave or not. Choices are hard. It's easier to let things roll on. But at last I packed my bags and came home. I'd been away so long I saw England quite freshly.'

# 10

# Back Home

We would sit with our backs to the Aga, huddled up in the wool from sheep, and go to bed at six o'clock because it was so cold.

Julie Christie

The film that should have re-established Julie Christie in her own country was *Agatha.* This most English of enterprises was David Puttnam's project and he had, remarkably, secured the services of Dustin Hoffman. With Vanessa Redgrave in the title role, the film would explore the real-life mystery surrounding the brief disappearance of the great whodunit writer. In 1926 Julie's illustrious namesake Agatha Christie went missing without trace only to be found several days later amidst much painful publicity in a Harrogate hotel room. Not surprisingly, the author's own family were dead against the project and there was more trouble ahead for Puttnam and producer Gavrick Losey when the British technicians' union reacted angrily to his plans to use top Italian cameraman Vittorio Storaro. Then Julie Christie had a rollerskating accident which kept her in the United States for six weeks longer than scheduled, to finish off *Heaven Can Wait.*

But even if heaven could wait, *Agatha* couldn't, and director Michael Apted called in stand-by Helen Morse to play the wide-eyed young woman who befriends *Agatha* on the run.

Christie was disappointed but not distraught. She was more concerned with the business of relocating herself back to Britain. She had finally decided that her Hollywood days were over. In the end, after months and years of growing unease about her peace of mind in the United States, it seemed the only logical decision to make. And once made, she was convinced it was right for her.

It was not that she had not enjoyed living there. 'I had some brilliantly happy times in America. At one time I lived right out in the country in New Jersey in a derelict house. I was looking for a house with this fella. He was a musician,' she said. Christie declines to name her one-time partner but was clearly entranced with their Bohemian existence together with a house-full of rowdy Princeton drop-outs next door. She says: 'It was a blissful time.'

Later she lived on the beach in Los Angeles but, as she was quick to point out, 'Not on the grand beach with the big houses. I'm not saying this to say "Gosh. Aren't I simple?" but I just don't like that stuff. The beach had tiny, very attractive wooden shacky things. It was called Dog Beach and you couldn't be grand on that beach because, basically, you were avoiding dog shit all the time. But it was heaven because it's the Pacific Ocean, which is a lovely, romantic ocean,

and every night you sat out there and got this incredible sunset. Behind you was Malibu Canyon,
which was full of hippies and completely alternative.  It was heavenly as well as being disturbing.'

She was honest enough to admit to friends that
she was leaving not so much because she had become disillusioned with Hollywood, but more to do
with her private life. She reflected that most of the
time she had spent in America she had been having
a love-affair with some man or other. She was just
as appealing to eligible and not so eligible men as
her most famous partner Warren Beatty was to
women. She just didn't flaunt her affairs. She always  felt she had been simply passing through
America and had stayed because of the men. A
particular relationship broke up very unhappily and,
with no other lover on the horizon, Julie came
home. But underneath she felt she had never really
even been  truly content in America.

When she came back for good, one of the first
things Julie Christie noticed was how stained the
pavements were in London, compared to the pris-
tine  walkways of Beverly Hills, which are mainly
unused  by people who regard walking as something done only on the way to your motor car. 'I
was also surprised to see people in England wearing clothes  that didn't look as if they'd just come
back from  the dry cleaners but looked as if they
might have  been worn for more than one day.
And I was pleased that we still had shops instead

of supermarkets. What I'm saying is, I just loved being back.'

She had already bought a home to come back to, her large farmhouse, the White House, at Cefn-y-Coed, near Montgomery in Wales. She flew back to Britain after filming *Shampoo* to complete the purchase and Jonathan and Leslie Heale, her San Francisco artist friends, quickly arrived to look after the place. It was remote and hard to find, which suited Julie just fine. She had been thinking longingly for the past years of the day when she could move in and hide from the world and now she delighted in the tranquillity. Julie was at her happiest there, clad in baggy old clothes and surrounded by friends and her growing menagerie of animals.

The first winters were very cold after her long sojourn in the sunshine and Julie recalled later: 'We would sit with our backs to the Aga, huddled up in the wool from sheep, and go to bed at six o'clock because it was so cold.' She and her friends rejected central heating because of their beliefs that a house should protect but not separate people from the elements. 'Weather is part of our life,' said Julie. 'I hear people talking about the horrible weather. Horrible? This is all we've got. It's like saying "horrible life". I am sure we used not to look at it in this angry, accusatory way. We live in this wonderful, crazy world where nobody knows what is going to happen next. Are you going to get cancer? Are you going to be run over? Are you going to meet a great love and be the happiest person in the entire world? Are you going to have a late baby? Nobody knows.'

Julie found solace in the remote hills of Wales where the locals quickly welcomed the famous face that did not seek any special treatment. Gradually they accepted her as one of their own and helpfully diverted visiting reporters and photographers away from their beautiful neighbour. Yet they were amused when they heard that her forceful views on the environment meant that ordinary toilet paper was banned on the grounds that it was a waste of natural resources. Old newspapers were provided instead, which certainly pleased the local odd-job man who was consequently called out very regularly to unblock The White House's drains. Julie Christie's not so highly prized Oscar, meanwhile, was dispatched to the attic.

'My place would be primitive to some Americans,' she said. 'It doesn't have all the modern electronic comforts, but I do have electricity, a telephone and a washing machine. It's a pleasure each time I go shopping because there are about seven people, like the man who runs the garage or the woman in the post office, with whom I can stop and chat. In fast city societies you just don't stop to interact with people.'

However, Christie did not absent herself entirely from 'fast city society'. At the end of 1978 she encountered charismatic rock musician turned producer

Brian Eno and the two fell quickly and passionately in love. Eno moved in a world that Christie hardly knew and she loved the vibrant energy and challenging attitudes of the music business. The relationship did not last long but the couple remained close friends.

Her London home in Selwood Terrace had been sold so Julie also found herself a new London base, a rented flat in a large rambling Notting Hill Gate house, long before the area developed its reputation for being fashionable. She was surrounded there by friends in a commune-like atmosphere that provided frequent stimulating respite from her isolated hideaway. But many old friends had moved on from the old days. Wives and husbands and children and mortgages had snared many old Bohemians into the trap of respectability and Julie did find her circle of 'mates' had shrunk. But this gave her exactly the space she needed, and although she agreed later that life was lonelier than it had been in the United States it gave her time to focus her increasingly political attitudes. She felt freer and re-energized and began to become involved more deeply in the causes that were closest to her heart.

In March 1979 Julie used her platform on the jury at the Berlin Film Festival to support the Communist countries' protests at Universal's big Vietnam film hit *The Deer Hunter.* She said the film showed the Vietcong as subhuman and sadistic but in the press her heartfelt statements were ridiculed as being inspired by the fact that *The Deer Hunter* was in competition for Oscars with her own film *Heaven Can Wait.*

But the publicity was quickly forgotten when a chilling tragedy hit Julie Christie's Welsh paradise. In an incident that closely resembled the horrific opening scenes of a child drowning in a garden pool at the start of *Don't Look Now,* little Harry Heale lost his life in the same tragic way. The twenty-two-month-old son of Julie's close friends had wandered off and somehow fallen into the pond. When Julie Christie arrived with Duncan Campbell, Leslie Heale was frantically searching for her son. Grimly Leslie suddenly spotted what looked like 'a grey rug' in the two-foot deep garden pond. In April, Leslie sadly told the inquest: 'I could see the figure under the water. I waded in and pulled him out and ran to the house. His face was blue.' In the living room Leslie and Julie desperately tried to revive the boy, but tragically the toddler was dead by the time the ambulance arrived.

Not surprisingly, Julie Christie has never spoken publicly of the dreadful accident but friends say she was totally traumatized by the child's death. She felt responsible because it happened at her house and haunted by the appalling similarity between the scenes in the film and the real-life events.

She was remote and hard to reach for a very long time afterwards. Her return to regular work was put firmly on hold as Julie tried to help the Heales get over the awful loss. Even when John Travolta pleaded with her to co-star with him in *American Gigolo* (before Richard Gere took over the role) she had no second thoughts about rejecting him and the movie. She was a European actress now and had no wish to go over old ground. She was offered a juicy part alongside Albert Finney and Martin Sheen in *Loophole,* but turned it down. Then Michael Klinger wanted her for his Caribbean caper *Blue,* and again she said No.

The first script to catch her interest, out of the many that continued to arrive, was a story in French called *Sophie and the Captain.* It was a sexually progressive and extremely passionate tale about a husband gradually drawn to become a transvestite, because his wife became obsessed by lesbians. Some advisers thought this could be a controversial success to rival *Last Tango in Paris,* but sadly it didn't turn out like that. Julie insisted she just agreed to play the part because she loved director Liliane de Kermadec's unusual script. The director had been trying to get the film off the ground for several years but the interest of a movie heavyweight like Julie Christie was enough to get the show on the road.

But after two months' work Julie found herself plunged into the middle of an angry row between de Kermadec and the producers Serge and Irene Silberman, which instantly stopped production. Cast and crew were paid off and Julie Christie eventually flew back to Paris to speak out in support of the director at a press conference organized by the Film Directors'

Association. She insisted forcefully: 'It is important that the cinema should not lose a talent like this.'

Unfortunately, the public perception was of Julie Christie's glittering screen appeal diminishing through the passing of time, so the whole experience was distracting and highly unhelpful to her career. But by then she had other things on her mind, a new love-affair with left-wing Scottish journalist Duncan Campbell, then the news editor of *Time Out* magazine. He was by her side during the *Sophie and the Captain* controversy and more enjoyably they holidayed together in Italy where Julie found herself more and more attracted to the writer's uncompromising liberal viewpoints and his forceful character. Friends noted that, not since she had been with Warren Beatty, had Julie been so relaxed and happy with a man.

She was horrified when she was, not surprisingly, pursued by the press at *Time Out'*s tenth birthday party, although afterwards she did reluctantly agree that Campbell had become very important to her: 'I'm terribly dependent on him so we travel backwards and forwards to see each other.'

Duncan Campbell was a very frequent visitor but not a resident. 'Duncan and I don't live together, but we see a lot of each other,' said Julie. But marriage remained firmly off the agenda. 'Of course someone can't get to my age and not want a stable relationship. There is nothing nicer than human love, and friendship. And I have had stable, permanent relationships. But I never wanted to get married. Never. When I was a girl I imagined myself wearing a beautiful white wedding dress and being the centre of attention, but, apart from that, not at all. I don't see any reason for marriage unless you are religious, and I am not.'

Asked in 1983 about having children of her own, Julie said firmly, 'No, I'm spoilt, I suppose. I like to pick and choose what I want to do, and when I want to do it, and I don't think I could bear to have someone encroaching on me twenty-four hours a day. The prospect of being a spinster without any family doesn't bother me at all. I think the ideal way for humans to live is with a group of people instead of in a tiny, closed-off nucleus like a family. Of course, it's terribly difficult to find the right people, and you have to discipline yourself to adapt to the others. I am very difficult to live with because I am quite rigid and strong-willed.'

When she was younger she had always talked of her plan to have children by the age of thirty. 'But every time it came up I didn't want them,' she said. 'My brother said, "Unless you want it with all your heart and soul don't do it; it's the hardest thing on earth." I didn't want it with all my heart and soul so I didn't.' As Julie grew older two of her major anxieties became over-population and over-consumption.

Julie was concerned that whatever film she did next would be without any of the sexism that had permeated so much of her earlier work. And the next project to fulfil her criteria was David Glapwell's *Memoirs of a Survivor.* Based on a Doris Lessing novel, it was a sardonic reflection on the prospect of looming nuclear destruction. And Julie Christie was so keen to be involved in a film that was so close to her heart that she played her part without demanding her usual film-star fee and settled for the same wages as the rest of the cast.

She played 'D', who looked down on a post-nuclear society in chaos. She could see violent gangs stalking the streets or she could step through the wall of her apartment – like *Alice Through the Looking-Glass* – into a peaceful, ordered world of Victorian England. She watches her young follower Emily, played by Leonie Mellinger, fall into the clutches of the vagrants' leader Gerald, played by Christopher Guard, before the film becomes seriously strange and impenetrable. It was widely slammed by the critics but Julie Christie's performance escaped vilification. *Photoplay* observed, 'a strong performance from Christie in one of the most mystifying films I can recall'. It went, as they say, almost straight to video.

Another of Christie's concerns was animal rights and she spoke out passionately against the use of live animals in experiments. She agreed to narrate Victor Schonfield's powerful documentary about the abuses of laboratory animals without payment. And *The Animals Film* shocked ITV viewers in 1982 with its sickening study of rabbits having eye drops of toxic substances agonizingly administered.

At the press conference to launch the documentary, Julie Christie arrived in black beret and combat trousers, with hooded members of the Animal Liberation Front at her side. She announced that she spent much of her time writing to soap-powder manufacturers demanding to know whether or not their products involved testing on animals and she suggested other people should do the same.

Julie showed that there were no hard feelings towards France and the French, after her recent bruising encounter in the *Sophie* affair, by returning to star in *The Roaring Forties.* She was pleased it was a fast turnaround, however, as she was anxious to get to Greenham Common in time for the concert in Easter 1981 when Julie said: 'I came because only by swinging public opinion are we going to make the government listen.'

*The Roaring Forties,* or *Les Quarantièmes Rugissantes,* was originally called *The Last Strange Voyage of Donald Crowhurst* and told the story of the 1968 round-the-world race in which the cheating sailor hung around in the Atlantic before doubling back. He committed suicide before he could be discovered and exposed as a fraud. Julie Christie played the wife of the mariner who is talked into the con-trick by an unscrupulous press agent. Sadly, watching it was about as much fun as being cast adrift in an open boat.

Christie was now spending much of her time as a committed campaigner for a variety of causes. She went to many meetings of Pandora, the anti-nuclear pressure group. She spoke with real passion when she declared, 'Nuclear bombs are not made by countries or governments or one individual. It's the huge multinational corporations that are in the business of arms production. They are internationalists and have no allegiance to anything except profit. They can't be expected to care that their activities are poisoning our world, our bodies and our minds.'

In March 1983 Julie led the marchers from Greenham Common through Brussels in a massive anti-nuclear rally. In November 1985 she was sending off War on Want medical supplies from a deserted container yard near Tower Bridge. 'I have been to Nicaragua and I have seen the suffering,' she said.

For her next film role, Christie was attracted not only by the script but by the prospect of acting with Glenda Jackson which Christie cited as one of the main reasons for her taking the part. Certainly her character was hardly alluring. 'I played a rather cold, rather selfish, upper-class woman who cares more for form than substance. It's an unsympathetic role.'

In *The Return of the Soldier,* based on a Rebecca West novel, she played the part of socialite Kitty, whose comfortable world is rocked when her husband (Alan Bates) returns from the trenches of the First World War shell-shocked and suffering from amnesia which has made him forget she exists. Instead he wants a reunion with his old lover (Glenda Jackson).

Christie gave an insight into the amount of concentration she puts into a role when she said: 'I can't do what Glenda Jackson or Alan Bates can do, which is to have a joke off the set one minute and the next minute play a big emotional scene. I need to work up a lot to suffer on screen. Acting is an incredible intimacy with people you don't know and you have to learn to deal with that.'

The critics liked the film rather more than the audiences. *Photoplay* praised 'a fine romantic picture about second chances and the impossibility of raising the past from its grave', and enthused over Julie Christie for 'working wonders with an underwritten role'. Although the movie was very well received at Cannes, the box-office returns were deeply disappointing.

The flurry of work brought the usual interview requests, which were largely resisted. 'It's a great strain, being interviewed,' said Christie. 'Two people who have never met before sit down and the person being interviewed is supposed to present an image which is full of wonderful things you want other people to think about you. It is impossible.'

One film that appealed both to Christie's politics and her sense of humour was *The Gold Diggers,* an outrageous take-off of all those macho swash-buckling adventure movies that were once the Hollywood mainstream. New director Sally Potter insisted on a mainly female crew and the whole project had unmissable feminist overtones. Julie Christie could hardly wait to say Yes, even though she again received the same low flat-rate as the other actors. The film was later retitled *Gold.*

In 1986 Julie starred with some style in Sidney Lumet's perceptive political drama *Power* alongside Richard Gere and Gene Hackman. This searing and well-researched exposé of the ruthlessness of campaigning across America earned considerable praise from the critics, even if it did not exactly set the box-office alight. While Gere was memorable as the supremely cynical spin doctor, Christie matched him all the way in her role as his philosophical ex-wife Ellen Freeman. She told friends she was delighted to play the 'conscience' of the movie as well as being mightily impressed with 'astonishingly handsome' Richard Gere.

The determination to act only in films she believed in was exemplified by Julie Christie's participation in *Miss Mary,* a film by Argentine director Maria Luise Bemberg. Christie played an English governess in service to a degenerate Argentine family in 1930 when the order of society was threatened by a looming military take-over. She loved the location filming: 'Buenos Aires has a very European history and background. But there's this vast Argentina which is another cup of tea: abandoned, depopulated and very poor. I found people very warm. They've been silent out of terror for so many years that it was like a dam opening. I was enthralled and horrified by their stories. They weren't hostile towards me as an Englishwoman as long as I understood their anti-colonialism in some way. Mind you, when you're at a political rally and suddenly all these anti-British slogans come out, you do feel a bit of a twerp.'

Christie's public profile was raised again when she was reunited with old mentor John Schlesinger and old friend Alan Bates for a television version of Terence Rattigan's double bill, *Separate Tables.* The high-quality end result was screened to great acclaim in America and Britain and Schlesinger announced that the experience had been a joy. 'She used to be as acquisitive as me, but she doesn't need the trappings of success any more – which I think is an admirable quality.'

Christie agreed to play the dual roles of ex-model Anne Shankland who was desperately concerned about her fading looks and Sybil, a plain and bitter spinster. She was slightly cautious about the Rattigan classic: 'At first I found it hard to relate to the morals and attitudes of the characters ... but I decided to go ahead because I really wanted to work with John and Alan again and once I started it wasn't a conflict for me.'

Schlesinger used disfiguring make-up and protruding teeth to disguise Christie's natural beauty and said: 'She surprised us all in her portrayal of Sybil. She lived the role so completely I almost didn't recognize her. It was a measure of how much she'd matured since I last worked with her. The simple life in Wales obviously suits her.'

An even more welcome work offer came from the distinguished Merchant – Ivory film-making team to go back to her birthplace, India, to star in their lavish and enthralling movie *Heat and Dust,* based on Ruth Prawer Jhabvala's novel which won the Booker Prize. Christie played a BBC researcher called Anne who was drawn to India to learn about her family's past and the actress found many personal echoes in the journey. 'Coming back to India is a voyage of discovery for me. I was born in Assam on my father's tea plantation. But because I left when I was eight I never got to know or understand it. Now I need to do that.

'Anne is eager and enthusiastic to learn. But she has a lot of Western conditioning that has closed off part of her mind. She is unfulfilled professionally and emotionally, but in India she ceases to be lonely. She does not do this by finding a person, but by finding a way of thinking that does not demand that you should have such and such a man and such and such a job.'

Christie loved India: 'I have never had this reaction to a place before.' She was helped enormously to appreciate the land of her birth by the fact that she could wander unrecognized for the first time in twenty years. She relaxed and let her hair down and became thoroughly at home. She rejected her fabulous five-star hotel room for much more humble lodgings in a traditional Indian hotel round the corner and felt spiritually at home.

But in the end it was a very emotional experience: while she was making her first trip back to India since she left as a child to go to school, her mother Rosemary sadly died. 'I had tried to persuade her to come with me, but she said No, she did not want to go back. It was a sort of strange, fateful coincidence, losing my mother while I was in the place where I was born. But I grew very fond of India.'

Julie Christie always has to have very strong reasons for accepting a role. In 1988 she graced a CBS television miniseries *Dadah is Death,* playing an Australian mother who waged a brave world-wide battle to save her son from a Malaysian death sentence for heroin trafficking. 'It was a very strong woman's part,' said Christie. 'For once there isn't a man with a woman sort of circling around him. Most of the American mini-series I have been offered had a strong streak of sentimentality. But this one doesn't.'

The drama was based on the real experiences of Barbara Barlow, who battled to save the life of her son Kevin and his companion Geoff Chambers. Christie said, 'The ghastly experiences of the two Australian boys might dissuade people from travelling in foreign countries with drugs. Too little attention is paid to the laws of Third World countries.'

Christie was happily reunited with her *Don't Look Now* costar and close friend Donald Sutherland in the 1992 television drama *The Railway Station Man.* She starred as a widow forced to move by the violence of the Irish sectarian troubles to a new village with her son where she meets a mysterious hook-handed

American (Donald Sutherland) who is determined to bring a derelict railway station back to working life. Based on a book by Jennifer Johnston, the love story with a political background drew compelling performances from both Christie and Sutherland.

In 1995 Christie accepted her first stage role in twenty-five years when she agreed to star in a revival of Harold Pinter's *Old Times* at Theatr Clwyd in Mold, North Wales. Her old friend, Australian director Lindy Davies was instrumental in persuading the screen star to return to the theatre and the play transferred to Wyndham's Theatre in London's West End. She later toured the south of England in *Suzanna Andler,* a play by Marguerite Duras, which was not nearly such a happy experience. 'It was the most difficult thing I've ever done in my life,' said Christie. 'She is a very, very, very extraordinarily strange writer.' The problem was Christie's notoriously unreliable memory, which is easy to cope with when filming as only brief snatches of dialogue are required at a time. And the famously spare Harold Pinter dialogue was something she managed with her friendly director's assistance. But *Suzanna Andler* was quite different. 'The play is something I should not have done,' Christie admitted. 'The lines go popping out of my head all the time. So it's perilous. I can see how other people learn lines, but I haven't got that mind. In six weeks, I haven't stopped working for a day, for a minute. I didn't think I could ever get those lines.'

Kenneth Branagh was delighted when, after much persuasion, Julie Christie agreed to play Gertrude in his 1996 film of *Hamlet.* 'I didn't know I had it in me to get to the truth of her,' said Christie. 'So I procrastinated about doing it until my friends told me I was being silly. You don't get offered Gertrude and a Kenneth Branagh film every day.'

'Julie's a very intelligent woman and a very considered artist,' said Branagh. 'She always takes her time before she makes her mind up to do something and then she commits to it absolutely. In this case she was nervous about doing Shakespeare and nervous about how Gertrude might be interpreted.'

As the widowed queen who quickly takes her husband's assassin into her bed, Christie felt strongly that Gertrude had not had an adulterous affair with Claudius before the play begins and doesn't know that he has murdered her husband. It was very important to her to get these views established. Branagh was impressed. 'She is an incredibly beautiful woman who told me things about the queen in a way that I had never seen before.'

Afterwards Christie was very pleased by the experience: 'It came off, and working with Kenneth is heaven. The film is like Errol Flynn – swash-buckling. He has made it so entertaining.' She went to Ireland to promote *Hamlet* and enjoyed a discussion with a party of schoolchildren. 'I told them I saw Gertrude as innocent, and one of the kids said, "Yes, but she's so lustful." And it's a point they kept coming back to.' She laughed: 'I said, "So what's wrong with that?" And they looked absolutely shocked.' She clearly enjoyed her first Shakespearean film role: 'Kenneth had an incredible will, not just to get the film made, but to make his cast and crew happy. Friends came on the set and said it was like school without the teachers.'

The news that Julie Christie had had a face lift surprised her many fans and followers and the hysterical reaction in the press irritated the actress more than a little. Julie had spoken out more than once about the importance of character and the irrelevance of beauty so there were audible howls of concern from more strident feminists, particularly. She said that she had a small modification of her jawline as a result of spending time in America where: 'People who are older than you appear to be younger. That is really undermining. You know they're older than you and you look like their mother. I had all these double chins and I thought, "Oh, I can't bear it." '

But when questioned further about the details of the operation she answered icily: 'It was very minor.' She said she was the last person of her age still working in films and added: 'I think I should be commended for hanging on in this world for so long instead of being slaughtered. I can't understand why there isn't all this emphasis on every person that's in the business.'

Julie Christie's bold ability never to take herself too seriously was well illustrated in 1998 when she accepted the leading role in *Afterglow.* Phyllis Mann, a blousy one-time Hollywood actress, is trapped in Montreal in an unhappy marriage to a philandering handyman played by Nick Nolte and enjoys a sudden fling with a young whiz-kid businessman, played by Johnny Lee Miller. Christie said that the two things that attracted her to the part were the prospect of working with Alan Rudolph, a director she greatly admired, and with Nick Nolte, whom she described as 'incredibly tasty'.

Phyllis spends long lonely evenings with a drink in her hand sadly watching videos of her old films. But for Christie, there was no fear of playing a character with elements of her own life and she gave a wonderful performance, particularly when Phyllis turns to the flirting would-be seducer less than half her age and says sparkily, 'What is this, some kind of mother thing?' And again when he tries to impress the bored Phyllis with the classic: 'You are the most fascinating woman I've ever met in my life.' She looks wearily at him and says grimly, 'Yes. I know.' The performance won Julie Christie a richly deserved Oscar nomination.

With age came more wisdom and the experience to explain herself more confidently. When interviewed about *Afterglow* she said, 'I shouldn't be talking about myself, I should be talking about something that really matters, like the fact that we're selling arms to Indonesia which are being used for genocide in East Timor.'

And she reacted with some humour to being constantly labelled a 'recluse' by the media: 'I resent it enormously because that is a special word for very special people. For the media it's now a word for people who don't go on chat shows and don't get married.'

Princess Diana's death upset her profoundly. She knew from painful personal experience how it feels to be hounded endlessly by the press. She looked back on the height of her fame as some sort of nightmare and said that she knew how Diana must have felt. And even added: 'I knew she was going to die. That's been clear for years. It was like watching a movie made for perverts, where people paid, and watched, and continued to watch even though it was quite clear she had to die.'

Julie Christie is delighted to stay out of the newspapers whenever possible. 'I think I was lucky. God, I'd hate to be really famous now. The beastly people with their horrible long-distance lenses, making dirt out of your normal, developing, evolving life. They seem to be only interested in who is doing what sexually to whom. That is the most private thing on earth, and it has got nothing to do with anyone else at all.'

# 11

# Reluctant Revival

In the three years that followed the making of *Afterglow,* Julie Christie deliberately distanced herself from the film world. Failing to win an Oscar did not bother her in the least but it did concentrate her mind. She redoubled her determination not to waste any of her precious time and that led her to turn down plenty of 'unworthy' film offers.

On the personal front, Christie's journalist boyfriend Duncan Campbell was relocated in 1999 to report for *The Guardian* from California and she followed him to the West Coast. But they did not head for the glittering showbiz mansions of Beverly Hills or the beachside elegance of Malibu. She lived in a very ordinary house in an unremarkable town called Ojai, some 75 miles up the Pacific coast from Los Angeles, while Campbell's work meant he was away for much of the time. Christie deliberately avoided going anywhere near Hollywood.

Her only involvement in movies was to lend her voice to an animated film about the life of Jesus called *The Miracle Maker* and to help newscaster Julia Somerville to introduce a film called *Different Strokes* for a charity helping stroke victims. The actress insisted she was not wasting a moment of her life.

She was indulging her dream to 'sit by the Pacific and watch the sea.'

But Christie did not spend all her time in California daydreaming. She threw herself into joining the campaign against California's tough 'three strikes' law which saw offenders jailed for life for a third offence. She was outraged at the heartless nature of the law, which often consigned very young offenders to a lifetime of incarceration. Campbell was delighted to see his lover so fulfilled and the couple were happy with their relationship and friends explained that they loved being together, without ever wanting to live completely in each other's pockets. The sunshine suited Christie but she still found plenty of time to travel to Europe. When in Britain she divided her time between her Welsh farmhouse and a modest London bolthole in the East End.

But even superstars need to earn an occasional film contract and Julie Christie loves to surprise her faithful fans. It was certainly a shock to see her turn up, speaking impeccable French, as a British Museum Egyptologist called in to assist when a ghostly spirit from the past escaped into the Louvre in the 2001 film *Belphegor*. Director Jean-Paul Salome was clearly delighted to cast Christie and announced excitedly: 'Julie Christie is an extraordinary woman and a rare person.' The light-hearted movie was a modern day update of a popular 60s French television series, which enabled the budget conscious producers to cut costs by using plenty of original footage. Christie's character, Glenda Spencer, became a romantic interest for the investigating detective played by veteran French actor Michel Serrault, but it was a forgettable project that was low on credibility.

The idea of working with director Hal Hartley appealed to Julie Christie and she agreed to take a small part in his film *No Such Thing,* which featured the discovery of an ancient Icelandic monster stirred from centuries of sleep by a curious young TV journalist. Young Canadian actress Sarah Polley played the journalist and she and Christie soon became firm friends. The film itself was not easy to follow. Christie noted afterwards: 'To be honest, I didn't completely understand the script but I didn't mind that because I trusted the film-maker and weird is better than predictable.' Julie Christie played an Icelandic doctor who nurses the journalist back to health after a plane crash. 'My part was miniscule,' said Christie afterwards. 'You blink and I'm gone. It isn't a realistic film, it's an unnaturalistic film, as it would be with a monster in it.' Iceland is a country Christie loves. 'It's one of the most beautiful countries in the world,' she said. 'It's like being in a fairy story in itself, with all the dangers and surprises and honesty in the people...and they're the biggest party givers in the world.'

In the summer of 2001 the opening of the Edinburgh Fringe was marked by calls for a boycott of the Perrier Awards for Comedy by a group of stars, including Julie Christie, Victoria Wood and Emma Thompson, who were all anxious to draw attention to the controversial sales of powdered baby milk to Third World countries by Perrier's parent company Nestlé. The organisers of the campaign believed Nestlé was violating World Health Organisation codes on the marketing of the infant formula. Perrier was also under attack from environmentalists concerned about the 'wastefulness' of the bottled water industry. Julie Christie made a statement saying: 'I hope that up and coming comedians will think about these issues and decline to support the Perrier Awards.'

Julie Christie went back to acting in the 2002 movie *I'm With Lucy.* Julie and *Ghostbusters'* star Harold Ramis provided cameo performances as the embarrassing parents of young bride to be Lucy (Monica Potter) who hitch a ride with their dippy daughter on what turns into the date from Hell. It was a far from memorable movie.

The public image of Julie Christie has long remained one of a glacially beautiful, highly principled actress who takes herself a shade too seriously. Readers of the *Guardian* in May 2002 were delighted to discover in a rare personally by-lined article that in fact she has a well developed and fully functioning sense of humour. She reflected wryly on the 'strange phenomenon of celebrity' and shot down in flames quite a few stories about herself that had proved just too good to check. She noted that a photograph that appeared in the magazine *Vanity Fair* caused no comment in the United States but caused a huge fuss in the British press. Julie thought the story should have been headlined: 'Actress Has Flattering Picture Taken Shock!' She explained that she had not known she was transgressing: 'Some new unwritten law that women over 60 should not wear low v-necks and should keep their legs covered.'

And in a rather more serious vein Christie went on to say in America she had done an interview with National Public Radio to publicise Hal Hartley's film *No Such Thing,* of which she was very fond. She had hoped she would be given the chance to talk about something other than herself but later realised this was naivety on her part. Not only was she not able to bring up the war on terrorism, but her familiar remarks about her poor memory were spun into a major health scare. She was alarmed to see British newspapers writing about her 'medical condition' but refused to take the nonsense too seriously. She wrote wryly: 'A doctor consulted by the press concluded that I had suffered a "trauma to the hippocampus" which sounds like a good name for a heavy metal band, but I had never heard of it before.' Concerned by the alarming headlines screaming 'Julie Christie suffers cruel memory loss', friends and relatives rang to find out the truth, which was rather different. She said: 'A few light-hearted remarks…were turned into some strange illness which I do not have, diagnosed by a doctor I had never met, and transformed by a reporter I have never spoken to, into a shock horror tale.'

The misinformation did not end there and stories, spread by news media and endlessly accelerated by the Internet, also suggested that Christie now shared her life with an invented son who was identified as 'Luke, a musician.' Julie Christie laconically remarked: 'Only a really bad memory would have made me forget I had a son. How "Luke" arrived on the scene remains as much of a mystery as my phantom "medical syndrome".'

Julie Christie's social conscience was again in evidence in September 2002 as she spearheaded an artistic protest to what she saw as American aggression towards the Middle East after the 9/11 attacks on New York the previous year. She headed the all star line-up at London's Royal Opera House for what she ambitiously described as: 'Three magical evenings of spine-tingling music, movement, poetry and human experience' which were intended to 'transform the horror and darkness of last September into practical action to address the root causes of terrorism.' Members of the audience were invited to pay up to £75 for a ticket with all proceeds going to the charity Peace Direct.

Later she joined the campaign to save historic Spitalfields Market from 'modernisation', which threatened to squeeze out long-standing stallholders. 'Living locally,' said Julie, 'I recognise the contribution that Spitalfields Market makes to London and support the calls to protect its special quality.'

The death of film director John Schlesinger in July 2003 moved and upset Julie Christie very deeply. He had played a crucial role in her early career and had remained a trusted confidant ever since. But with a typical lack of sentimentality she was determined her friend and one-time mentor was remembered the right way and she said: 'John was rude and irreverent, and that's why I'll miss him.' The reverential obituaries, which were widely published, seemed odd to Christie. She recalled him as a provocative, mischievous character who, as she bluntly put it, 'delighted in taking the piss out of everything and everyone, including his friends.' She wrote about his kindness and his generosity and she also told an anecdote which perhaps said more about Schlesinger than all the tributes. Julie Christie wrote: 'In *Far From the Madding Crowd* I had one scene where I had to open the coffin of the dead mistress of my husband Captain Troy, played by Terence Stamp. I knew the coffin contained a terrible secret about my husband and I had to prise it open dramatically to discover it. I went into one of those actorly things: I needed to be very intense and serious and be on my own to get into the mood. I was getting very ratty with everyone who made a noise on set. We eventually got round to shooting after I had been indulged...I slowly prised the lid off the coffin and inside, instead of a dead mistress and baby as there should have been, there was a small, smirking props man holding a huge dildo.' John liked to create an atmosphere of irreverence even in the process of film-making, recorded Julie Christie.

Julie Christie might have no children of her own but she made a marvellous matriarch in the lavish

£70 million movie of *Finding Neverland* as Mrs du Maurier, the protective grandmother of the Llewelyn-Davies boys who were J.M. Barrie's inspiration for Peter Pan. Some critics said she gave the performance of her life but Christie insisted she was only playing a 'minor, supporting role' and shrugged off the renewed acclaim. They did agree it was a fitting project for an actress who appeared to have led a charmed life, on screen at least. 'I've had a good run,' she said. 'I've loved every minute of my life.' Christie's appearance certainly impressed star of the movie Johnny Depp. He said: 'When I laid eyes on Julie Christie the first day she came to the set I almost wet myself. She's so beautiful.' Director Marc Forster deliberately cast actors playing against type. He recognised that it was very hard for Julie Christie to play the prudish, interfering grandmother because she is 'so warm and lovely' in real-life. 'But she was very committed to the character and did beautifully,' said Forster. Some descendants of the Llewelyn-Davies family did criticise the move for rewriting history and one relative suggested that having Mrs du Maurier angrily waving a coat hanger and becoming the inspiration for Captain Hook was 'really rather ridiculous.'

Christie said *Finding Neverland* was not a part she felt at all sure of at first. She admitted she had never been interested in the work of J.M. Barrie but had a friend who was really into it. She got on well with director Marc Forster and came to be very supportive of her character because although she did not always behave well, Christie remained convinced she was 'a very nice woman.'

Christie remained as in demand as ever and she agreed to a small role in the 2004 epic *Troy*. It was a £150 million 'swords and sandals' movie very loosely based on Homer's Iliad. The movie starred Brad Pitt as Achilles and was crammed full of acting talent as Orlando Bloom, Sean Bean and Brian Cox also appeared and Christie made a two minute appearance as Achilles' mother Thetis.

Christie also featured in *Harry Potter and the Prisoner of Azkaban* as Madame Rosmerta, a big hearted barmaid from the Three Broomsticks pub, who came close to stealing the few scenes she appeared in.

Duncan Campbell's job with the *Guardian* was relocated back to Britain in 2004 but the couple stayed as solid as ever. Both decline to discuss personal matters but Christie was quoted as agreeing that it was: 'A wonderful relationship.' Then she laconically added: 'Now we just have to hope neither of us goes bananas.'

Christie made a surprise visit to Edinburgh in July 2005 to play her part in the public commemoration of those who died in Iraq. Julie was a speaker at the Naming of the Dead Ceremony, which was attended by 2,500 people on Calton Hill. Around one thousand names of people who lost their lives were read out by some 70 speakers at the event which was organised by the Stop The War Coalition. Julie Christie had already made her opposition to the Iraq war very clear and she said that their lives had been 'wasted.' She said: 'The troops should never have gone to war at all. The names being read out were wasted deaths. Sending troops to Iraq was just feeding the greed of Bush and Blair.'

Just when she might have been expected to forget the mercenary business of movie-making altogether she received an offer she simply could not refuse. No matter how hard she tried. Brilliant young Canadian actress Sarah Polley built up a mutual respect and a close bond with Julie Christie when they worked together on *No Such Thing* and on *The Secret Life of Words.* 'We became really good friends,' says Sarah. 'She was someone I felt instantly connected to and very grateful to meet.' Flying home from a long filming session Sarah read something that would later affect both their lives deeply. Alice Munro's sublimely sensitive short story *The Bear Came Over the Mountain* is about a loving and long married couple whose relationship is devastated when the wife develops Alzheimer's. Would-be director Sarah Polley instantly recognised the movie potential and she recalled later: 'My first thought was, "How amazing would it be to see Julie play this role?" For me, the opportunity to watch her give this performance is the reason I wanted to make this film in the first place. So it was pretty much impossible for me to imagine anybody else. The role was pretty much adapted and created for her. The point of me doing it was to get her to play this part. It wasn't like, "I want to make this move and wouldn't she be great for it?" She was the central reason I thought of it as a film in the first place.'

But Sarah Polley had a battle on her hands to convince Julie Christie to take the role. 'It's hard to get Julie to act,' said Sarah. 'It's not for the faint of heart. She's always certain there is somebody else who is better for the role.' Polley knew that even after all her success Christie did not think of herself as a particularly great actor, so to convince her to work was a very difficult challenge. Polley pestered and pleaded and endlessly persuaded. 'It definitely took some convincing but I stayed with it and tried not to let go and hoped she would give in,' said Polley. 'Eventually she did, and I'm so glad because her performance is the heart of the film. I think it just took her a long time to get used to the idea.'

Christie said she formed a strong friendship with the younger woman when they worked together on *No Such Thing* in 2000 and is a great admirer of her talents. But that did not mean she was a pushover. 'Of course when she sent me this screenplay I said No,' said Christie. But the determined director-to-be would not take No for a final answer and began what Christie later called a 'seven month courtship' to win her agreement to take part.

'The fact is I don't really want to do anything,' admitted Christie later. 'I usually find the stories out there don't really interest me, and if you're going to take on a project, you should care. There's just not all that much out there that's worth caring about.' But gradually Christie saw that Sarah Polley had a story that desperately needed to be told. She knew Sarah was a fine actress but she wanted to make sure she was truly committed to the film. Christie said: 'You know, I made Robert Altman wait for seven months too before I agreed to do *McCabe and Mrs Miller* all those years ago. As an actress you have to believe the director is passionate, almost obsessive, about the work because it's so hard, you can't do it half-heartedly.'

Polley kept on and on. She said she felt like a stalker. 'In the end I thought, if I don't do it, I'll miss the opportunity of being with her on her first feature film,' said Christie. She had personal experience of the terrible impact of Alzheimer's and her sympathy with the project grew. In the end the No turned to Yes. And once Christie had committed to the powerful, and at times uncomfortable, script she hurled herself wholeheartedly into the project. Julie Christie was happy to play a woman older than herself and to be filmed without make-up in close-up. The young director later revealed: 'We had to age her a little. Julie is this stunning natural beauty who hasn't had 8,000 facelifts so you can see her face as it is. But the way she looks in everyday life makes it extremely difficult to believe she could be going into any kind of retirement home.' So in the film she wears a wig and the film-makers had to go to some effort to make her look old enough. Face to face, Julie Christie looks remarkably young for her age and she moves like someone years younger. Friends agree that she has the most agile and flexible and youthful presence. 'So we had to do a lot to make it convincing that she could be suffering from this disease,' said the young director.

Sarah Polley faced another search to find an actress who looked like the young Julie Christie to play the character in flashback sequences in the film. Sarah Polley said: 'We're looking for someone stunningly beautiful but no acting experience is necessary.' The very pretty Stacey Laberge filled the bill.

*Away From Her* stars Christie and veteran Canadian actor Gordon Pinsent as Fiona and Grant Anderson who have been married for 40 years when she starts to reveal symptoms of the disease. Anxious to protect her partner from becoming a full-time carer Fiona persuades Grant that she needs to go into a nursing home. He reluctantly agrees and they choose a lavish care home, where the rules forbid him from visiting for a month. When he is at last permitted to visit, Fiona seems to have forgotten their great love and is showing great affection to another man. Grant is heartbroken but determined not to do anything to disturb his wife's happiness.

Julie Christie knows that not all Alzheimer's sufferers finish up in homes as kind and comfortable as the one portrayed in the film. 'Patients seem so protected there, not like some of the homes they have in England,' said Julie. 'When I first walked in there, I said, "This is fantastic. It's so nice." Canada where the film was made is a different place. Canadian compassion built that place.' Christie also knew she had made the right decision to go ahead with the difficult, demanding movie after she sat through the Canadian premiere. 'It's very rare that you feel you can give an audience something meaningful when you're acting in motion pictures. While I was watching the film at the premiere I found my real pleasure came in watching the audience react to the film. Everything came together, the music and the images and the whole thing was lovely. I'm so proud and happy for Sarah because she put so much into it.' Julie Christie was delighted to see the film strike such a strong chord with the audience. 'It's an experience you don't often get in this business,' she said.

Privately as well as professionally this was a very happy time for Julie Christie as the news broke that she had quietly married Duncan Campbell in India. Her brother Clive confirmed the event had taken place and all concerned were delighted to have avoided the media spotlight. Julie Christie had spoken about the irrelevance of marriage in her life but friends insisted that after much thought and consideration she and Campbell had decided together to put their long relationship on a more permanent basis. 'They are very much in love and they're both very pleased to have taken this step,' said a pal.

For many viewers of *Away From Her* there were powerful echoes of Katherine Hepburn's memorable performance in *On Golden Pond* and the movie earned a range of awards, and writer Sarah Polley and Christie were both nominated for Oscars. Not surprisingly with her previous experience of Hollywood's glitziest occasion, this was not an occasion for any personal celebration. The moment the word 'Oscar' is mentioned she said later: 'Anxiety sets in.'

In fact after much hype and speculation Christie did not win. She looked unmoved and later almost relieved as she missed out on a second Oscar, as the best actress award went to 32-year-old French actress Marion Cotillard for her role as singer Edith Piaf in the biopic *La Vie En Rose.* For the occasion Christie wore exactly what she pleased, a knee length burgundy dress, which she designed herself, with elbow-length chiffon gloves and beige shoes which appeared to be several sizes too large for her. The outfit was widely thought not to be a fashion success and in the *Daily Telegraph* writer Jan Moir said harshly: 'Julie Christie looked like the Saturday night cabaret turn in a Swansea hotel.'

# 12

# Epilogue

Julie Christie was always determined to be an actress but her route to stardom was never a zealous thrust for fame. The extent of her ambition was to be a good actress, yet by the age of 26, she had won a Best Actress Oscar for only her fifth film and had starred in *Doctor Zhivago,* one of the best-loved movies of all time.

For an actress who has always valued the quality of her work rather than any personal fame or glory it remains a remarkable achievement. From the outset Julie Christie always cared more about her acting than about her celebrity status, and those feelings have strengthened over the years. She did not set out to be identified through *Billy Liar* as the quintessential sixties woman; sensitive, independent and adventurous. She was embarrassed that her alluring looks should have encouraged talk of a screen sex symbol, and she was bemused by the fuss that surrounded her emergence as a sexually predatory female in *Darling.* She never expected *Darling* to fling her into instant orbit as a global star, the very incarnation of the new British woman. Her natural inclination was reticence when the spotlight fell so brightly on her in *Doctor Zhivago,* adoringly filmed by David Lean. She was not fooled by the title bestowed on her of 'the face of 1965', realising that she had barely started her acting career and still had to earn her stripes. The title, she was fully aware, had almost everything to do with her looks and little to do with her ability. She likened her early fame to a leaf in the wind, conscious that the Oscar elevated her to Best actress when really she had only just begun. But she was soon to prove beyond doubt her ability to act with intelligence, depth and conviction.

Christie rightly considers herself a much better actress now, with a much fuller understanding of the process of filmmaking. But, beautiful and beguiling, exuberant and enigmatic, wilful and rueful, Christie can now look back on a film career in which she has portrayed some of the most significant and complex of women. The irony is that filming still does not come easily. 'I almost never say Yes to a part,' she said. 'That's because I view films as interruptions of my life.'

It is not the learning of lines, the exploration required of the character she is playing, or the physical process of acting in front of a film camera that she dislikes. It is everything that surrounds a movie, the socialising it entails, the hours spent discussing a scene she is about to do with other actors and actresses, all of which she finds difficult. There have been many occasions when she has wished it all came to her more easily since, as she points out, there are so many more enjoyable things to do than making a movie: reading, researching for the many causes she supports, watching films and going for long walks.

Julie Christie has long been in the fortunate position of being able to pick her roles. She is serious about movies and politics, knows the directors she likes and chooses carefully. But if she is a reluctant film actress these days, the redeeming feature for Julie about taking on a new film is the chance to travel on location and see places she might otherwise never get to. She loves travel and nature and by her own admissions she is greedy for sensations – flowers, beauty, food – and goes to a great deal of trouble to experience these things. At home in Wales she is likely to save reading a letter she has just received from a dear friend until she has lit candles and settled by the fire with a glass of wine. It is a moment and an experience to be savoured.

Julie Christie does not have a huge number of friends in the film world and her hesitancy over whether or not to make a film can tax even the most patient. Sarah Polley is only the latest in a long line of directors who have experienced the extraordinary lack of Christie confidence. Weighing up in her mind whether the role, the subject, the film's message or the director is right for her is not the only hurdle. Communication can be difficult because Christie has an aversion to telephones. When, in 1983, the director Joe Losey was trying to interest her in a new film project, *Wild Palms,* and was having difficulty tracking her down, Julie sent him a Christmas card from the wilds of New Jersey with a letter inside which tantalisingly revealed a noncommittal reply and the explanation: 'I'd ring you if I hadn't such a 'phone phobia.'

Julie Christie hates making decisions and she particularly hates making decisions in a hurry. She said recently: 'I don't like that bit of panic and hurry. I'm very bad at making decisions, so the easiest thing to do is not to make them. I like things to stay as they are – perhaps that's it, and perhaps that's why I haven't got a computer, and perhaps that's why I don't have a mobile phone.'

Alan Rudolph, the director of *Afterglow,* explained: 'Julie never says Yes to anything. She'll never actually agree to do your film. You just have to assume that, if she doesn't say No, she'll be there when shooting starts.' Despite her glowing record as a film actress, Christie's fear of failure lingers just under the surface when it comes to movies.

But in the real world she is much more decisive. In February 2008 Julie Christie was proud to be named as an ambassador for Survival International, the worldwide movement to support tribal people. It is a cause very close to her heart and she has supported Survival for more than 30 years. In a passionate radio appeal she said: 'I've been involved because Survival fights against the extinction of many groups of human beings.' Christie narrated a film for Survival's new 'uncontacted tribes' campaign which featured some previously unseen footage of some of the world's most remote and endangered peoples. She has been particularly outspoken on behalf of the Kalahari Bushmen, who were evicted from their ancestral lands to make way for diamond mining.

A sixties icon despite herself, Julie Christie has become resigned to being forever asked about those heady days. But she says, because of her poor memory, it can be uncomfortable when people start talking about the past. Often, she says, the people who ask her about the sixties know more about that era than she does. 'I don't know the person they are asking about,' says Christie. 'She is a stranger.'

Yet happily she does recall some of the offbeat moments. At perhaps the height of her fame, after the London premiere of *Far From the Madding Crowd* her mother and stepfather accompanied her and afterwards they went to a disco. 'My stepfather had never been to a disco before,' she said years later, 'and he put a couple of peanuts in his ears once he got there to protect himself from the noise. Well, he couldn't get one of them out so we had to take him to see a doctor! That's what I remember about the premiere.'

But in fact Julie Christie would much rather talk about the causes she has become committed to than the movies she has appeared in. Over the years she has spoken out over nuclear waste, animal rights, factory farming, human rights in places as varied as Central America, Nicaragua, Palestine, East Timor and Cambodia, feminism and many other causes. Occasionally she has been mocked or sneered at but always she has been sincere.

Julie Christie never wanted fame and her considered view is that: 'Celebrity is the curse of modern life. And I don't like being part of something dirty.' But as she has the stardom she uses it as positively and as honestly as she can. In spring 2008 she said that it was perfectly possible she might never make another film – but she will never stop campaigning for the causes she believes in.

# Filmography

## Major films

## *CROOKS ANONYMOUS, 1962*

British comedy about an organization run by ex-convicts who set out to reform and watch over their less fortunate brothers and return them to the straight and narrow. Main object of the team's attentions is safe-breaker and compulsive jewel thief, Captain 'Dandy' Forsdyke (Leslie Phillips). His despairing girlfriend Babette La Verne (Julie Christie) won't consider marrying him unless he takes the cure. With Stanley Baxter, Wilfred Hyde White, Michael Medwin and Pauline Jameson. *Director:* Ken Annakin

## *THE FAST LADY, 1963*

British comedy about an obstinate, over-patriotic, young Scottish civil servant (Stanley Baxter) who sets out to learn to drive a vintage Bentley sports car called the Fast Lady in order to ingratiate himself with the gruff tycoon father of Claire Chingford (Julie Christie), a girl he has fallen for. With James Robertson Justice as the tycoon and Leslie Phillips as a wolfish car salesman.
*Director:* Ken Annakin

## BILLY LIAR, 1963

Billy Fisher (Tom Courtenay) is a young daydreamer who leads an irresponsible life as a funeral director's clerk. He fiddles the petty cash, rows with his parents and is involved with two women who share an engagement ring. Above all he is an incorrigible liar who retreats into his own invented world. Then into his life comes freewheeling Liz (Julie Christie) who offers him the chance to escape his drab life. She persuades him to run away with her to London but at the last moment his nerve fails him. With Wilfred Pickles and Mona Washbourne.
*Director:* John Schlesinger

## YOUNG CASSIDY, 1965

Biopic of Irish playwright Sean O'Casey based on his autobiographical *Mirror in My House.* Rod Taylor starred as the rebel who comes up the hard way but rises to literary greatness. Maggie Smith is his one love who leaves him so he can achieve more without her. Julie Christie plays prostitute Daisy Battles who seduces young Cassidy. With Edith Evans, Michael Redgrave and Flora Robson. *Director:* John Ford (Jack Cardiff took over when Ford fell ill).

## DARLING, 1965

Julie Christie as amoral fashion model Diana Scott who leaves her husband and sleeps her way to the top of chic London society, ending up as the lonely and disillusioned wife of an Italian nobleman. Her conquests along the way include TV reporter Robert Gold (Dirk Bogarde), sleek advertising executive Miles Brand (Laurence Harvey) and fashion photographer Malcolm (Roland Curram).

*Director:* John Schlesinger BEST ACTRESS OSCAR FOR JULIE CHRISTIE

## DOCTOR ZHIVAGO, 1965

Epic screen adaptation of Boris Pasternak's Nobel prizewinning novel with Omar Sharif as the idealistic Russian doctor – poet who finds himself in sympathy with the ideals of the Revolution but is unable to adjust to the new society, Geraldine Chaplin as his wife Tonya, and Julie Christie as Lara with whom he falls in love. With Rod Steiger, Alec Guinness, Tom Courtenay, Ralph Richardson, Siobhan McKenna, Rita Tushingham.

*Director:* David Lean

## FAHRENHEIT 451, 1966

A setting some time in the future in which to own books is a crime and the state has a squad of firemen with flamethrowers to destroy the illicit literature. Fahrenheit 451 is the temperature at which books are reduced to ashes. Montag (Oskar Werner) is an obedient, honest and ambitious fireman who does his book-destroying job with efficiency, and has a law-abiding wife (Julie Christie). Then a young pro-bationary school teacher (also played by Julie Christie) plants the first seeds of doubt in Montag's mind and from then on he steals the odd book, starts reading them secretly and ultimately challenges authority. With Cyril Cusack and Anton Diffring. *Director:* François Truffaut

# FAR FROM THE MADDING CROWD, 1967

Based closely on Thomas Hardy's book, the story of independently minded sheep-farmer Bathsheba Everdene's multifaceted love for the three men in her life. They are arrogant, dashing Sergeant Troy (Terence Stamp), ever-reliable shepherd Gabriel Oak (Alan Bates), and Squire Boldwood (Peter Finch). *Director:* John Schlesinger

# PETULIA, 1968

Tragi-comedy set in San Francisco and based on John Haase's novel *Me and the Arch Kook Petulia* with Julie Christie as Petulia Danner, the unhappy wife of a sadistically weak, psychotic husband (Richard Chamberlain), who decides to have an affair with Archie Bollen, a nice, rcently divorced doctor, played by George C. Scott.
*Director:* Richard Lester

# IN SEARCH OF GREGORY, 1969

Julie Christie as the daughter of an incurably romantic Swiss financier (Adolfo Celi) who is invited to her father's latest wedding in Geneva. She lives in quiet domesticity in Rome and her real attraction in coming to Geneva is her dad's calculating description of Gregory, his house-guest from San Francisco whom he describes as a tall, handsome 'likeable maniac'. At the airport she spots a giant poster of an auto-ball champion and in her imagination he becomes the physical embodiment of her romantic fantasies about Gregory.

*Director:* Peter Wood

# THE GO-BETWEEN, 1971

Adaptation of L.P. Hartley's novel with Michael Redgrave as Leo Colston looking back at an incident from his boyhood during a long hot summer in a lavish country home when he becomes emotionally involved as the go-between for illicit lovers, Marian (Julie Christie), the uppercrust daughter of the house, who is betrothed to a member of the aristocracy, and the tenant farmer Ted Burgess (Alan Bates). With Margaret Leighton, Michael Gough, Edward Fox, and Dominic Guard as the boy Leo.

*Director:* Joseph Losey

## McCABE AND MRS MILLER, 1971

McCabe (Warren Beatty), an ambitious small-timer, amiable braggart and roving gambler opens a bordello in a turn-of- the-century Western boom town. Constance Miller (Julie Christie) becomes his partner in the flourishing exercise as the whorehouse madame who prefers her opium pipe to McCabe's amorous overtures. With Shelley Duvall and William Devane.

*Director:* Robert Altman BEST ACTRESS OSCAR NOMINATION FOR JULIE CHRISTIE

## DON'T LOOK NOW, 1973

Psycho-horror thriller from a Daphne du Maurier short story. Julie Christie and Donald Sutherland play a young British married couple who go to Venice to forget the tragic drowning of their child. A chance meeting in a restaurant with two sisters, one of whom is blind and says she has 'seen' and spoken to the dead child, sets off a mosaic of mystery. With Hilary Mason and Clelia Matania.

*Director:* Nicolas Roeg

## SHAMPOO, 1975

Warren Beatty as a Beverly Hills hairdresser who adopts a camp façade to mask affairs with his women customers, including a bubbly young actress (Goldie Hawn) and a bored wife (Lee Grant) whose husband

(Jack Warden) keeps a mistress (Julie Christie) on the side.

*Director:* Hal Ashby

# NASHVILLE, 1975

A kaleidoscopic portrait of twenty-four different characters over a period of a few days in the country music capital of America including Ronee Blakely as a Country & Western star on the brink of a nervous collapse and Gwen Welles as as an untalented waitress hoping for a break. With Geraldine Chaplin, Karen Black, Shelley Duvall and Keith Carradine. Julie Christie has a cameo role as herself on a personal appearance tour.

*Director:* Robert Altman

# DEMON SEED, 1977

Futuristic thriller about a computer system which seeks to perpetuate itself in human form. Julie Christie stars as Eve with Fritz Weaver as her scientist husband. They live near an advanced computer centre and their marriage is crumbling because of his commitment to a new machine, Proteus IV designed to do almost everything except think.

*Director:* Donald Cammell

# HEAVEN CAN WAIT, 1978

Fantasy comedy-drama with Warren Beatty as Joe Pendleton, an American football star who has died prematurely in a road accident but is allowed back to inhabit another body temporarily. The only one available is that of an ageing wealthy industrialist whose death is plotted by his wife (Dyan Cannon) and his secretary (Charles Grodin). Julie Christie as Betty Logan falls for the rich reincarnation whose main aim is to resume his sporting career. With James Mason and Buck Henry.

*Director:* Warren Beatty

# MEMOIRS OF A SURVIVOR, 1981

Julie Christie as 'D', the diarist of Doris Lessing's novel, surviving in a not-too-distant future Britain which is spiritually, politically and economically bankrupt. An attractive middle-aged woman, she lives alone in the midst of the chaos around her in which horses and dogs are set upon for food, people queue in the streets for water and packs of wild children huddle in the underground. With Leonie Mellinger, Nigel Hawthorne and Christopher Guard.

*Director:* David Gladwell

# THE RETURN OF THE SOLDIER, 1982

A soldier (Alan Bates) comes home from the trenches of World War I, shell-shocked and suffering from partial amnesia. He does not remember his unfeeling wife (Julie Christie) but does recall his doting cousin (Ann-Margret) and a lower-class call-girl (Glenda Jackson), now married, whom he loved as a young man and whom his wife now allows him to see once again.

*Director:* Alan Bridges

# LES QUARANTIÈMES RUGISSANTES, 1982

(Also known as *The Roaring Forties*) Drama prompted by the story of yachtsman Donald Crowhurst's attempt to trick his way to victory in the 1968 round-the-world yacht race by idling in the Atlantic and doubling back. Julie Christie stars as the lone mariner's wife. *Director:* Christian de Chalonge

# HEAT AND DUST, 1983

Julie Christie is a very modern English woman researching and to some extent reliving the Indian past of a great aunt. Greta Scacchi portrays the great aunt as a young bride of scandalous behaviour whose life is in turmoil as her affections oscillate between her loyal husband and an Indian potentate. With Christopher Cazenove, Julian Glover and Susan Fleetwood.

*Director:* James Ivory

# THE GOLD DIGGERS, 1983

Experimental feminist drama and musical adventure about two women. One is working in a bank investigating money and gold and its relationship to imperialism. The other is Ruby (Julie Christie), daughter of a gold-rush entertainer delving into her mother's life.

*Director:* Sally Potter

# POWER, 1986

Story of big-time politics and the media involving Pete St John (Richard Gere), a peripatetic public relations man and amoral image-maker, whose services practically guarantee success. Two who still care  for Pete even though he has dumped them both are his ex-wife (Julie Christie) and his former mentor (Gene Hackman).

*Director:* Sidney Lumet

# MISS MARY, 1986

Julie Christie as a severe English governess who comes to Buenos Aires in 1938 to care for the young daughters of a prominent Argentine aristocrat and his wife and ensure that the girls are properly prepared for the very proper business of being properly married.

*Director:* Maria Luisa Bemberg

# FOOLS OF FORTUNE, 1990

Historical saga about the Quinton family who reside in their grand rural home in Ireland until the British-employed soldiers, the Black and Tans, burn down their house during the Irish war of independence. The only survivors of the massacre are Quinton's wife

(Julie Christie), her son Willie (first Sean T. McClory and then Iain Glen as an adult) and their maid (Niamh Cusack). Willie becomes withdrawn and his mother becomes a manic depressive and chronic alcoholic. With Michael Kitchen and Mary Elizabeth Mastrantonio.
*Director:* Pat O'Connor

## HAMLET, 1996

Updated to ninteenth-century Denmark, Shakespeare's masterpiece starred Kenneth Branagh as the Prince set upon revenge after the ghost of his father appears to tell him of his murder at the hands of his own brother. With Derek Jacobi as Claudius, Richard Briers as Polonius, Kate Winslet as Ophelia and Julie Christie as Gertrude.
*Director:* Kenneth Branagh

## DRAGONHEART, 1996

Dennis Quaid stars in tenth-century epic as an itinerant dragonslayer who decides to team up with his prey to rid the land of an evil ruler who has betrayed them both. Julie Christie as Queen Aislinn, with David Thewlis, Pete Postlethwaite.
*Director:* Rob Cohen

## AFTERGLOW, 1997

Julie Christie as Phyllis, a melancholy ageing B-picture actress living in Montreal, mourning for her runaway daughter and looking back over her career. Nick Nolte is her handyman

husband whose affairs she overlooks until he really falls for another woman. She then allows herself to be drawn into a relationship with a young businessman played by Jonny Lee Miller.

*Director:* Alan Rudolph

BEST ACTRESS OSCAR NOMINATION FOR JULIE CHRISTIE

## *BELPHEGOR – LE PHANTOME DU LOUVRE, 2001*

Julie plays Glenda Spencer, a noted Egyptologist who is brought in by the curator of the famous Louvre museum in Paris after a ghostly spirit escapes from a sarcophagus into the

museum's electrical system. The sarcophagus was part of a collection of artifacts brought to the Louvre from an architectural dig in Egypt and Glenda reveals that the mummy inside the coffin was the evil spirit Belphegor – with chilling results. *Director:* Jean-Paul Salome

## *NO SUCH THING, 2001*

A young guileless television journalist called Beatrice (Sarah Polley) is sent by her ratings-obsessed boss (Helen Mirren) to follow up a story about a monster on the loose which has been on a killing rampage. During her assignment, Beatrice wins the trust and protection of Dr Anna (Julie Christie) as she develops an unlikely friendship with the monster.

*Director:* Hal Hartley

# SNAPSHOTS, 2002

Burt Reynolds plays the reclusive middle-aged owner of a second-hand bookshop in Amsterdam whose memories of a lost love are revived when a beautiful young woman called Aisha (Carmen Chaplin) walks into his shop. After Aisha's mother Narma (Julie Christie) arrives for a visit, Aisha throws a party which is attended only by Larry and Narma – and he finds romantic fulfilment in unexpected ways.

*Director:* Rudolf van den Berg

# I'M WITH LUCY, 2002

One hour before she is due to wed, a young bride called Lucy (Monica Potter) tells her inquisitive best friend what has led to her choosing to marry. She relates her experiences with each of the five men she has dated over the past year. Julie has a small role as Lucy's mother.

*Director:* Jon Sherman

# TROY, 2004

Action-packed historical epic with a big star cast led by Brad Pitt as Achilles in the famous story of the face that launched a thousand ships: the Greek armada which sailed to war with Troy after Trojan prince Paris (Orlando Bloom) convinced Helen, Queen of Sparta, to leave her husband Menalaus and return with him to Troy. Julie Christie played Thetis, mother of Achilles.

*Director:* Wolfgang Petersen

# HARRY POTTER AND THE PRISONER OF AZKABAN, 2004

Julie plays Madam Rosmerta, landlady of the Three Broomsticks pub, in further adventures of Harry Potter (Daniel Radcliffe) whose life is in danger after Voldemort's trusted aide, convicted murderer Sirius Black, is out to kill him after escaping from prison.

*Director:* Alfonso Cuaron

# FINDING NEVERLAND, 2004

Johnny Depp stars as the writer J.M. Barrie who encounters Sylvia Llewelyn Davies (Kate Winslet) and her four young boys just at a time when his latest play has bombed and he is at a low creative ebb. He strikes up a friendship with the family and through them is inspired to write *Peter Pan.* Julie Christie plays Sylvia's mother, the bitchy Mrs Du Maurier, who is suspicious of Barrie's involvement with her daughter's family and wants him out of their lives.

*Director:* Marc Foster

# THE SECRET LIFE OF WORDS, 2005

A love story centred on Hanna (Sarah Polley), a torture survivor from the Bosnian conflict who undergoes counselling in Copenhagen. There, her terrible torture and its after effects are documented by Inge (Julie Christie). As a trained burns unit nurse, Hanna volunteers to care for Josef (Tim Robbins), a badly burned worker on an oil rig who gradually coaxes her terrible story from her. But it is only from Inge that he finally learns the true extent of Hanna's appalling suffering.

*Director:* Isabel Coixet

# AWAY FROM HER, 2008

Grant and Fiona Anderson are an Ontario couple who have been married for over 40 years. But their lives change dramatically when Fiona (Julie Christie) suffers from Alzheimer's and Grant (Gordon Pinsent) finally agrees to put her in a nursing home. Once there, Fiona rarely remembers her husband and he has to watch as she transfers her affection to another man, a wheelchair-bound mute, who is also a patient at the care home.

*Director:* Sarah Polley

BEST ACTRESS OSCAR NOMINATION FOR JULIE CHRISTIE

# Major Television Roles

## A FOR ANDROMEDA (BBC), 1961

Science fiction series about a menacing computer controlling earthlings from an outer space constellation called Andromeda. Julie played Christine, a brunette laboratory assistant, who is killed and by molecular reconstruction recycyled as a blonde android.

## DANGEROUS CORNER (ITV), 1963

Julie Christie and Tim Seeley as a married couple are invited to a dinner party given by his sister and her husband, played by Pauline Yates and William Lucas. The party takes a disturbing turn when the conversation gets around to the suicide of Lucas's brother.

## SEPARATE TABLES (HTV West), 1984

Terence Rattigan's two-play classic set in the genteel, rather second-rate hotel, the Beauregard, in primmest Bournemouth in the early 1950s. In play number one *Table by the Window,* hotel resident John Malcolm (Alan Bates) is a one-time politician whose promising career has been wrecked by booze and on to the scene comes Anne (Julie Christie), his vain and petulant former wife who divorced him on the grounds of cruelty. But her arrival is not the coincidence she pretends. In *Table Number Seven,* Sybil (Julie

Christie), is the mousey, timorous daughter of a domineering tyrant of a mother (Irene Worth) and afraid to respond to the attraction of a self-styled retired major (Alan Bates).

*Director:* John Schlesinger

# A LONG WAY FROM HOME, 1988

Australian mini-series based on a heroin-smuggling incident in Malaysia, a dramatized version of the real experience of Kevin Barlow and his mother Barbara Barlow, played by Julie Christie. Kevin and companion Geoff Chambers were sentenced to hang in 1986.

# THE RAILWAY STATION MAN (BBC 2), 1993

Drama based on a novel by Jennifer Johnston, in which Julie Christie plays an artistically inclined woman who has been widowed by sectarian violence in Ireland prompting her to move away with her son to a small village. There she meets an American (Donald Sutherland) who is determined to make a disused railway station usable again.

As they grow closer, a local man warns her that the station is being targeted by activists as a storage site for their weapons and that her son is connected to the group.

324

# Bibliography

Dirk Bogarde, *Snakes and Ladders* (Penguin) Kevin Brownlow, *David Lean* (Faber and Faber) David Caute, *Joseph Losey, A Revenge On Life,* (Faber & Faber) Britt Ekland, *True Britt* (Prentice Hall) Michael Freedland, *Michael Caine* (Orion) Allan Hunter, *Faye Dunaway* (W.H. Allen) Brian McFarlane, *An Autobiography of British Cinema* (Methuen) John Parker, *Warren Beatty* (Headline) Rex Reed, *Conversations in the Raw* (World) Mark Sanderson, *Don't Look Now* (British Film Institute) Terence Stamp, *Double Feature* David Thompson, *Warren Beatty and Desert Eyes* (Vintage) Adrian Turner, *Robert Bolt, Scenes From Two Lives* (Hutchinson)

336

# Books For ALL Kinds of Readers

At ReadHowYouWant we understand that one size does not fit all types of readers. Our innovative, patent pending technology allows us to design new formats to make reading easier and more enjoyable for you. This helps improve your speed of reading and your comprehension. Our EasyRead printed books have been optimized to improve word recognition, ease eye tracking by adjusting word and line spacing as well as minimizing hyphenation. Our EasyRead SuperLarge editions have been developed to make reading easier and more accessible for vision-impaired readers. We offer Braille and DAISY formats of our books and all popular E-Book formats.

We are continually introducing new formats based upon research and reader preferences. Visit our web-site to see all of our formats and learn how you can Personalize our books for yourself or as gifts. Sign up to Become A **RHYW** Registered Reader.

**www.readhowyouwant.com**

Printed in Great Britain
by Amazon

10842128R00201